DIRTY LITTLE
SECRETS
OF THE
TWENTIETH
CENTURY

ALSO BY JAMES F. DUNNIGAN

How to Stop a War (with William Martel)

A Quick and Dirty Guide to War (with Austin Bay)

How to Make War

The Complete Wargames Handbook

Getting It Right (with Raymond M. Macedonia)

Dirty Little Secrets (with Albert A. Nofi)

Dirty Little Secrets of World War II (with Albert A. Nofi)

Dirty Little Secrets of Vietnam (with Albert A. Nofi)

Victory and Deceit (with Albert A. Nofi)

Victory at Sea: World War II in the Pacific (with Albert A. Nofi)

Digital Soldiers

Way of the Warrior (with Daniel Masterson)

The Pacific War Encyclopedia (with Albert A. Nofi)

DIRTY LITTLE

SECRETS

OF THE

TWENTIETH

CENTURY

JAMES F. DUNNIGAN

Quill
William Morrow
New York

Library of Congress Cataloging-in-Publication Data

Dunnigan, James F.
Dirty little secrets of the twentieth century
/ James F. Dunnigan.
p.   cm.
Includes bibliographical references (p.) and index.
ISBN 0-688-17068-4
1. History, Modern—20th century—Miscellanea.
I. Title.
D422.D788   1999
909.82—dc21   99-15807
CIP

Printed in the United States of America

First Edition

1   2   3   4   5   6   7   8   9   10

BOOK DESIGN BY NICOLA FERGUSON

www.williammorrow.com

For Catherine Howell, Doris Nelson,

and Phyllis Lindemann,

who saw most of the century

and helped make it a better place

ACKNOWLEDGMENTS

*Thanks to Al Nofi and Bob Bateman,
for catching stuff I missed.*

CONTENTS

Contents

OPERATING INSTRUCTIONS

THIS is the fourth *Dirty Little Secrets* book to be published since 1990. All have used the same format and approach. So if you've read any of the others, you'll know what to expect here. For those who haven't seen the earlier books, just enjoy and illuminate yourself. The series stresses an easy-to-read format (each item is self-contained and rarely more than a page or so in length) and easy access (all the items are grouped in chapters and indexed). Because each item is meant to be self-contained, there is some repetition. You can open the book to any page and read an item without reference to the one before or after it. But all the items do come together as a whole.

And the dirty little secrets? These are items the average person doesn't know about, or is simply misinformed about. I don't cover everything here; my publisher gave me only so much space. So I tried to select those items that would be most useful to the most people. Not the obvious stuff, like politics, wars, or headline news, but things we all bump into. There's a lot on how we lived, worked, ate, partied, and died in the twentieth century. Not a lot on the more arcane aspects of economics, politics, and similar items that caused eyes to glaze over throughout the century. I could have gone on about why the Great

Depression occurred (a weak banking system and psychological shock, but even the experts don't all agree), celebrity scandals (Fatty Arbuckle and O. J. Simpson in the same book?), or party politics (you really want more scandals?). But why?

The items are written from an American point of view. The world is a big place, and the twentieth century meant different things depending on where you were. Most of the planet, by American standards, had barely entered the twentieth century by the 1990s. So we use America, which most readers are familiar with, as our reference point for exploring the twentieth-century experience.

Much of what passes for common knowledge is wrong. This book corrects a lot of the misinformation going around and clearly explains many things that have always been vaguely known but never fully understood. In other words, some real dirty little secrets.

If you have a comment, criticism, rant, or compliment for me, I can be reached via E-mail at jfdunnigan@aol.com. My web page is at www.jim.dunnigan.com.

DIRTY LITTLE

SECRETS

OF THE

TWENTIETH

CENTURY

ONE

THEN AND NOW

SINCE people first began keeping track of things thousands of years ago, you couldn't help but notice that each century had its own special character. The century just ended could arguably be called the most special of all. Several phenomenal characteristics made the twentieth century stand out. There was the enormous growth in population; it more than tripled between 1900 and 2000. More people lived in the twentieth century than during the previous several hundred years. More people were killed in wars during the twentieth century than in any other. But there was also more medical, material, and scientific progress. More scientific advances than in any other century. Most of the scientists who ever lived did so in the twentieth century. More books were published than in any other century. At the end of the century many, if not most, people on the planet were better off than their ancestors in 1900.

It was a century to remember, and to know a little better.

Note: All dollar amounts are given in terms of year-2000 dollars. That is, they are adjusted for inflation and represent the dollar value at the end of the twentieth century. If you want to see what the actual money values were for a year, see the Appendix.

——The View from There——

The approaching twentieth century looked a lot different for someone in 1900 than it did for someone reflecting on the recent past in the 1990s. The nineteenth century, in general, was itself a rather shocking event, for so many things changed so quickly. This had never happened before. So it was suspected that the twentieth century would move even faster into unknown territory. Because the nineteenth century had begun in war and ended in peace and material progress, the feeling was that the good times could just keep on going and that change was positive. Rarely had humanity faced a new century with that attitude before.

As much of the world celebrated the new century on New Year's Day, 1900, few had any idea how violent life would be for the next three or four generations. If you were a toddler in 1900, you stood a good chance of dying in World War I and its related conflicts. If you survived that, or even if you didn't, your children would be caught up in an even more violent World War II. Your grandchildren had a wide assortment of little wars to keep them terrified. Only your great-grandchildren would encounter a world at peace, more or less.

While no one could imagine the scale and extent of the coming violence, it was even harder to picture the changes in day-to-day life. In 1900 most Americans lived without indoor plumbing, electricity, or modern medicine. No radio or TV, and only silent movies, for those few living in cities that contained a movie theater. Cars were new technology, and quite rare. Phonographs and telephones were also new, and used by just a small segment of the population. Most people went to bed when the sun went down, for the only artificial light was from candles or kerosene lanterns. The average life span was a mere forty-seven years, and minor infections or a bad chill could easily cause death. A century ago people read more, walked more, talked more, worked longer hours, and went to bed earlier. Quite a change. And we can expect equally dramatic changes going into the next century. So hold on to your hat. Well, no, that won't work. Wearing hats was much more common a century ago. Hang on to your cell phone instead. . . .

——Life Has Changed——

Even for those of us who have lived through most of the twentieth century, it's hard to comprehend how much life has changed in a hundred years. Never before in the history of the species has so much changed in such a short period of time. Not only are we living more than twenty years longer than at any other time, but we are living more comfortably. While natural calamities still come by occasionally, reminding us of our place in the scheme of things, most of the time we have the means to live like kings. Indeed, that puts it into perspective, for as far as creature comforts are concerned, more people lived more comfortably in the twentieth century than at any other time in the past. Middle-class consumers, who comprise a majority in some industrialized nations, have access to luxuries aristocrats in the past could not even imagine. Automobiles, video, recorded music, airplanes, malls, telephones, computers, and a host of drugs and medicines that actually work as advertised.

No aristocrat of the past could travel as fast and safely as we can today. Entertainment in the past had to be live or in your mind; today we have movies, television, recordings and radio. For thousands of years, the nobility could travel about in a crude carriage, litter, or boat. Today, just about everybody can drive themselves anywhere they want in a comfortable (especially by pre-twentieth-century standards) automobile. And people today do wander about in their cars, "recreational travel" having become a major segment of the economy. Via telephones and computers we can communicate instantly with billions of people anywhere on the planet. Change has been speeding up for several centuries now. But few adults alive in 1900 believed there would be so much change in the next century. It seems likely that there will be even more in the century to come.

One thing Americans in 1900 did have a clear view of for the new century was America's role in the world. In 1898 the United States had fought a brief war with Spain and acquired an overseas empire. But it was more than colonies, for America had increasingly been doing a lot of business with foreigners. In 1900, foreign trade was only about 12 percent of the GNP. By the end of the century that had grown to 25 percent. A quarter of Americans owed their economic well-being to overseas trade. So it should be no surprise that at the end of the century the U.S. Navy was by far the largest in the world and that America took a keen interest in what happened in faraway places. American jobs depended on it.

What you have to stop and think about is that we have gotten used to change in this century, a rate of change unprecedented in human history. You can make a case that many of us have not adapted to the rate of change, and this would explain the higher level of anxiety (and use of drugs to deal with it) in the late twentieth century. But humans are very adaptable critters, and we've certainly proven it again and again in the last hundred years.

——The Population Explosion——

There are a lot more people on planet earth now (about 6 billion) than there were a century ago (1.6 billion.) That's over three times as many, and the human population has never grown that fast before. Why so many more? Simple—more food and clean water. Simple as that. But the implications are something else.

In 1800 there were 900 million people on the earth, and it didn't quite double up to 1900. Before that, growth was even slower. Two thousand years ago, the planet's population was only about 200 million. The population grew to about 360 million by A.D. 1200, then stalled for two centuries because of wars (the Mongol invasions), climate change (it got colder), and disease (the Black Death).

The huge population growth in this century, despite losses of over 200 million dead from wars, was largely due to increased knowledge of simple things. Better sanitation (clean water more than anything else) and more efficient farming methods were behind most of the increase. But the increase was uneven. Europe went from 390 million to 720 million, while Asia began with 970 million and increased to 3.6 billion.

In Africa, population soared from about 100 million to 700 million. This is one reason that Africa is currently the poorest continent. While

African farming methods were primitive in 1900, there was not as much land capable of growing crops. Much food was imported, and the population soared without any way to feed it with local farm production. Western technology was better at keeping people alive than it was at enabling them to feed themselves, especially in Africa. Political problems made it difficult to sort things out. In 1900, most of sub-Saharan Africa consisted of European colonies. In the 1960s, most of these areas were set up as independent nations. The new governments proceeded to use the Soviet Union as an economic model, thereby destroying most of the productive business enterprises they had. It took thirty years for most Africans to accept this error, and as the century ended, progress was being made.

Throughout the century, there were many who warned that the rapid population growth would lead to disaster before the century ended. The doomsayers had a point, for never in human history had there been such a rapid increase in population. But the twentieth century was also a time of explosive growth in technology and knowledge. This is what kept food production ahead of population growth. The population crash never came, and as the century ends, population growth is declining. This is another side effect of the growth of technology, for as people gained more education and income, they had fewer children.

This was not a new trend; it had long been noted among families that made a lot of money or were simply better educated. The ancient Romans, two thousand years ago, complained about it, and it was always a problem among the well-off nobility. But what was once considered a curse among aristocrats trying to keep the line going is now considered a positive development. When couples have more wealth, the women avoid having children, and the men, who are often more enthusiastic about it, can't do much about the situation. It was long thought that women were mainly trying to avoid the risk of death or injury in childbirth. This always was a serious consideration until this century. But it turned out that women were also eager to avoid all the work that went into having children, and as soon as a nation has economically well-off women, there are fewer children. The women don't have to be middle class, simply better off than their parents. Once that starts happening, the birthrate declines.

But the planet is still in uncharted territory, for never have so many people lived on so little land. In the past we know of regions that became overpopulated, followed by a failure of the local agriculture and a sharp drop in the population from starvation, civil war (over the declining resources), low birthrates, and migration. We are already seeing starvation and civil wars in Africa, and migration throughout the nonindustrialized nations. We don't know where it will end, and even with declining birthrates, the population explosion is set to continue into the next century. For many parts of the globe still have large families. We can take some comfort in the fact that humans have tended to overcome worldwide population pressures so far.

So while humans are ahead on points, we don't always win the race with mass starvation from overpopulation.

——Moving Every Five Years——

Why have Americans been the best-paid people in the world throughout the twentieth century? One of the most important reasons is one you probably never thought of.

Americans are better trained, and they work harder and do so for longer hours. All true, but one of the key economic advantages has been Americans' willingness to move. The American economy's explosive growth in the twentieth century has meant new businesses often starting where the climate, raw materials, or transportation were suitable, but often where the labor supply was not. Fortunately, Americans are the most mobile population in the world. We move a lot, in contrast to people in other industrialized and developing nations, where most people resist moving away from the place they were born. From the 1950s through the 1980s, about 20 percent of Americans changed address each year. By the end of the century, people began to settle down a bit, with only about 16 percent moving each year. A lot of this had to do with the increasing trend for both husband and wife to have careers, and moving both at once can be expensive. But for the young, unmarried American workers, the willingness, even eagerness, to move far and often to advance their job prospects has given the American economy an advantage no other industrialized nation has.

It's not unusual for masses of poor, uneducated workers to move, desperately looking for new work. But more of the American workers relocating turned out to be the best trained and educated. Indeed, it was generally the poorest and least-educated American workers that were most resistant to moving.

Not all the moves have been work-related. Throughout the century, there has been an enormous internal migration as people moved from the farms to the urban areas. This was for jobs. Now that is reversing, as people move back to rural areas for a more pleasant lifestyle. Improved communications, "telecommuting," has made this possible. A similar trend has reversed the enormous movement of people from cities to the suburbs in the three decades after World War II. As many commercial areas of cities get emptied out by companies moving south or overseas, these old buildings are recycled as apartments. Couples who had earlier moved to the suburbs from the city neighborhoods they grew up in now come back to the city after the kids have grown up and moved away. And then there is the American custom of moving up to a larger home as one's economic condition improved. A lot of the moving was within the same town, from your "starter" house to a larger one.

But employers have long offered incentives to move workers to their work. Transportation costs, of course, were paid or subsidized for many immigrants entering the country. Once they were in the country, even more generous inducements were offered to get people to where the jobs were. In the early part of the century, when so many people were entering the country, few inducements were needed. Most of the jobs were along the new railroad systems built in the last few decades of the nineteenth century, or next to the port cities. Cheap rail and water transportation was available, and people looking for a job were quick to move.

The second half of the twentieth century was a somewhat different story. The people most frequently being moved around were managers, professionals, and technical experts. And most of these people owned their own homes. It cost money to sell your house and then buy a new one. It also cost a lot to ship the household goods. Plus there was the uprooting of the family from school and friends. Companies took care of more and more of the financial burden, with some large companies starting their own real-estate divisions to deal with the growing portfolio of employee homes they were buying and selling. Companies began to examine the idea of saving substantial costs by not moving people so much.

For the World War II generation, especially those who were the first in their family to graduate from college courtesy of the G.I. Bill, the frequent moves were taken in stride. Most of the moves were caused by a promotion within a large corporation, or simply by a new and better job in another city. Most wives stayed home and took care of things there, making the frequent moves more manageable. Wives were known to joke that IBM really stood for "I've Been Moved."

By the 1980s, more and more of the wives had jobs, and the idea of moving every few years was getting a bit tiresome. While earlier generations could use the example of their parents' or grandparents' picking up and moving to find better economic prospects, decades of prosperity had induced many to settle down. All those moves were stressful, leaving a trail of divorce and troubled children in their wake. America still has the world's most mobile labor force, but without quite as much enthusiasm for the nomadic life.

——The Shaving Revolution——

One simple invention simultaneously eliminated millions of minor wounds, saved millions of wasted hours, and revolutionized marketing. You'll never guess what it was.

In 1901, King Gillette invented the modern safety razor. Before that, you shaved, at some risk, with a straight razor. In a pinch you could shave with a very sharp knife. As a result, many men didn't shave, or at least didn't shave every day. It was particularly dangerous to shave when you had a hangover. Gillette's invention didn't really catch on until World War I, when many American troops noted how convenient it was to shave in the trenches with a safety razor. Doing it with a straight razor could be unpleasant if you were startled by some incoming enemy fire. Gillette saw to it that 3 million razors and 36 million blades were shipped to the troops.

Centuries of experience with straight razors suddenly disappeared as it became fashionable to use the safety razor. Boys faced with their first shave needed little encouragement to forgo the fearsome straight razor for the much less risky safety razor. Indeed, the name Gillette gave his invention, the "Safety Razor," was meant to capitalize on the reputation of the more dangerous straight razor. Nevertheless, straight razors continued to be sold, and bought, until the 1960s. Today, the only ones that still use straight razors are barbers, who are expert in its use (they normally have to successfully shave the lather off a balloon to graduate from barber school) and can get a closer shave with it than with a safety razor.

Gillette's blades were made of tempered 40-gauge steel and measured about 9/10ths of an inch wide and .006 inches thick. The blades were light—four hundred of them weighed a pound. The safety razor consisted of two parts: a shaving head, which included the protective plate, the blade, the flange, and a post with a screw to hold it all together and attach the head to the second part, a molded handle, made of either metal or wood.

The double-sided razor blade was screwed into the blade holder, which itself was topped with a metal plate that allowed only a small portion of the blade to be exposed. Under the blade, a metal flange guided the razor over the skin.

Gillette also invented the "razor blade" principle for marketing expendable items. The blades were only good for twenty to forty shaves, depending on how thick your beard was. Initially, they cost from fifty cents to a dollar each. This was a high-profit item. To encourage men to adopt the safety razor, the razor and a small supply of blades were sold for under ten dollars. Gillette knew that it paid to sell the razor cheaply, for the real money was to be made on the blades. This principle was later adopted by many other manufacturers throughout the century.

At first, few women had any use for the razors. Long dresses had been women's customary attire for centuries, and even their bathing suits had skirts. Women were not supposed to show their legs. But this changed in the 1920s, as short dresses and sleeveless blouses became the fashion. Then a fashion photographer decided to shoot some models dressed to look like classical statues of women. This meant sleeveless dresses with short skirts. But to look like statues, the models had to have smooth skin on their legs and armpits. Now, no woman had ever been crazy enough to shave her armpits in the past, not with a straight razor. In cultures that preferred the hairless look in their women, plucking was the preferred (if painful) method. But the photographer knew how to use a safety razor, and soon his models had shaved legs and armpits. For whatever reason, the shaved look caught on. Slowly at first, among the more fashion-conscious. But by midcentury, most American women shaved. By the end of the century, most middle-class women worldwide did so also. By the 1970s, most of the shaving gear sold in the United States was bought by women.

The company King Gillette founded is still thriving, and selling lots of razor blades.

──The Taming of the Curse──

For half the planet's population, the twentieth century brought some relief in an unexpected way. But the biggest challenge was in letting people know about it.

One of the less well known developments of the twentieth century was how women were provided with better ways to deal with menstruation. The monthly "curse," as many women called it, was, early in this century, dealt with as it had been for thousands of years. Rags were kept handy, and these were washed out and reused until each period of menstruation was over. Inconvenient and not foolproof, this had worked for thousands of years. But it all changed during World War I, when some American army nurses noted that the new types of very absorbent bandages being provided by the Kimberly-Clark corporation could, if worn correctly, do a more efficient job of soaking up menstrual blood. After World War I, Kimberly-Clark set up the Kotex company to manufacture and distribute this new approach to dealing with the curse.

In the early part of this century, talking about something as feminine, sexual, and personal as menstruation was difficult. Thus the advertising of the new Kotex products was always a major challenge. A lot of code words were used, and the medical (as bandages) origins of the menstrual pad were invoked by putting a cross (similar to the red or white cross used to designate medical supplies) on the packaging. The pads were white, and made of the same material as bandages (and could be used as bandages in a pinch). Many mothers still explained menstruation in the ancient terms of "purifying" the body of toxins. The Kotex company did nothing to disabuse young girls of this myth when "what is happening to me and why I should use Kotex products" pamphlets were distributed in the 1920s and '30s. The magazine ads for menstrual pads were discreet, the perfect example of targeted advertising, aimed at women, who immediately understood the ads, while most men had only a vague idea of what it was all about.

Pads were slow in gaining wide acceptance, partly because of the cost. In the 1920s and '30s, pads cost fifty cents to a dollar each, and the Great Depression made it easy for women to stick with, or go back to, the ancient practice of using less absorbent, but washable cloth pads. But after World War II, with prosperity returning, most women rapidly adopted the more convenient disposable pads.

Then, in the 1970s, along came an even more convenient way to deal with menstruation: tampons. These absorbent cylinders were worn inside the body, eliminating the external pads and the belts needed to hold them in place. By the 1990s, about a third of women had switched to the new tampons.

Then it was "back to the future" time. First there was the toxic-shock scare. In a very few cases, some women who wore tampons too long were poisoned by a common bacterium. The cause appeared to be the depletion of the antibodies, because of the absorbing action of the tampon, that normally keep this bacterium in check. In some cases the infection was fatal, but the major effect was to cause many women to rethink their approach to dealing with menstruation. Many women were also shocked by the ecological implications; by the 1990s, North American women (the major users) were disposing of over 20 billion pads and tampons a year. The volume of this was greater than that of disposable diapers. In addition, many women noted that pads and tampons were made largely of synthetic materials (rayon, most commonly) and cotton grown with the use of many chemicals. There was great fear that these chemicals in tampons were being absorbed. So a movement began to eliminate all this waste, as well as the threat of toxic shock. This provided a market for several new products. First, there were pads made from organic cotton (grown without the use of chemicals). Then came the natural rubber cup, inserted like a tampon but shaped to hold up to six to twelve hours of menstrual flow (before being taken out, washed, and reinserted). Finally, there is the washable pad, which is an updated version of the ancient loincloth used to catch the menstrual flow.

But these new developments are not gaining many adherents. The pads and tampons are too convenient for most women. The new washable cloth and the rubber cup may catch on in less wealthy nations, though, where five or so dollars a month for tampons or pads is an onerous expense.

Controversies aside, the twentieth century saw convenience and comfort come to something women have had to cope with for as long as there have been women.

The Real Reason We Live Longer

A century ago, the average American lived about forty-seven years. Today, we manage over seventy years. Most people think all the medical gadgets and medicines developed in this century are the cause. No, most of those added years come from something as prosaic as large pipes, which carry water to people and sewage away. For thousands of years, outbreaks of waterborne diseases made cities very unhealthy, and cities grew enormously in size during the nineteenth century. But medical research in the nineteenth century had also confirmed that dirty water was the cause of most of these diseases, many of which would periodically grow into epidemics. So starting late in the nineteenth century, most large cities in the industrialized nations began cleaning up their water supplies and installing sewage systems.

It wasn't until the middle of the century that most of America had completed building all those sewer and water pipes, and it has taken until the end of the century to build sewage-treatment plants to clean up all those lakes and rivers the sewage was dumped into. Other countries are not so fortunate. India still has a sanitation problem, and with a population of over a billion, it is a *big* problem. In the late 1990s, about 8 percent of Indian children died before reaching the age of five. But twenty years earlier, it was 20 percent. Industrialized nations lose only a few percent at most. This has to do with good sanitation more than anything else.

While these improvements gained much praise where they were built, they rarely got their deserved credit for enabling so many people to live longer. That glory tended to go to the new medicines that began to appear with great frequency early in this century.

While the antibiotics did not appear until the 1930s (inorganic sulfa-based) and 1940s (penicillin), their theoretical application was discovered much earlier (1908 for sulfa drugs and 1928 for penicillin). Of all the thousands of new drugs developed in this century, the antibiotics, particularly penicillin, saved the most lives. Bacterial infections—including flesh wounds "gone bad," blood poisoning, pneumonia, and many venereal diseases—were often fatal before antibiotics came along. Even so, while antibiotics have saved millions of lives, clean water and sanitation have saved billions.

Let us never forget the true medical miracle of the twentieth century—the sewer pipe.

——Where Modern Medicine Came From——

What we think of as modern medicine—the high-tech hospitals, endless miracle drugs, emergency rooms, and such—is a rather recent development. And American medicine in particular was to become something unique in the world, and not for all the right reasons.

A century ago, there were few doctors who were specialists, and hospitals were decidedly low-tech. There were no antibiotics and few drugs of any kind. Aspirin was an exciting new development, while morphine and heroin, discovered in the nineteenth century, were seen as potentially more than painkillers.

What changed everything was organization, drug research, health insurance, and lots of money. In 1900, few doctors belonged to the American Medical Association or any other professional organization. Many "doctors" had talked their way into the job, rather than having attended a medical school and passed rigorous tests. But the trend through the last half of the nineteenth century was to restrict the practice of medicine to those who really knew what they were doing. Setting up standards like this had always been difficult, because so much of medicine was nothing more than hand-holding and psychology. That actually worked in many cases. Indeed, it still works in many poor countries like India and China, where people cannot afford real doctors but feel quite comfortable going to someone who says he's a physician, has a few medical skills, and puts on a good act. The accreditation mania got into high gear after 1900, and by the 1920s most states had passed laws forbidding the practice of medicine without a license. This last requirement would indicate that a doctor had gone to a medical school accredited by an association of licensed doctors.

In 1900, the medical profession was still in the process of getting rid of quacks and adopting basic medical techniques we all take for granted. Things like stethoscopes, keeping things germ-free (using antiseptic substances like soap and alcohol), and taking a medical history were still new procedures a century ago. There were no miracle drugs. The lack of highly effective drugs meant that other forms of medicine, like homeopathy, chiropractic, and what could best be described as "folk medicine" still had many followers. And for good reason, as back then these other forms of medicine were not much less effective than mainstream medicine. Indeed, many doctors took a dim view of all the drugs in the works. It was somehow felt that chemists were trying to take over the profession. Those doctors were right, for in the next half century it was chemistry that provided many of the most potent cures yet created.

While bacteria are the biggest killers of people, the first drugs synthesized or extracted from natural substances were painkillers and mood-altering compounds. Morphine and cocaine were developed in the nineteenth century, as was the use of ether as an anesthesia. With the danger of infection so great, hospitals were still considered places to treat the poor inexpensively. Anyone with money stayed away from hospitals as much as possible. Women had their children at home, and operations were justly feared because of the danger of incurable infections in the germ-ridden hospitals. It wasn't until the 1930s, after hospitals had proven they had diligently enforced antiseptic medicine, that upper- and middle-class people began to lose their fear of what had once been called "pest houses."

The big revolution in medical practice was World War II, which saw the widespread introduction of antibiotics (penicillin and the like). World War II had also caused hundreds of military hospitals to be set up. Over 700,000 men were wounded, and many more became sick or injured. These hospitals, and the thousands of civilian medical personnel (drafted, like everyone else) who ran them, created an atmosphere of confidence in hospitals and the new miracle drugs. The antibiotics were indeed miracle drugs, for bacteria had been not only the biggest killers for thousands of years, but also the biggest impediment to the more widespread use of surgery.

With antibiotics, surgery was much less dangerous and as a result became much more common. Another major impetus for more surgery was the perfection of blood banks during the war. Until the late 1930s, when the Russians demonstrated that one could safely take blood from corpses and reuse it, there was no practical way to collect large quantities of blood and distribute it to where it was most needed. American doctors worked out the details (there were many) to make it possible to collect a lot of blood, store it for the few weeks it was still usable, and get it to where it was most needed. During World War II, this meant the combat zone, where thousands of wounded American soldiers would otherwise have died of shock or blood loss had there not been whole blood and plasma available. After the war, with surgery less risky because of ample blood for transfusion, the surgeons saw many more lifesaving possibilities for their skills.

There was, however, a dark side to this. American medicine had developed differently from medicine in Europe. While most of the advances in medical practice had come from Europe over the last two centuries, Americans adopted this knowledge in a unique fashion. America had become the home of "aggressive medicine." To Americans, sickness was something that was to be attacked with all available remedies. Until the middle of the twentieth century, this led to the popularity of many different forms of medicine. If mainstream medicine didn't cure you, then you could try one of the others, which included homeopathy, chiropractic, faith healers, herbalists, or whatever. To the average sick American, the search for a cure wasn't over until you were dead. And with the recent development of cryogenics (freezing bodies for later revival), many believe that even death does not end the hope of a cure.

But from the 1940s on, there were not only more cures available but more reliable ones. There was grounds for optimism, for by the middle of the century most epidemic diseases had been tamed by improved public-health methods. Bacteria were under control with antibiotics. With surgery less risky, and thousands of surgeons at the top of their form from all that wartime experience, more surgery was being done and new techniques were being developed.

In the 1950s, open-heart surgery got its start (just one example of complex procedures that would have been hopeless before antibiotics), with the help of new electromechanical tools. In that same decade, polio, the disease that had crippled President Franklin Roosevelt, was cured. People were beginning to think anything was possible, and the medical community was eager to make it so.

The 1950s also saw the introduction of tranquilizers on a large scale. These medications (Miltown and Equanil in the 1950s, followed by Librium and Valium in the 1960s) revolutionized mental-health care, and very cheaply too. But this was the exception. Medicine was to become more and more expensive as the century wore on.

Going into the 1960s, it became obvious that while all this new medicine was working, it was getting more expensive. Health insurance, which had been around for a while, suddenly became a lot more popular. At first it was relatively cheap, for people were healthier than in the past, and not many people needed many of the new technologies. But that changed as more people became aware of what the new medical technology could do. And especially as the new medical treatments lengthened everyone's life span.

At this point, there developed a considerable difference between the way medicine was practiced in the United States and the way it was done in other industrialized nations. America, with its tradition of aggressive medicine and explosion of new medical technology, with a booming economy and a health-insurance system that spread the costs, basically went after a limitless approach to medicine.

While European countries adopted one form of universal health insurance or another and then treated the expense as another item in the national budget, the United States put the burden of insurance payments on individuals or, more accurately, on organizations. Large corporations were forced by competitive pressures to offer health insurance to their employees. So did governments. Those without health insurance were covered either by government insurance (if they were poor or on Social Security) or the essentially free care hospitals offered to anyone coming into the emergency room with a problem. The expense for this was absorbed by charging those with insurance more. It was a makeshift system, but it worked. Unfortunately, the insurance premiums kept going up as more cures were discovered and, in the tradition of aggressive medicine, more Americans demanded the cures.

The European countries had always been more frugal when it came to health care, and their costs per person after World War II were lower. By the end of the century, the average American was spending nearly twice as much on health care than the average European. At the same time, the average European had a slightly longer life span. Moreover, Europeans felt healthier. Granted, this was largely what people were telling poll takers. But Europeans were spending less on health care and living longer, so something was going on.

What was happening in America was the availability of hugely expensive medical techniques and the willingness to use them. The growth in health spending was astounding. In 1929, when such records were first kept, health spending was 3.6 percent of gross domestic product (GDP). Even the Great Depression did not slow down growth in this area. By 1940, it had grown to 4 percent of GDP. Growth was slow after World War II, for in 1955 it was 4.4 percent. But then, as Americans realized how much effective health care was out there, costs really took off. By 1965, it was 5.9 percent; by 1975, 8.3 percent; by 1985, 10.5 percent; and at the end of the century, it was 15 percent and still growing. The GDP itself was going up enormously during the century, so the dollar amounts were growing even faster. In 1929, some $36 billion was spent, about $300 per capita. An estimate of per capita spending in 1900 was about $200, largely because doctors had few tools to work with. At the end of the century, the health-care bill was $1.4 trillion, or $4,600 per capita. In 1900, the average life span was forty-seven years; in 1929, it was fifty-seven years; at the end of the century, it was seventy-seven.

By the end of the century, the pattern for most Americans was to get hit with the bulk of their lifetime health costs in the last six months of their lives. In Europe, when a person is near the end, the doctor orders painkillers and sedatives to make the patient comfortable and tells the family to prepare for the end. In America, the doctor orders heroic, and very expensive, procedures, and the patient often dies sooner than if the European approach had been taken. Even if Americans don't want the expensive, heroic procedures, doctors and hospitals often don't comply. Fearful of lawsuits for not doing everything possible, the medical professionals do all they can, and bill for it.

Health-maintenance organizations (HMOs) were another post–World War II health-insurance variation that caught on toward the end of the twentieth century. Rather than just pay for health care when something is wrong, HMOs seek to keep people healthy before something goes wrong, and make greater profits the more successful they are at this. But HMOs soon ran into the American tradition of aggressive medical care. This made for great headlines when a patient wanted a very expensive procedure that had a slim chance of success. HMOs, like most European doctors, won't allow such things to be paid by the insurer. Making the situation worse is the growth of lifestyle medical treatments. Many of these are drugs that make older patients, or those who have chronic conditions like arthritis, more comfortable. Hard to argue with that, but these medications and procedures (including plastic surgery) are very expensive and getting more so. The impotency cure, Viagra, introduced in the late 1990s, was the classic lifestyle drug, and many agitated for it to be covered by health insurance.

In America, aggressive medical care is seen as a right, even if it's likely to cripple the economy eventually. On this last point, there is little argument. Already, major American corporations, faced with worldwide loss of competitiveness due to rampaging health-insurance costs, switched over to HMOs. Some states began rationing care for those on taxpayer-funded health plans.

But the American attitude toward health care remained one of aggressive optimism. No one knows where this will lead, but so far it has obtained slightly less benefit for twice the cost.

——The Microbes Strike Back——

Antibiotics not only provided a cure for most bacterial infections but also led to the evolution of bacteria that are immune to antibiotics. All in less than a century. This, it turned out, was not a good development for many people.

As far as disease goes, you could divide the twentieth century into three parts. In the first third of the century, the microbes were supreme. The least little cut could turn into incurable (except for amputation) infection. Pneumonia, a bacterial infection of the lungs, was usually fatal. Bad water could bring people any number of deadly microbes. Cleaning up the water supply and getting rid of garbage helped a lot, but the microbes were still largely incurable. This changed in the 1930s, when microbe-killing sulfa drugs were developed. These drugs had limited effect, but they were a big step forward. Just as World War II was starting, penicillin was perfected, and production grew throughout the war and after.

Up through the 1960s, it appeared that microbes were down and out as a menace to human health. But scientists knew better. Microbes, and all other living creatures, adapt to anything that hurts them. By the 1960s it was clear that the microbes were evolving into strains that were resistant, and even immune, to penicillin. New antibiotics were developed, as science tried to stay one jump ahead of the microbes. But by the end of the century it appeared that the microbes might be pulling ahead in this race.

There were several reasons for this, the main one being that in some countries, especially the United States, antibiotics were overused. In Europe, antibiotics were given only after it was clear that the patient's immune system was not resisting the microbes successfully. In America, antibiotics were given much more frequently, often when a bacterial infection was just suspected.

Although the doctors know that overuse of antibiotics is causing these problems, the fear of getting sued for malpractice, or just having to deal with insistent patients, keeps the unneeded prescriptions for antibiotics coming.

Research into the matter turned up yet another curious side effect of the American war on microbes. The appearance of more cases of allergies, including cases of people allergic to just about everything, was traced to "excessive cleanliness." People who wash more frequently when young and generally avoid germs more diligently are more likely to get allergies, and more of them, when they get older.

The way this works can be seen more clearly if you look at how the use of antibiotics, and standards of personal hygiene, differ between France and the United States. The French feel that having some germs around actually protects you from infection. French doctors agree with this attitude, and prescribe far fewer antibiotics. And the French live longer and have fewer allergies than Americans. Not only that, the French are much less prone to getting "traveler's diarrhea" when they venture abroad. The French, and their doctors, attribute this to what they consider a healthier relationship with, well, dirt. Americans simply consider the French a little grungy.

Perhaps the next American health craze will be, "Get Dirty."

——AIDS Before AIDS——

AIDS hit the late twentieth century like a plague, especially among homosexuals and drug addicts. This incurable viral infection was seen as an unprecedented epidemic. Not so, for decades of immunity provided by antibiotics had caused everyone to forget an earlier sexually transmitted killer. Syphilis appeared in Europe right after Columbus discovered the Americas. There were similar diseases in Africa, but syphilis was a true horror. Transmitted primarily through sexual contact (or from mother to child), it initially caused painful sores and then took decades to kill by destroying the victim's nervous system. The terminal stages of syphilis often left a victim a babbling idiot. Not a pretty picture, and incurable until antibiotics came along. Unlike AIDS, which is transmitted largely through the blood (homosexual sex and drug addicts sharing needles), the syphilis bacteria needed only heterosexual sex to spread, and spread it did. Like AIDS, syphilis took a long time before it killed you, providing ample opportunity to be spread around. Early in the twentieth century, "a cure for syphilis" was as eagerly sought as a cure for AIDS is today. But back then, there was no track record of medical miracles to look back on with confidence. Despite that, in 1906 the Wassermann test, a blood test to detect syphilis, was developed. Now it was possible to detect the disease accurately. In 1910, arsphenamine was developed to treat syphilis, and then antibiotics came along. Antibiotics could cure syphilis, rather than just treat it. At the beginning of the century, mankind was faced with a host of incurable killer diseases. Most of these have been brought low by various medicines only in this century. Diseases like AIDS are nothing new, and AIDS is actually a lightweight compared to the plagues of the past. But it's all relative, for after all the medical miracles of the twentieth century, AIDS is the only active plague we've got.

——The New Immigrants——

America is a nation of immigrants. Nothing new in that. But the twentieth century has, from the beginning right up through 2000, brought more twists and turns to the story of immigration than anyone could have imagined.

Let's talk real foreign invasion. Imagine if, in the last decade of the twentieth century, over 30 million foreigners entered the country. We're talking a number representing over 10 percent of the population. What kind of effect do you think that would have? No need to wonder; it already happened in the first decade of the century. America is a nation of immigrants, and most of the immigrants entered the United States in the twentieth century. In fact, more entered in the first decade than in any other decade. The first three decades of this century saw so many people enter the country that by 1930, nearly a quarter of the population were immigrants or the children of immigrants. It was a shocking development in so many ways.

First, there was the sheer number of people coming in. Most were from Italy and Eastern Europe. This added to the shock, since immigrants from these areas had been relatively rare before the 1890s. In the first three decades of this century, Eastern Europe and Italy each had over a quarter of a million people entering America per year for many years. Two things propelled this tidal wave. It was known by all potential immigrants that America had the highest wages in the world and that there were plenty of jobs. America, if not exactly welcoming immigrants, did not actively repel them like most other nations. Second, there was the price and safety angle. Since the introduction of the steamship in the last few decades of the nineteenth century, it was possible to get across the Atlantic safely and relatively cheaply ($300 to $800 a head). These two factors set off a stampede.

After the 1890s, more and more of the immigrants were urbanites, whereas during the nineteenth century a much higher proportion had been farmers. The timing was perfect, as America was beginning its great shift from an agricultural to a manufacturing economy. In 1900, 34 percent of the workforce was in agriculture; by 1940, it was 16 percent; and at the end of the century, it was less than 3 percent. The jobs were in the cities, and this is where the new immigrants went.

The immigrants were disproportionately young men and women. Although most had few skills, there really was no training for many of the new jobs being invented in America. The first two decades of the century saw the development of mass-production techniques and methods for training workers quickly to become productive. This was a major benefit for the United States, as the young-adult immigrants were people in their prime added to the workforce without the usual burden of family dependents (children and elderly). These young immigrants did not marry and have children until they were economically secure, at least by their own standards. There was not much of a welfare system back then, so you did not have a family until you could pay for it.

In the first half of the century, this made the American economy even more productive than it was to begin with. In the second half of the century, it became more common for college-educated immigrants to arrive in large numbers. The rest of the world, noting the success of the highly educated United States workforce, increased the number of college graduates. But many of these nations were unable to provide jobs for all the new grads, and these bright folks quickly figured out that if they were going to find jobs, America was the place to be.

There was a downside to this youth-and-education angle. American immigration laws were changed in the 1960s, making it easier to bring relatives into the country. In the past, it had been rare for parents to follow adult children to America. But now this changed, and a higher and higher proportion of immigrants were no longer highly productive young adults. The immigrants quickly figured out that they could bring over their parents and grandparents, sign them up for Social Security (and other benefits), and let the government pay for everything. Immigrants also found a generous, at least by the standards they were used to, welfare system. You bring a family in and you'd be supported by the state. So more families came. By the 1990s, the laws were changed to eliminate a lot of this. But the entry of multigenerational families was a change that reduced the economic benefit (to America) of traditional immigration patterns. Canada and Australia, in a similar situation, dealt with the problem by setting economic and educational standards for prospective immigrants. If you wanted to come in, you had to show the money or degrees at the door.

The term "brain drain" entered the vocabulary, as college-educated immigrants left their homelands in droves. But there was something else going on here. Immigrants were noted for their hard work and diligence, which was largely a result of going from a place of little opportunity to one of vast possibilities. Native-born Americans had a different attitude, for America was all they had ever known. Some native-born Americans knew better. Those that went to other, especially

Third World, nations to live (not as tourists) came home with an immigrant's sense of appreciation for what America is and the rest of the world is not. But most native-born Americans tend to be more laid-back. When immigrants became parents, they passed on this sense of urgency and opportunity. But after a generation or two, the old country was forgotten and everyone went after the good life. Much of the late-twentieth-century research on why some immigrant children did better in school than others revealed that the major factor was attitude toward the value of education and how much homework the kids did. Even if the parents did not understand English, they could still get after the kids to bear down and do their homework. This worked amazingly well, but only if the parents and kids bought into the idea.

One of the less inspiring aspects of the brain drain was that it exposed a "brain deficit" in the United States. Native-born Americans were reluctant to do the hard work required to get advanced degrees in science and engineering. By the late twentieth century, most of the people teaching these subjects in American universities, as well as most of the graduate students, were foreigners or the children of immigrants. This simply spotlights a little-discussed aspect of America's economic predominance in this century. By attracting the better-educated and more ambitious immigrants, America improves the overall quality of its workforce. Look at America's high-tech industries in the late twentieth century and you will see a disproportionate number of immigrants working there, and running the companies as well. America has provided a better place for people to work and start businesses in this century, so it should not be surprising that so many people the world over have arrived to do just that. But the downside is that America, land of the free, provides ample opportunity to simply have a good time. And a lot of people do just that, and often lose sight of the fact that it's the constant flood of new immigrants that makes the good life possible.

The immigrants tended to move into neighborhoods, or create new ones, composed primarily of people from the same nation. By 1920, most major American cities had bustling Italian, Polish, Hungarian, Jewish, Russian, and other ethnic neighborhoods. You could walk down street after street in these areas and not hear a word of English spoken. It was quite common for many of these immigrants, especially the women who stayed at home with the children, never to learn English, or never learn to speak it very well.

Many native-born Americans took a dim view of all these odd-sounding, and odd-looking, foreigners. What few realized was that the immigrants from different countries cast a wary eye on each other as well. It wasn't until the first or second generation of their children born in this country that it was considered acceptable to marry members of the other immigrant groups (even of the same religion). Coming to America was a lot easier than becoming Americans. The children of the immigrants grew up bilingual (often reluctantly; the kids wanted to "be American" and speak nothing but English), and their children learned only a few words of a foreign language to keep their grandparents happy.

The first generation or two of the immigrant experience was rough. As always, the immigrants got the lowest-paying jobs, partly because of the language barriers, partly because the newcomers didn't know their way around, and partly because their own countrymen were ready to take advantage of them. From the beginning, each immigrant group developed its own leadership, and some of those leaders promptly set up sweat shops, where they paid very low wages for very long hours. Getting exploited and cheated by someone who looked and talked like yourself was somehow more bearable than having some native-born American do it.

Some groups were better off than others when it came to getting themselves organized. Jewish immigrants from Eastern Europe benefited from the presence of an earlier wave of German Jews. The latter had become quite successful in America and, despite some embarrassment at the strange dress and customs of their "East European brothers," vigorously organized social and educational groups to speed the process of turning the newcomers into Americans.

The majority of the early-twentieth-century immigrants were Roman Catholic, and the Church mobilized its resources to get the new arrivals settled in. Churches and schools were set up, as well as social agencies. But unlike the case of the Jewish immigrants, there were far greater differences among the Catholic ones, differences that greatly influenced the success of the different groups.

The Italians, in particular, had a very hard time of it. Many were from the countryside and had more difficulty adapting to urban living. Immigrants from rural backgrounds were less enthusiastic about taking advantage of the free public education available in America. They preferred to get their kids out of school and into a job as soon as possible. This was not that much of a problem early in the century, but after World War II, it was noted that Italians were among the least likely to send their kids to college. Only toward the end of the century did that rural antipathy to education disappear. Meanwhile, the rural-versus-urban-origins pattern was played out with other groups. This was rather obvious in the last two decades of the twentieth century, as America admitted many refugees from the Vietnam War. Those refugees coming from ethnic Vietnamese families had the traditional respect for the benefits of education. But the tribal groups, coming from a rural tradition that paid little attention to formal education, did not take advantage of America's educational benefits, and the children fared much less well than the Vietnamese who hit the books.

There was more to it than attitudes toward education. Experience in urban living was a big advantage. Many Latin American immigrants came from rural cultures that did not put a lot of faith in formal education. As a result, it took several generations before the parents and kids became true believers in education and skillful in the ways of urban life.

Italians had another burden—organized crime. In a pattern repeated in Ireland later in the century, a patriotic revolutionary movement had developed into a criminal organization. The "Black Hand" evolved from centuries-old resistance movements against foreign control of Italy. It was only in the 1860s that Italy became a united country, after fourteen hundred years of being split into a multiplicity of smaller states and kingdoms. During that period, the French, Spanish, and Germans often occupied parts of Italy. The Italians, like the Irish, resisted. Like the IRA, the Black Hand (and many similar organizations) stole and extorted to keep the resistance going. When Italy became unified, the Black Hand did not go away, for many of its members had long been spending more of their time as gangsters than freedom fighters. The Black Hand turned into the American Mafia when the Italian gangsters began to prey on all Americans rather than just Italian-Americans. This happened in the 1930s, and a new generation of American-born Italian gangsters resolved to do what the Black Hand had always done, but with American organization and efficiency. The next generation went even further afield from their Black Hand origins and made a large and fatal (for the Mafia) mistake: They did not keep their heads down, and "Mafia" became a popular term. That brought sustained attention from the police and courts. By the end of the century, the Americanized Black Hand was in ruins, but not before millions of law-abiding Italian-Americans had to endure decades of shame and embarrassment because of a relative handful of well-organized thugs among them.

The Italians were not the only immigrant group to go through the gangster phase. The Jews, despite the ministrations of the solicitous German-American Jews, saw many Jewish immigrants, or their children, turn to crime to make their mark. And that they did, although most were out of the business by the 1960s. But the Jewish immigrants also had an advantage, an enthusiasm for education. Their German-American mentors were living examples of how this worked. Through the last decades of the nineteenth century, America's best colleges were turning out Jewish graduates (despite anti-Semitic quotas). One of the ironies of all this was that a popular anti-Semitic belief was that these alien-looking (the beards and articles of religious clothing) Eastern European Jews were mentally deficient. This seemed to be confirmed when, in 1917, the IQ test was used on a wide scale for the first time to test the mental abilities of army recruits. The scores of Jewish recruits were below average, and the anti-Semites had a field day with it. The low scores were later discovered to be a result of so many eager Jewish recruits, with flimsy English skills, plowing through the test anyway. The guys wanted to get into the war and fight, not muck about with paperwork.

Meanwhile, the Eastern European Christians did quite well for themselves in America. They didn't get much attention, except for all those irritating "Polish jokes." The Poles had the last laugh, because when the census takers tallied the score of how well each group of immigrants had done, the Poles were right up there at the top of the list with the Jews from Eastern Europe.

Many of those ethnic neighborhoods formed in the early part of the century, as a means of protection against native-born Americans and all those other foreigners, remain. Although most of the descendants of those immigrants have dispersed to the suburbs and married outside their ethnic groups, many of the "old neighborhoods" survived. This was accomplished by a hard core of people who simply would not leave, no matter how rough and decrepit their old neighborhoods became. Eventually, the neighborhoods revived, with children and grandchildren moving back in from the suburbs and distant cousins from the old country coming to America and looking for familiar faces and a friendly place to get started. History repeated, or rather paraphrased itself, as it often does.

The 18 million immigrants who arrived in America during the first three decades of this century changed the face, and mind, of America for the rest of the century. The effect was much magnified because so many of these immigrants settled in the cities, especially New York City. This is where the new electronic mass media had their network operations. So local New York City stories often became national news. New York was also the national center for publishing and theater. Although the U.S. film business was centered in Southern California, it was founded by many young Jews from New York, who went back east for writers, ideas, and local color. The World War II movie, which set the standard for many other genres, always managed to have an ethnically mixed group of soldiers fighting for the American way. There was invariably an Italian and a Jew from a big city, a Pole and a fellow from the Old South or out West. The officer or senior sergeant would often be of old WASP (White Anglo-Saxon Protestant) stock, descended from someone who came to America several centuries earlier.

Italians went on to dominate many industries, while wincing at the unflattering attention the Mafia, and Italians in general, were getting in the mass media. In another one of those American ironies, many of the principal prosecutors, judges, and politicians who put the Mafia out of business in the last few decades of the century were themselves of Italian ancestry and no doubt relished being able to do what their grandparents had often muttered about doing (quietly, usually in Italian) if they had the chance.

There was an enormous fall in immigrants in the middle of the century. A 1924 law eliminated million-immigrant years and restricted the number of Eastern Europeans and Italians who could get into the country. The Great Depression, World War II, and the Cold War all cut off many of the usual sources of immigration. There were only half a million immigrants in all of the 1930s, and only a million for all of the 1940s (including the many refugees allowed in after World War II). This is in sharp contrast to 1905–7, 1910, 1913–14—all years in which over a million people arrived in America. Immigration increased year by year in the latter part of the century until, in 1989, we had a million-immigrant year again. But the United States population was now over three times what it was in the first three decades of the century, so that million did not have the same effect as the earlier millions.

But there were other factors working to radically change the patterns of immigration to America. For the first six decades of the century, the most common way of reaching the United States was by ship. Jet passenger aircraft changed all that in the 1960s and '70s. Intercontinental travel now became common, and by the 1980s few immigrants arrived by ship. But because of population pressures in Central America and a large, open border, many immigrants were now arriving by foot.

America's southern border has always been wide open. But official immigration from Mexico had numbered only a few hundred people a year for most of the nineteenth century. That began to pick up after 1900, as civil war and general unrest became more common. But there was another form of immigration from Mexico that had been going on longer than the U.S. border had been there. Many Americans in the border area were of Mexican ancestry and had kin in Mexico. Visitors went back and forth regularly, usually avoiding the official crossing points. And just as regularly, unofficial immigrants came north, settled in Mexican-American neighborhoods, and were never noticed. Well, they were noticed, not in the United States, but rather down in Mexico. As population and poverty grew in Mexico, jobs and prosperity flourished up north. Especially after World War II. Millions of Mexicans sneaked into the United States in the last three decades of the twentieth century and took refuge in a growing number of Mexican or Latin American communities around the nation. There came a point in the middle of the twentieth century when these communities were drawing an increasing number of immigrants from Mexico each year. Although it became harder and harder to get across the border, once immigrants were across, all they had to do was make it to the neighborhood where relatives or friends from back in Mexico would be waiting to get them started in their new life. No accurate count can be made of how many Mexicans came across the border illegally this way, but it was apparently in the millions. And Mexicans were not the only ones. Because of the high wages and generally better standard of living, at the end of the century people from all over the world were willing to pay tens of thousands of dollars to get into the United States. From as far away as China and India the illegal refugees came. Spending $20,000 to $50,000 for transportation and guidance by criminal gangs that specialized in this kind of smuggling was actually a good investment.

How good an investment is obvious only if you look at it like an immigrant. Most Americans have lost sight of how cheaply one can live. Recent immigrants from Third World countries have not. Living really cheaply (a dozen men, sleeping in shifts, in a low-rent apartment) and working two jobs fills up the bank account very fast. In fact, many come for just a few years to make a lot of cash and then go home to live off it for the rest of their lives. This is nothing new, but early in the century, pay was not as high nor the ambience as welcoming as it is today. Back then, if a young man did not return to his homeland within ten years (and probably without a huge amount of money) he would have to wait much longer, usually until after he had married and raised children, to return home. For those who came over early in the century, the Great Depression and World War II intervened as well. For the Eastern Europeans, the Cold War and Iron Curtain kept them out of the old country even longer. But many elderly Italians who returned in the 1950s and '60s found themselves strangers in the land of their birth. Their childhood friends were often dead or barely recognizable by now. The Italian-Americans discovered that they had developed a heavy American accent when speaking Italian. The locals soon came to refer to this elderly fellow in their midst as "the americano," even though he had been born in their village at the turn of the century. But that was so long ago, and this was now.

It's not just the fact that America is the richest country in the world that brings people—although one must not forget this has always been the principal reason—but it is also one of the few nations that tolerates a lot of different people. We are all minorities in America. The three biggest ethnic minorities at the end of the century—German (23 percent), Irish (16 percent) and English (13 percent)—barely constitute a majority. And the Irish- and English-Americans still go through the motions of not getting along because of all the nasty things England has done to Ireland over the centuries.

People keep trying to get into America not just to make money but also to have a pleasant place to spend it. That means tolerating a lot more differences than we generally give ourselves credit for. We all came from somewhere else, and whether or not we think about it much, we can't get away from it.

—Crime—

America has always been a violent country. But then, so has the entire Western Hemisphere. Something to do with the frontier mentality and the clash of cultures. But as the century went on, America got more violent. You can get an idea of the scope of this violence from what we spent on police. In 1900, the national spending on police was $1.2 billion (about $15 per capita). By the end of the century, it was over $100 billion ($361 per capita). Why? Apparently the main cause was a change in policing methods. Some of the change was technical, some psychological.

From the 1920s on, more and more police operated from cars rather than foot patrols. The police began to lose contact with the people they were policing. Other industrialized nations kept more police on foot and in touch with the population. But Americans felt it was more efficient to have the police mobile and better able to rush to emergencies. After World War II, the police got radios for their cars. They no longer had to stop and use a telephone. With the radio cars, the police could be controlled from a central office. At first, the new methods seemed to work. Criminals were also using cars, and the radio-equipped police cars were able to chase down the bad guys. It looked good.

We also know from the historical record (which is often ignored in these matters) that crime increases when the economy is booming, while the crime rate is actually lower when times are bad. This was especially true during the Great Depression, when the crime rate came down from the heights it had reached during the prosperous 1920s.

But the biggest causes of increased crime were the ill-conceived post–World War II theories about what caused crime and how best to deal with it. These new theories were accepted by most major police departments until the 1990s.

For example, the experience during the 1920s led to the theory that when we try to prohibit something popular—like alcohol from 1919 to 1934—criminal activity increases. This was certainly the case during the 1920s, and again from the 1960s onward, when the heat was on illegal drug use.

Another theory held that the more young males (eighteen to twenty-four years old) were around, the higher the crime rate. This was seen to happen during the 1960s, as the huge World War II Baby Boom generation came of age. But then the crime rates just kept going into the 1980s, even as the proportion of younger men in the population declined. This was blamed on crack cocaine, a drug that made users violent, as opposed to earlier drugs that brought on a drowsy euphoria. The age angle is interesting, especially since a far higher proportion of the population was young earlier in the century than after World War II. In 1900, the average age of the population was twenty-one. By the end of the century it was thirty-three.

Moreover, in the 1990s, when the crime rate began to decline, one of the areas most responsible for the decline, New York City, was going through an increase in its eighteen- to twenty-four-year-old male population. There was still a lot of crack cocaine around in New York City.

But if we look back further, as many countries have centuries of records on criminal activity, we find that the crime rate also goes up and down with political stability as well as economic prosperity. But basically it fluctuates. A generation or two of high violence leads to a generation or two of much less crime and violence.

Apparently, the biggest cause of lower crime rates at the end of the century was the changes in policing techniques. Effective technology, lots of money, and common sense finally caught up with criminal activity.

In 1900, it was rare for someone to get arrested. Police would administer on-the-spot warnings, or even beatings, to malefactors. This power was sometimes abused, but as long as the peace was kept, no one got too upset about wise guys or an occasional innocent getting hit upside the head with a nightstick. Arresting someone was expensive, because jails were expensive to build and maintain, so if you locked too many people up, you would have no place to put them. Moreover, there were few police cars in 1900, and the average cop walked a beat (less than a square mile) in the more crime-prone urban areas. These cops got to know who was naughty and nice in their areas. The famous line from the 1939 movie *Casablaca*, "Round up the usual suspects," was a bit of early-twentieth-century police wisdom that still applies today.

Late in the twentieth century many police departments noticed that a small number of criminals accounted for the majority of the crimes. These fellows (most were men) were dubbed "career criminals," and special efforts were made to take them off the street. What is interesting is that the concept of "career criminals" was well known to police early in the century, and the line "Round up the usual suspects" made a lot of sense when you knew that the same small group of people were committing most of the crimes.

But once the police got their automobiles (in the 1920s) and then their two-way radios (1940s), there was a lot less contact with the people, and with the career criminals. Police work became less policing a beat and knowing who was out there, and more responding to telephone calls from distressed citizens. After several generations of the police-car business, cops were put back on the beat and modern technology, like cameras and computers, was used to keep better track of who was misbehaving.

But there was a potential pitfall with the cop on the beat, or what later became known as "community policing." The biggest such potential problem was corruption. For the cop to get to know the neighborhood, he had to spend a lot of time there. But the longer a cop was on a particular beat, the more temptation he would face from locals who were willing to pay a little, or a lot, of money if the beat cop would look the other way while some illegal activity was going on. Once a cop got a little corrupted, he could be turned into a criminal himself.

But crooked cops are nothing new, and it was eventually realized that keeping the crime rate down by having the beat cops back was tolerable even with a greater risk of police corruption. Besides, the 1990s crime-fighting methods were not identical to those of the early 1900s. Computerized record keeping (of criminal activity and police resources) allowed police commanders to move cops rapidly to where the criminal activity was. The crooks were not as organized as the cops, and while the bad guys would gravitate toward better criminal opportunities, the better-organized cops were getting there first and in greater numbers.

By the early 1990s, people were desperate for solutions to the growing crime rate. As crime-counting methods became more accurate, the problem loomed even larger, with some 35 million separate crimes being reported annually. About 25 percent of American households had someone who was a crime victim in any given year.

It actually looked worse than it was, for city residents were twice as likely as rural residents to be victims of crimes. Since cities were where the media were, people saw more crime than really existed. Crime had become so pervasive by the last decade of this century that some half of all violent crimes, two fifths of all household crimes, and slightly more than one quarter of all personal thefts were not even reported to the police.

Many people, especially the police, noted some other characteristics of these crimes. Men were more likely to be crime victims than women. The same was true with young people in general, who were more likely to be crime victims than older people. There was also a difference by race, with blacks more likely than any other racial group to be crime victims. Class also made a difference. Lower-income families were more likely to become victims of violent crimes than were members of middle- and upper-income families. On the extremes, young males were most likely to be involved in violent crimes (as perpetrators or victims) and elderly females the least likely. The most likely victims of crime were young black males.

New York City cut its crime rate in half in a few years by, in effect, going back to hundred-year-old policing methods and using computers, statistics, and common sense to go after the career criminals and drug dealers who generated most of the crime. New York had to build a lot more prisons, but the police had the statistics to show how much crime these guys committed when they were out of jail and how much less when they were locked up. The emphasis on arresting people for minor infractions discouraged, as it did a century ago, many young men from going on to more serious crimes. Many other cities followed New York's example, and the national crime rate plunged throughout the 1990s.

More effective policing did not receive universal acclaim for bringing the crime rate down. Criminologists, those academic crime experts who explain to us why crime goes up and down, did not accept the "better police work" explanation. They had good reason not to, for the criminologists had developed enormous influence over police operations in the twentieth century, and the crime drop of the 1990s indicated that many of the criminologists' favorite theories were wrong.

Criminology had gone through a lot of changes since it first appeared in the nineteenth century. Indeed, the criminologists' theories and proposals led to the formation of the first big-city police departments. For thousands of years before that, police work had been done by an assortment of other government officials, from judges, sheriffs, and—when muscle was needed—government troops. But really large cities were something new, and so was their crime rate. Early in the twentieth century, the theory of criminal behavior was that career criminals were mentally defective or physically different. This fell out of favor during the 1920s, to be replaced by the new discipline of sociology. The new theories, which held sway until the 1950s, proposed that criminals were the victims of their own environment. Out of this came the theory that poverty caused crime. Many police took a dim view of this theory, as they noted that crime went down during the Great Depression, when the number of poor people was much greater.

From the 1960s to the present, various theories of criminal behavior proliferated. Some were based on Marxist class struggle, while feminists had their own theory based on gender differences. Criminologists had largely agreed that police efforts would have little effect on crime rates and that nothing less than fundamental changes in society (elimination of poverty and race/gender/sexual orientation discrimination) would be needed to make a dent in the crime rate. All these theories were directly threatened by improved police methods, largely a return to the methods common before the city officials began to implement criminologists' theories in the 1950s. It took a few years before many of the criminology experts would admit that, perhaps, new police methods could reduce crime.

The arguments over what causes, and contains, crime will go on into the new century. Meanwhile, most people are happy enough to discover that there is an effective way to deal with it.

——Dressing Up, and Down——

More money makes people more clothes-conscious, right? Nope. Fashion mania peaked during the Roaring Twenties, at least to the degree that everyone was running out to buy more clothes than they had ever done before. For the rest of the century, the clothing business was trying to play catch-up. It got so bad that completely new styles of clothing had to be invented, using radically new materials, along with aggressive marketing methods to move the goods.

We entered the twentieth century with very different attitudes about clothing. For one thing, people had a lot less to wear. There were basically two types of clothing for most people: work and dress-up. The latter was usually restricted to a suit or good-quality dress for church and special occasions. Few people went to work in suits, which were quite expensive. It was difficult enough to keep clothes clean, there being no washing machines or dry cleaning.

This all began to change in the first decades of the century. New developments in clothing design changed what we wore and how we wore it. The zipper came along in 1913, although buttons still remained dominant for several decades, until the cost of zippers came down. While the zipper changed how clothing was held together, the 1957 invention of Velcro changed it still more. But zippers and Velcro were practical items, and high fashion tended to use the more stylish buttons.

Through the end of the century, high fashion fought a losing battle against the practical and, in effect, antifashionable. From the 1950s on, many of the young, increasingly the biggest consumers of clothes, sought high fashion in low places. This was a unique trend; in previous centuries, it was adults who spent the most on clothes. But in the twentieth century there was more money to spend, and a lot of it was spent on clothing for the kids. Adolescents were also able to get jobs and spend the money on themselves. They bought a lot of clothes.

In the 1950s, it was the "greaser" look, the clothing of someone who spent a lot of time tinkering with a hot rod in a garage. From the 1960s on, it was the "downtrodden" look. You were in fashion if you looked poor. Naturally, the people who were really poor preferred to dress up, especially with brand-name clothes. But the second half of the twentieth century was a time of a huge middle class, and their slovenly attired progeny were by far the majority. The kids were always looking for something new. The more radical the better. The "youth look" changed clothing from a primarily adult-oriented product to something very different. Aggressive promotion, another twentieth-century phenomenon, made trends in fashion travel faster and more broadly.

What most defined twentieth-century clothing was innovation in how clothing was put together and the materials used. But what changed the look and feel of clothing more than anything else in this century was the development of so many artificial fibers. The first was rayon, appearing just before World War I. It was made from wood pulp and was in many ways superior to existing cotton and woolen fabrics. Rayon was highly absorbent, soft, and comfortable, and it draped well. Because it was synthetic, it could be manufactured in versions possessing different characteristics. Rayon was basically a superior replacement for cotton and wool in clothing, blankets, and many household items. It took a few decades for the price to come down, but when it did, in 1948 per capita annual use of fibers had rayon in second place (6.3 pounds), behind cotton (27 pounds) and ahead of wool (4.9 pounds).

But rayon was only the beginning. Acetate fiber was invented in the 1920s (also made from wood pulp). Once woven into cloth, it had a luxurious feel and appearance, could be modified to possess different lusters, was soft, and it draped well, was fast drying, and shrink-, moth-, and mildew-resistant. Acetate proved most popular for women's clothes (blouses, dresses, linings) and for draperies and upholstery. Because it was new, high-tech and useful, it was very popular.

Nylon came along in the 1930s, and in 1950 there were acrylic fibers. These, like nylon, were made from oil. Acrylic had another set of useful characteristics. It had excellent wickability (drying quickly to move moisture from body surfaces), could be made to have characteristics of both cotton and wool, was resistant to moths, oil, and chemicals, and was very resistant to sunlight damage. Acrylic became a popular replacement for wool in the design of sporting clothes.

Perhaps one of the most famous, or infamous, of the synthetic fibers came along in 1953. It was polyester, and it looked like the perfect fabric. It was strong; resistant to stretching, shrinking, and most chemicals; quick-drying; crisp and resilient when wet or dry; wrinkle-, mildew-, and abrasion-resistant; it retained heat-set pleats and creases (permanent press); and it was easily washed. It was also relatively cheap to make. But it was such a good fabric that it was distinctive, and all over the place. It had a special feel, and many began to associate that feel with cheap, synthetic clothes. This was not meant as a compliment, and at the end of the century it still wasn't.

While the new synthetic fibers attracted some derision when they were used as replacements for traditional fibers, they still attracted positive attention from those looking for something new and different. But the greatest success of synthetics was in new clothing categories. Sport and leisure-time clothing, a category unique to the twentieth century, grew up with synthetics, and entire new forms of fashion were created as a result. Leisure wear and sportswear grew into a major clothing category because of the synthetics. One might say, without too much exaggeration, that these categories are the main ones at the end of the twentieth century. These lines of clothing were designed for comfort and utility, and this approach to lifestyle has defined the latter half of the twentieth century in the United States. People are exercising less, but they still like to wear the clothes.

The twentieth century was, in general, full of clothing improvements that made women's lives more comfortable. For example, in 1914 the brassiere was patented and became a common form of women's underwear from the 1920s on. Although 1920s female fashion featured flat chests, most women in the first half of the twentieth century relished the added comfort bras provided. The invention of the bra didn't come out of nowhere. It was a response to the popularity of the blouse-and-skirt combination that had appeared in the late nineteenth century. Previously, the only ways to keep the breasts in place were the ancient ones of binding (cheap), corsets (expensive), or wearing a close-fitting chemise under the blouse and skirt. None of these solutions were very comfortable; the bra was. However, the bra has been invented, and then fallen out of fashion, many times over the centuries. The "new" one was invented specifically to solve the problem of what to wear under a strapless gown. The inventor was the lady with the dress problem, and she ran with the idea because she saw the commercial possibilities. Twentieth-century engineering techniques led to much better designed bras, something engineers get little credit for.

Nylon stockings went on wide sale in 1940, providing most women with the synthetic equivalent of silk stockings. Four million pairs were sold in the first four days. These were something women really, really wanted because they were comfortable and looked so good. Spandex appeared in 1959. This was a highly elastic fiber that continuously conformed to the body, stretching and then snapping back into place. Nylon hose, and later pantyhose, made use of spandex to produce a very form-fitting and popular product. In the sixties, as hemlines rose, pantyhose fashion became imperative. In the years since, pantyhose have come to dominate women's hosiery.

Women have a thing about shoes. Men just don't understand it. From the beginning of the century, women were offered an increasing number and variety of shoes. And they sold. In 1900, the common fashion for women's shoes was a high-heeled, high-top shoe that sold for $50 to $100 a pair. Low-cut oxfords cost about the same. Black was the most common color. From the 1920s on, the styles of women's shoes proliferated enormously, especially as more women got involved in sports. In the last third of the century, there was a virtual explosion of women's shoe styles. It became noticeable, a dirty little secret finally revealed to the world. Women looked a little embarrassed, shrugged, and kept on buying shoes. Most prices were still $50 to $100.

Clothing purchases grew early in the century, peaking at $918 per capita in 1929. Then the Great Depression came, and by 1934, clothing spending had fallen by half. It wasn't until the late 1940s that the rate of clothing purchasing regained its 1929 level. But then a strange thing happened: Clothing purchases did not keep up with per capita income increases for the rest of the century. By 2000, people were spending only about 50 percent more than they did in the peak year of 1929. This did not take into account the millions of mothers and grandmothers who, until after World War II, made a lot of the clothing for their families. Inexpensive sewing machines became quite popular in the first half of the century. And the sharp decline in clothing purchases during the Great Depression made it mandatory for many women to sew their own clothes to keep their families dressed. The sale of cloth and patterns became a huge business right through the 1950s because of this. So when you take into account the larger families and the higher proportion of children to adults in 1929, the adults at the end of the century come off as less clothes-conscious than their great-grandparents.

For dressing up, the twentieth century was an embarrassment of riches, and in the second half of the century, most Americans just took it for granted. Clothes became disposable as never before. It was common for people (especially women) to buy clothes that they would never wear. Little known by most Americans is the use of much thrown-away or donated-to-charities clothing that is cleaned, jammed into shipping containers, and sold by the ton to wholesalers in poor countries. Which explains why you see so many Asians and Africans on the TV news wearing last year's American fashions.

So, in the end, America dresses not only itself but much of the world.

──Freud Takes a Pill──

Many people may not have noticed it, but in the late twentieth century, the psychoanalyst has been largely replaced by pills. In the first decade of the century, one of the hottest things in medicine was Dr. Sigmund

Freud and his psychoanalysis technique. Freud was one of the leading thinkers in the field of psychiatry, that field of medicine that deals with the mind, and the medical treatments are called psychotherapy.

This has always been a dicey area of medical treatment.

Until 1900, the most effective medical practices had been those that fixed something you could see or feel. Stitching up wounds, setting broken bones, and various forms of surgery were cause-and-effect medicine. Mental problems were less obvious in their causes or treatments. This was especially true of mental problems that did not send people completely over the top. Those poor souls were locked up somewhere to protect both them and the public (usually to the detriment of the patient, but that's another story). But for many people, the best way to deal with their troubled minds was to talk to someone. For thousands of years, friends, family, and clergy had dealt with this. As medicine became more of a profession, doctors got involved in dealing with mental illness. Freud developed a theory that many of these mental problems were due to past, now forgotten, events that were still there in the patient's subconscious. Freud developed a therapy in which the doctor (a psychiatrist) talked to the patient in one-hour sessions, often for years, to help the patient recover these lost events and deal with them. Thus was born psychoanalysis, which was all the rage among those who could afford those weekly sessions with their psychoanalyst.

The only people who *could* afford psychoanalysis were the middle class and the rich, and it became fashionable to have your own "analyst." Film celebrities did so, and the psychoanalyst and his (it was usually a he, a father figure, very Freudian) couch entered the popular culture. While psychoanalysis became fashionable and popular, there was no scientific basis to support it. People did it largely because it was popular to do, and many felt that it did help.

In the 1950s, drugs began to appear that addressed various forms of severe mental distress in a direct way. The drugs worked, and people who had been written off (and locked away in asylums) for years were suddenly cured. Well, not completely. The early drugs had side effects for some users that caused them to stop taking their medication, thus prompting the mental condition to return. At the same time, more drugs arrived that dealt with anxiety and depression. Bit by bit, patients discovered that a faster, cheaper, and more certain cure was available from pills.

The psychoanalysts fought back for several decades, but they could not refute the number of cures resulting from the new drugs versus the endless psychoanalysis sessions that kept the patient under control (and a lot less affluent), but never cured. By the end of the century, fewer than 2 percent of mental patients underwent psychoanalysis. Two thirds of medical schools that train psychiatrists no longer teach Freud's techniques.

While Freud and his techniques have been somewhat debunked and largely replaced by drugs, one must remember that Freud was proposing a technique that had worked for thousands of years. One person, through interest and conversation, can, and often does, change the mind of another. But drugs can deal with pervasive problems like anxiety and depression. Indeed, drug-based psychiatry has since launched a search for many conditions that no one knew existed before. In the 1950s, the treatable (and billable) psychiatric conditions listed by mental-health professionals numbered a few dozen. Now there are over four hundred, and more drugs to obtain quicker cures, although sometimes there are cures for conditions no one is sure even exist.

So we are right back to where we started when Freud came along a century ago.

——Good Eating——

You think a hundred years have changed America's eating habits? Think again. A century ago, people consumed a lot of meat. But we did a lot more physical work. As the century went on, we adopted a healthier diet. But here's the catch: Our diet has come full circle since 1900. At the end of the century, we had about the same eating habits we had in 1900. A lot of meat and potatoes. Eating healthy was no fun; steak was. In 1900, the per capita consumption of meat was about 170 pounds. In 2000 it was also 170 pounds. But there were a lot of interesting changes between the two 170s.

In 2000, people eat 20 percent more fat than the 1900 crowd, and

15 percent fewer carbohydrates. Same amount of protein, but less fruit, vegetables, and bread. We're a bit larger these days too, not just in height but also in girth. In a word, we are overfed. A lot of it has to do with lack of exercise. In 1900, there were few cars, and people thought nothing of walking a mile or so to get somewhere. More jobs involved strenuous labor, and housework had few machines to ease the physical burden. First radio, then television, kept people, especially children, inside and immobile. Sopping up what the TV offered was often accompanied by a side order of high-fat junk food.

But it wasn't just more opportunities to eat and fewer to exercise. The kind of food we ate changed. In 1900, most food was bought raw. As the century went on, more and more food was available already "processed." Now, processed food was not new to the twentieth century; it was one of the great developments of the nineteenth century. Canning and flash-freezing made it possible to provide more nutritious food during the long winters, and this was a truly beneficial innovation. But after 1900, we had the century of "fun foods."

Some snack items were available in 1900. Popcorn was here before the Europeans arrived, as were peanuts and sundry fruits and berries. But the development of refrigeration in the twentieth century gave us more readily available ice cream. People are eating over ten times as much ice cream in 2000 as they were in 1900. Then came the realization by food manufacturers that you could manipulate the taste and texture of foods to enormously increase their sales. Thus was born the snack-food industry, which went on to provide the basis for the junk-food diet many Americans adopted in the latter half of the twentieth century. If something is crunchy, salty, and sweet, people will keep eating it. This lesson was not lost on other food businesses. Fast-food chain restaurants became a major force in American eating habits from the 1960s on. Aside from offering lower prices, faster service, and more attractive premises than what came before, they also offered the same addictive taste sensation as did the snack-food manufacturers.

Another often unnoticed aspect of the fast-food revolution was the demise of many diners, greasy spoons, and family restaurants. The fast-food outlets took away so much business that these older eating establishments no longer had enough customers to keep them going. These older forms of eating out faded away gradually, only rarely being noticed after they were gone. But with them went some healthier eating habits.

By the end of the century, we have come back to one urban custom that was beginning to disappear in 1900: eating out most of the time. In 1900, this was because many living accommodations in cities did not have kitchens, so you had to eat out. In 2000, most everyone has a kitchen, but many also lack the time or inclination to cook. It doesn't cost much more just to subsist on a fast-food diet. And that has not increased much in cost over the last century. In 1900, fifty cents or a dollar got you a cup of coffee and a piece of plain cake (now replaced by a pastry or doughnut). A few dollars got you some stew and bread, or some meat with veggies on the side. Even in 1900, ethnic food was beginning to show up in the big cities. Some of it was quite cheap and nutritious, especially if Italian or Chinese.

There's a lot more to eat today than there was in 1900, and unfortunately, too many of us try to eat it all.

___ Olympic Feats of Bureaucratic ___ Development

Physical fitness has been a big deal this century, and it shows in the constantly falling athletic records. Or does it? What has increased athletic performance in this century has less to do with working out and more to do with paperwork.

A hundred years ago, athletes were much less capable than the year-2000 jocks. Not only did this century see an unprecedented increase in life span, but also a dramatic increase in athletic performance. The Olympic Games were revived, after a fifteen-hundred-year hiatus, in 1896. Except for interruption by major wars, these games were held every four years. The table on page 45 shows the results for three events that were run in all the years indicated. The marathon is a supreme test of endurance, a run of some 40 kilometers. Results show hours, minutes, and seconds to finish. The 100-meter dash is the ultimate test of human speed. Results are shown in seconds. The 1,500-

EVENT	1900	1924	1936	1952	1972	1996
Marathon	2:59:45	2:41:22	2:29:19	2:23:03	2:12:19.8	2:12:36
100 meters	11.0	10.6	10.3	10.4	10.14	9.84
1,500 meters	4:06.2	3:53.6	3:47.8	3:45.1	3:36.3	3:35.78

meter run is rather in between. Results are shown in minutes and seconds. From 1900 to 1996, the top marathon time declined 26 percent, the 100-meter dash 11 percent and the 1,500-meter run 12 percent.

Actually, all the increased performance was a result not of the entire population's becoming stronger and faster but mainly of better selection and training. Nowhere was this more evident than in the communist nations from the 1950s to 1990. Before the end of the Cold War, the communist countries made it a major objective to win the greatest number of Olympic events. In typical communist fashion, this was to show the superiority of the socialist system, and of course, any means available were to be used. This included illegal drugs to enhance athletic performance. The main reason these drugs were outlawed was that, while the athlete would perform better for a while, there was long-term damage to the athlete's health. But for the communist coaches, the ends justified the means. All the coaches had to worry about was getting caught by the Olympic officials. If the athletes later got sick, that was the price they had to pay to build socialism. Or at least socialism's reputation.

The performance-enhancing drugs became a major factor only in the last decades of the century. The real advantage the communists had was their ability to comb their entire population of children for potentially world-class athletes. The chosen kids were generally taken away from their parents and raised in special schools for young athletes. The parents were paid off, and the kids themselves were made to understand that the rewards were great for those who won Olympic medals. For the losers, there might be jobs as coaches in second-rate schools. But the winners did win big by the standards of the ramshackle communist economies.

Other nations did not examine every child to find and develop those with athletic talent. In fact, most athletic endeavors in the West were seen as a part of one's education, to be put aside once schooling was finished. The communists demonstrated that this selection and training process was an excellent method for producing exceptional athletes and breaking performance records. Noncommunist nations provided incentives only in some sports, and few of these were Olympic events. Moreover, this selection process was unique in history and the major reason records were broken again and again in this century.

The communists had a further advantage in that for most of this century the Olympics were only for amateur athletes. Even though the communist athletes worked full-time at developing their athletic skills, technically they were amateurs (often, on paper, military officers or trainers). It was an open secret that the Olympic officials addressed (by allowing professionals to compete) only about the time these communist nations collapsed in the late 1980s. But as long as it was "amateurs only," the best noncommunist athletes could not compete, thus allowing the communist athletes to walk off with a disproportionate number of medals and world records.

The marathon race, and the vast increase in number of participants and decrease in running times, demonstrates another twentieth-century trend. The marathon was basically a twentieth-century invention, first run in 1896, when the Olympic Games were held for the first time since the fourth century A.D. Such long-distance running had never been practiced as a sport, although some tribes used it as a hunting technique (literally running their prey to death). After 1896, many amateur athletes took up marathon running as a sport. After World War II, better shoes and training methods improved times, and from the 1970s, the introduction of large purses in major races prompted many of the better amateurs to go professional and train to an even higher level of performance.

In the last few decades of the twentieth century, many Olympic sports became commercial events. The larger and larger prizes enabled more athletes to turn pro and break more records. This trend also forced the Olympic officials to drop the ban on professionals, lest the Olympics turn into a contest between second-rate athletes.

The twentieth century did not suddenly create a lot of super athletes; it simply provided the money and time for those ever-present natural athletes to train harder, and break more records.

TWO

ENTERTAINMENT

THE twentieth century was the century of entertainment. Never before was there so much of it, and everyone enjoyed themselves as never before. Most of us take all the entertainment for granted, but in 1900 there was not much to be had. People pretty much had to entertain themselves. No radio or TV, and live entertainment was expensive and not generally available outside the cities. Movies were just getting started, but they were without sound, only in black and white, and wildly popular. The phonograph was also an expensive, and primitive, gadget for the middle and upper classes. Folks might not have had much entertainment back in 1900, but they could see what was coming, and it probably felt really good.

Note: All dollar amounts are given in terms of year-2000 dollars. That is, they are adjusted for inflation and represent the dollar value at the end of the twentieth century. If you want to see what the actual money values were for a year, see the Appendix.

——An Avalanche of Media——

Nothing defined the twentieth century more than mass media. It not only described what went on, but also went a long way toward shaping events. And that shaping was going on from the first day of the century.

Mass media is not a twentieth-century development. Mass media arose in the early nineteenth century as a result of the industrial revolution and the introduction of steam-powered machinery. Before this, printers could do only 250 one-sided impressions an hour using mostly muscle. This made possible a lot of expensive, small-circulation papers. Introduction of the steam-powered rotary press in the early 1800s changed that, as there were now economies of scale. The publishers that could afford the expensive new steam-driven presses had a price advantage, and soon there were fewer newspapers, but each with a much larger circulation. The new mass-circulation papers quickly discovered that their vastly increased number of readers attracted more advertisers, who placed a lot more ads than they would have placed in the older, smaller-circulation newspapers.

Politicians also noted the difference large-circulation newspapers had on public opinion. Before the steam press, the smaller-circulation newspapers were read mainly by the better-educated and wealthier people. Indeed, until the nineteenth century, only property owners could vote in the United States. But after the Civil War, it gradually changed so that all adult male citizens could vote (women did not get the vote until 1919). At that point, all those new voters reading all those inexpensive daily newspapers began to behave rather differently than the previous generations of voters. Since they were less educated and more easily swayed by what they read in a newspaper, it was soon realized that newspapers, now a mass media, had become a major political force. American participation in the Spanish-American War was driven by several newspaper chains that were trying to increase circulation. One publisher, William Randolph Hearst, replied to one of his illustrators in Cuba who was complaining that fighting had not broken out yet, "You furnish the pictures and I'll furnish the war." Hearst proceeded to do exactly that.

But these newly minted media moguls were not just warmongers, they were shaping public opinion in many areas. Influencing politics was always popular, for certain new laws could directly affect the newspaper business. Getting the right people elected and the right laws passed became a sometimes blatant intention of newspapers. In most nations, the newspapers were frankly partisan, and often owned by the government or political parties. Even seemingly independent newspapers were commonly bought off. If the paper could not be bribed, individual journalists could. This practice has continued until the present. Only in America did the concept of an independent press take hold, and even then many newspapers identified, openly or via the tone of their reporting, with one political party or another. While the American style of journalism gradually became popular in other nations throughout the twentieth century, America remains the one nation where the concept of an independent press has really taken hold. More or less.

A century ago, the terms "muckraker" (one who digs up scandals for hot stories) and "the yellow press" (sensationalism for the sake of making a buck) were common. It all sounds familiar, doesn't it? But that was only the beginning. Mass-circulation newspapers were already there a century ago, but in the twentieth century, print was cut down to size by totally new media.

First came video, in the form of silent movies. These first began to appear in the 1890s. Thomas Edison had invented the basic technology a decade earlier. At first there were what we would call peep shows. But by 1908, the film projector had been perfected and put into wide use. There were some ten thousand movie theaters operating in the United States in that year. Half the population saw at least one movie a week. There were over a hundred thousand people involved in making and showing movies in America. And it would be another twenty years before movies went from silent to sound. The movies were mainly an entertainment, although some films were made with the intent to change people's opinions. It wasn't until sound came in that newsreels became common and more movies began to carry a really powerful "message." Nevertheless, movies exposed millions of people to information and entertainment they would otherwise have never seen. This began changing the world.

Next came the radio. The "wireless telegraph" was developed during the 1890s, and by the first decade of the twentieth century, there were primitive versions of what we now know as radio. It wasn't until the 1920s that the first commercial radio stations began to appear. But by the end of the 1920s, radio was a mass medium. Radio sets were relatively cheap, costing a few days' wages. By the 1930s, most of the population of America could be reached by radio broadcasts. Radio began to replace newspapers in some respects, for no newspaper could get out a story on a breaking news item as quickly as radio. Moreover, radio could take you right to the scene of a breaking story. This was first done with sporting events, followed soon by natural disasters and political speeches and even advertising.

Even as radio was proliferating, television was invented. While, technically, TV was ready for public use in the late 1920s, the Great Depression of the 1930s, then World War II prevented this from happening until the late 1940s. But once TV did become available, it spread even faster than radio did. The newspapers' ability to mobilize public opinion was quickly overtaken by radio and its ability to provide immediate news. TV didn't have immediacy at first, for the broadcasting equipment took several decades to become as portable as radio reporters' gear. But TV did add the enormous impact of pictures. On-the-spot radio reporting was filtered through the reporter; TV video and sound were the real thing, and people took notice. TV quickly became the principal transmitter of sports, disasters, political events, and, of course, wars.

But TV did not replace newspapers and radio; it simply added another huge wave to all the mass media people were being hit with. The three forms of mass media worked together, each adding its own special element. Newspapers continued to provide depth to the reporting. If you wanted all the words, and a lot of the opinions, you read the newspaper. If you wanted breaking news immediately, you listened to the radio, which soon had twenty-four-hour news stations and could be listened to anywhere, especially in a car or while you were walking around.

By the 1980s, a new method of delivering television programming became widely available: cable. Broadcast over the air, there was a limit to how many TV channels could be delivered in any one area. There were only so many frequencies available. Cable made it possible to deliver many more channels, and with much better clarity. One result of cable was twenty-four-hour TV news stations. The first was CNN, but more followed, as well as cable channels for every conceivable interest. This turned out to be more promise than performance. As cable channels proliferated, you heard a lot of people saying, "Five hundred channels and nothing to watch." Like many new technologies, cable was oversold. But there was still something there that people wanted: better reception and some additional channels.

A more riveting development of the 1980s was lighter TV broadcasting gear. Now TV reporters could lug around a portable satellite dish to send their pictures out in real time. So when the 1991 Gulf War got hot with the United States bombing campaign, people worldwide were able to watch the bombing live from Baghdad. Still, many people heard the news first while listening to a radio in a car or simply as a common form of background noise in the home or at work. And if you wanted all the details, you grabbed a newspaper the next day.

There were other ways in which the older forms of mass media developed. Radio, in particular, constantly developed new uses. Since most of the world's population is still illiterate, as it was in 1900, radio was the perfect way to reach these people with news and, all too often, propaganda. As radios became cheaper after World War II, many isolated villages full of illiterate people could afford a radio. It became a form of entertainment and a way for the government to get the official word across cheaply. In the 1960s, transistor radios became common. The big advantage of transistor radios was that they were inherently cheaper than the older models that used vacuum tubes, and they could economically run off batteries. In many parts of the world, the one industrial "luxury" the locals would scrimp and save to buy was transistor radios and the batteries to run them.

Radio also developed a hobbyist following, something neither cinema nor TV could do because the equipment was so expensive. Indeed, the first radio stations were created by hobbyists using equipment they often built themselves. These "ham radio operators" still exist, although the World Wide Web has cut into their ranks. Hams used longer-range shortwave frequencies. If the conditions were right, hams could reach anywhere on the planet. Some of the earliest government-sponsored radio stations used shortwave, the better to send their version of the news worldwide. It was considered another form of diplomacy. And it worked, for in many nations with a government-controlled, and often quite biased press, the locals sought shortwave broadcasts from other nations, particularly Britain's BBC World Service, for a more balanced version of the news.

Many dictatorships in this century jammed foreign shortwave broadcasts (by sending out a stronger signal on the same frequency) to keep their people in the dark and under control. Even owning a shortwave radio receiver became a crime in some nations, particularly the communist ones. But no jamming is effective all the time, and the BBC and other stations got through. This was one of the many reasons most communist governments, and dictatorships in general, had disappeared by the 1990s.

Another offshoot of transistors was the portable tape recorder. Various forms of voice recording had been available since the late nineteenth century, but all were cumbersome, bulky, and expensive. But by the 1970s, portable magnetic tape players had become almost as cheap as portable radios. Opposition politicians in nonindustrial nations found that they could distribute tape cassettes full of speeches and other information to their followers. Such a technique was a key element in overthrowing the shah of Iran in the late 1970s. An Islamic country, Iran had a tradition of Muslim religious leaders preaching sermons against a secular government, and it was these recorded sermons that mobilized the largely illiterate and devout population against the Westernized shah. This technique continues to be used in Muslim nations, and any others where there is a tradition of compelling public speaking. If you can't get in via radio, you can sneak in cassettes. No one has come up with a way to stop cassettes from being passed from hand to hand.

As if there weren't enough news available, in the 1990s the Internet arrived, and it grew even faster than the earlier mass media. It took radio thirty-eight years before it regularly reached 50 million people. It took television only thirteen years to do the same. Cable TV took only ten years. It took the World Wide Web only five years. By the end of the century, in less than ten years, nearly half of all Americans had access to the Internet and its easy-to-use World Wide Web of information and news.

The Internet began in the 1960s as an experimental system able to survive a nuclear war. The system turned out to be robust enough to survive the anarchy of the commercial networks that had developed since the late 1970s. The World Wide Web tied everyone together and, more important, allowed anyone with simple (and cheap) software tools to become a "publisher."

By the 1990s, it became common to hear of "data overload." The World Wide Web was the last straw, and the end was not in sight. Newspapers and magazines put up Web pages with all, or much, of their paper content on-line. For news junkies, it was paradise.

By the late 1990s, radio stations were feeding their material over the World Wide Web for anyone on the Web to hear from their personal computer, or PC. At first this seemed something only a geek could love, or use. But it soon became useful for a lot of people traveling or now living far from their previous favorite radio stations. Web radio became very popular with sports fans wishing to hear the hometown sporting events or people desiring news from other regions or countries. Even many foreign radio stations were putting their feed onto the Web.

PC manufacturers were openly upgrading their hardware and software so they could handle TV via the World Wide Web. This won't become common for another year or two, but it will make information overload more obvious.

Ironically, the World Wide Web, which provided more information than any of the previous mass media, also provided a means to navigate the ocean of data. "Search engines" became an entirely new media tool on the World Wide Web. These were Web pages using powerful software to constantly search out new Web pages and index them so that users could easily find specific bits of information. By the late 1990s, there were at least half a dozen major search-engine sites (Yahoo, Excite, HotBot, etc.) as well as several "super-search engines" that used all the available search engines to find something. The search engines were not perfect, but they enabled the overwhelmed user to find the elusive bits of information among over a hundred million Web pages.

The media flood showed no sign of subsiding as the century ended. People are learning how to cope better, but it's still a wall of information that just makes many feel helpless.

——Great Unknown Innovators of Cinema——

Humans are visual creatures. Our memories are visual, and most people's most vivid memories are from movies they have seen. This is something unique to the twentieth century, and what is often forgotten are the people who invented the techniques and have since been overlooked. It was a series of individuals who came up with the hundreds of specialized techniques and ideas that make movies work.

Movies got started in the 1890s, with the development of the Kinetoscope. Thomas Edison invented this, and it was meant to be viewed by one person at a time, sort of an early peep show. The first commercial use of these devices was in New York City in 1894, where for about $1.50 you could watch a few minutes of what would today be called home movies. In France, the same technology projected onto a large screen in front of an audience proved much more popular. By 1900, cinema (what the French called movies) was all the rage, the latest and most popular bit of technology for a new century.

Movies developed in strange ways. In 1933, the first drive-in movie opened in New Jersey. Capacity was five hundred cars, admission was $3.30 per car. Eventually the drive-ins became a victim of television and affluence. Smaller families and larger-screen TV sets took away the economic incentive to view movies at a drive-in. Television was a catastrophe for the movie business, initially. But until TV hit the market, no one knew.

Movies had about half a century to get big—really, really big. Then TV cut into their business, but it also made the movie-production companies even larger once TV stations realized that it was more profitable to use filmed shows rather than live ones.

The history of American filmmaking is pretty simple. Americans began making movies, a lot of them. Americans developed techniques that made their movies generally better than anyone else's and quickly took over the international film market. But what is little known are the handful of innovators who created many of the techniques that gave United States movies their competitive edge. To correct that oversight herewith some of the **great unknown innovators** of American cinema.

Thomas Edison, the inventor of American movie technology, didn't like motion pictures and believed they would never catch on as a popular entertainment. But **William Kennedy Laurie Dickson**, an English engineer, disagreed. Knowing of Edison's work on filmmaking technology, Dickson convinced Edison to hire him in 1883. In 1888, Edison had Dickson look into what everyone else was doing in filmmaking. Dickson went after the assignment with vigor. By late 1890, he had put together a crude movie camera and photographed a trial film featuring a fellow researcher moving about. He called the film *Monkeyshines* and showed it to Edison. His boss was impressed, and this led to the first commercial American movie business, the Kinetograph company, showing short peep-show films. Despite the commercial success of the Kinetoscope viewers, Dickson knew he could do better. He convinced a skeptical Edison to acquire superior filmmaking patents and move toward longer movies that could be displayed for audiences. Edison was on record as considering this a dead end. In 1895, Dickson produced the Vitascope, a large camera and projector system that made it possible to film and project longer movies. At this point, Edison tired of his eager subordinate. Dickson took the hint and went off on his own. He founded the American Biograph Company and developed an improved version of the Vitascope. Dickson released its first film and eventually became a major producer of films. He then sold most of his shares in American Biograph and returned to England, but not before single-handedly starting the American film industry and creating much of the technology and the filmmaking techniques needed to get things started.

———

Edwin S. Porter came to America in 1895 and obtained work with Edison's Vitascope company. He was in charge of setting up the equipment for the first movie screening in 1896. He left Edison for other film jobs for a few years, but returned in 1900, this time as a producer and director. Porter proceeded to invent or perfect many basic filmmaking techniques. These included night photography, time-lapse filming, mixing documentary film with new footage, and the use of a story line and film techniques to enhance the drama. Porter directed the first dramatic American film, *The Great Train Robbery,* in 1903. Among the modern techniques pioneered here was the dramatic climax, jump shots (from one viewpoint to another), low-angle shots, perspective setups, close-ups, vantage-point shots, cross-cutting to different scenes to give the audience a feeling of being led through the story, contrast shots to show cause and effect, and the use of a script. This movie had a cast of forty, huge for the time. Most important, Porter demonstrated the importance of editing all the footage shot. Before this, what was shot was generally what was shown. The twelve-minute *Great Train Robbery* electrified everyone, including Edison. Investors lined up to back additional films by Porter. But Porter had shown how it could be done, and many others began making hugely popular movies. This caused a flood of films. Porter tired of the grind and left Edison in 1909 to form his own company. He sold that after a year and became an independent producer. But the thrill was gone, and the film pioneer retired from the business in 1915. He established all the basic techniques of modern filmmaking in a few years, and nearly every film made since has followed the patterns set by Porter.

———

Twenty years after *The Great Train Robbery,* movies were a major leisure-time activity in America. Some 40 million Americans were going to the movies each week. About half of them were kids (under eighteen years). But most films were made for an adult audience, and this was a major draw for adolescents. Sex, crime, and not-so-happy endings were becoming more common themes. Moreover, many film stars behaved just as badly offscreen, leading to a number of highly publicized scandals featuring real-life rape, murder, adultery, drugs, alcohol (now illegal), and all manner of bad examples for the youth of America.

The heads of the major studios noted the rising clamor from morally correct interest groups and sought to head off possible government regulation by forming an organization (the Motion Picture Producers and Distributors of America, Inc., or MPPDA) in 1922 to rein in the unsavory content of many films. They enlisted a prominent Republican lawyer and politician, **Will Hays,** to head the organization. Hays jumped in with both feet, drawing up blacklists of Hollywood regulars who were making offensive films, calling for morals clauses in studio contracts, and maintaining a highly visible public-relations campaign for the changes he had in mind. Some powerful directors did not go along, so some racy (and very profitable) films continued to be produced. Finally, in 1930, Hays decided that persuasion was not working and pushed through the Production Code (or "Hays Code"). This was a detailed list of what was not allowed in films. It was now easy for any censors to decide what was an acceptable movie and what was not. The distributors would simply not allow any film that was not code-compliant to be shown in the theaters they controlled. From 1930 to the mid-1960s, the code determined what could be shown in a movie. Among the no-nos were dead bodies, narcotics, drinking, sex, gambling, suggestive dancing, frilly lingerie, the bad guys winning, and the ever-popular inside of a woman's thigh.

Like the prohibition of alcohol from 1919 to 1934, the prohibition of racy filmmaking was not popular with most moviegoers. But it was politically correct for public figures and politicians to back this self-censorship. Also like the prohibition of booze, film censorship didn't last. Directors constantly tested the code, and over the years wore it down. In the 1960s, the code had become a toothless tiger and was replaced, in 1968, with the current G, PG, R, etc., series of ratings. The Hays Code slowed down, and cooled down, Hollywood. It also gave foreign films a better opportunity to compete, although once the

Hays Code died in the 1960s, Hollywood roared back in the raunch and ribaldry department, rolling over the foreign competition.

Oddly enough, the indelicate movies were not the most profitable ones. The most profitable films continued to be those that were generally compliant with the Hays Code. But the extra zing the non-code films added helped make American films the most popular, and profitable, in the world.

———

All the basic techniques for making cartoons were developed before 1920 by **J. Randolph Bray** and **Earl Hurd**. Bray created the first cartoon with a structured story (rather than just a lot of disjointed actions) in 1910. Four years later, he developed the cel system. This approach took one background illustration, printed it hundreds of times on translucent paper, and then superimposed these static scenes over the illustration of the moving characters and filmed them all, one shot at a time, to produce the animation. Earl Hurd developed a similar system independently, using transparent celluloid (thus the term "cel" system) sheets. Bray and Hurd soon got together and collaborated. They refined their system even more, using different celluloid sheets with different graphic elements. Thus cels could be laid over each other to produce many different scene variations.

By 1922, the Bray system had revolutionized cartoon production. But Bray and Hurd did not stop there. They established an assembly-line process for animation that remains in use to the present. There were different departments for inking, painting, and assembling the final cels, thus enabling the director of each cartoon maximum speed and flexibility. By breaking the work down into simple steps, they could quickly bring on more staff (without having to spend a lot of time training them) to increase production. Bray and Hurd also developed most of the techniques used in cartoons for the rest of the century. In addition to the use of cells, they used gray tones to add more texture, camera dissolves between scenes, various types of close-ups, an endless array of clever stunts, titles, and mixing of live action and animation. While Disney grabbed most of the glory, innovator Bray lived to see his techniques become the standards in the animation industry. He died in 1978.

———

Herbert and **Natalie Kalmus** made color movies a reality. Herbert invented and perfected the process known as Technicolor in the early 1920s. But the movie companies did not beat a path to his door. Despite the superiority of the Technicolor technology, producers had been burned too many times by the poor quality and extra expense of color film. They were not eager to spend any time or money on Technicolor, which was tricky to use and required experts to implement. Then Natalie came up with a solution. She went out and aggressively pitched the studios. More to the point, she turned Technicolor into a service rather than just a process. She developed and offered a package deal, providing equipment, specially trained cameramen, and other specialists to advise on how to best use color in makeup, costumes, and sets to get the most out of the Technicolor process. This was all provided at a flat rate, which appealed to producers. Out-of-control shooting costs are an old problem. Natalie was a consummate dealmaker. She brought Disney into the fold by offering them a seven-year exclusive deal for Technicolor use in animated films. Her plan succeeded. While only about 12 percent of all films were in color between 1925 and 1950 (Technicolor patents expired in 1949), virtually all of them were made in Technicolor. While Herbert invented the process, it was Natalie who made it sell, and made both of them rich.

———

Johann Gottlob Wilhelm ("Billy") Bitzer invented the craft of the movie cameraman. Starting out as an electrician for the Biograph company in 1901, he quickly moved on to become a cameraman and learned the basics of his craft. But when he went to work for D. W. Griffith in 1915, he exploded in a torrent of innovation. He worked on all of Griffith's major films between 1915 and 1920. He perfected the use of filming indoors in a studio, using artificial light. He went further and developed many of the special lighting effects in use today, including backlighting. It was Bitzer, not Griffith, who perfected the close-up and long shots. Bitzer also was the first to use freeze-frame. Every movie cameraman since has had to learn the basic techniques invented by Billy Bitzer.

———

André Bazin put movie directors in their place, as the true "authors" of films. The question of who could claim authorship of films had been fought out in court cases since the 1930s. But in 1951, when Bazin founded his French journal *Cahiers du Cinéma*, he proceeded to make a very convincing case that it was, indeed, the director (not the producer, actors, cameraman, screenwriter, etc.) who was the author of a film. Bazin did this by publishing articles in his journal pointing out the distinctive styles of the different directors. You would have thought this would be obvious, but generally it wasn't. But the articles Bazin wrote or edited made it clear that each director did have a distinct style, and this revelation caused a revolution in how many people viewed films. With the coming of television and VCRs, it was possible for the growing number of movie buffs to appreciate the films of a director over many viewings. Bazin died in 1958, but not before he opened the eyes of millions and got directors the respect they deserved.

———

One of the early moviemakers, **Thomas Harper Ince** worked as an actor before getting into producing and directing. In 1912, he set up a studio to produce short films to meet an insatiable demand by an American population madly in love with these newfangled movies. But Ince set up his operation in a unique fashion, one that was to be copied by nearly every movie company since those early days. Ince created an 18,000-acre facility in southern California that was the first Hollywood studio compound. He had the indoor stages, offices, outdoor sets, dressing rooms, cafeteria, equipment warehouses, and maintenance shops all on one lot, the very first studio lot. It was called Inceville. But Ince's organizational talents went futher than the way the buildings were arranged. He set up multiple shooting units so he could have several projects going at once. He had set managers who scheduled who used which set when. He hired accountants to make sure all involved kept to their budgets.

But perhaps Ince's greatest contribution to moviemaking was the continuity script. This was a master plan for filming, containing every detail of a film. Things like listing (and consistently referring to) scene numbers, suggested camera setups, projected costume and prop needs, recommended camera angles, lighting requirements, and projected postproduction works like special effects and titles. While Ince's continuity script sounded like suggestions, he let everyone know that they were to be treated like orders, and via these scripts and his auditors he was able to effectively control many projects at once and get them out on time and on budget.

After a few prosperous years, Ince formed a new company with Mack Sennett and D. W. Griffith. But Griffith's 1916 opus *Intolerance* cost a bundle and did not play well before the public. So Ince went to work for Paramount and MGM as the first independent producer. The other studios knew that Ince could bring projects in on budget, and they took him on to do just this with his marvelous methods.

Ince was mysteriously shot dead aboard William Randolph Hearst's yacht in 1924, ending a career that had already changed Hollywood forever.

Linwood Gale Dunn started out as a cameraman at RKO in 1928. Fascinated with a crude device called the optical printer, he turned it into the first tool for creating special effects. The optical printer is a camera synchronized with a projector. The projector shines images directly onto the unexposed film in the camera. Dunn added controls to the camera and projector to automatically do fades, dissolves, and wipes. He would skip one or more frames to speed up action, or film the same frame twice to slow things down. Before Dunn's innovation, these effects were done by putting a piece of paper in front of the camera and moving it. Crude, especially when compared to Dunn's smoother, automated effects. Dunn did freezes by duplicating a scene as often as needed for the effect. He could also combine shots on the optical printer by masking part of a frame, then shooting it again with additional material.

For twenty-eight years, Dunn worked his magic for RKO, on such notable films as *King Kong*. When RKO went out of business in 1957, Dunn founded a company to produce the first commercially available optical printer. He added new features, such as blue-screen photography. This was the most powerful special-effects technique in Hollywood until CGI (computer-generated images) came along in the 1980s. The *Stars Wars* movies made great use of Dunn's techniques. The optical printer is still in use, and Dunn received two Oscars in recognition of his pioneering work.

Thus did a lot of generally unknown artists and engineers provide the tools that made movies look so good.

Great Hits and Misses in Movie Technology

Technology, especially major advances like sound in the late 1920s, color in the 1930s, wide screen in the 1950s, and CGI in the 1980s, increased the audience for movies. A lot of new movie technology was never seen in action, only the results. New cameras, lighting systems, special-effects techniques, and better management methods were the behind-the-scenes-technology that made more of a difference than many viewers realized. The whole point of the behind-the-scenes stuff was to *not* be obvious.

Many technologies did not work. In the 1950s, 3-D was introduced with great fanfare and vigor. Also tried between then and the 1990s was Smell-O-Vision (different aromas released during the film), vibrating seats (great for earthquake scenes), and viewer feedback (to decide in which direction the plot should go). None of these worked, and even the wide-screen technology went through some unexpected changes before it sort of settled down. The strange journey of wide screen is a good example of how Hollywood deals, or misdeals, with technology.

Cinerama was the first wide-screen format, using three cameras, and three projectors in theaters, to produce an amazing expanse of action. Multiprojector systems had been available since the 1920s, but until Cinerama, making such films was too tricky and expensive. Cinerama showed that you could make movies in a wide-screen format on a regular basis (although at a higher cost). Cinerama also made use of multichannel high-fidelity sound.

The push for wider-screen movies was a direct response to television's keeping people away from movie theaters. TV screens, like the conventional movie screen, had a 1.33:1 ration (one third wider than tall). Cinerama, and competing systems other studios promptly came out with, was shown at a 2.55:1 ratio. When the initial fascination with this "letterbox" (named for the standard #10 envelope shape) began to fade, the ratio began to shrink. After forty years, and forty different wide-screen systems, we currently have most movies being shown in a 1.88:1 format in the United States (European theaters use 1.66:1). The Panavision system won out, so you no longer see movies making much of other formats (like CinemaScope, Actionscope, VistaVision, Cinepanoramic, Dynavision, Todd-AO 35, Warnerscope, Cinetotalscope, Fujivision, etc.).

In response to the competition from television, much behind-the-scenes work went into developing better cameras, film, sound, and all manner of technology. This is one reason that movies from different decades "look" different. As for television, there evolved two approaches to getting wide-screen movies onto the 1.33:1 (or 4:3, same thing) ratio screens. At first, the wide-screen image was simply cropped to show the most important part of the action. This cropping was an artistic decision that did not please all viewers. So a second option was added, especially for movies released on higher-resolution media like laser discs and DVD, letterboxing. This showed the movie in its original format, and in doing so blacked out portions of the TV screen above and below the action. This worked particularly well on the large-screen television systems many video enthusiasts were buying toward the end of the century.

There was also a technological revolution in the theaters. Not just larger screens and new cameras capable of using them, but also many new theaters, better sound systems and more user-friendly theaters in general. In the 1970s, theater owners finally discovered that if you make the theatergoing as pleasant as possible, more people will come and keep coming back. Since TV took away so much of the movie theaters' audience in the 1950s and '60s, many theaters had closed or become shabby and lackadaisical in their treatment of customers. When these problems were addressed, movie attendance began moving up once more.

Special effects (FX) became a major factor from the 1970s on. Part of this was the success of the old-fashioned (blue screen and models) FX in films like *Jaws* and the *Star Wars* series.

Microprocessors came along in the 1970s and developed into powerful workstations capable of turning out computerized special effects quickly, if not very cheaply. Special effects had been around since the first movies, but lack of adequate tools restricted what could be done. Try to get too ambitious with the FX and you end up with a cheesy effect. Computers began to change that in the 1970s, as the crude PCs of the day were used to coordinate the execution of traditional FX involving models and trick photography. Then in the 1980s, powerful workstation PCs arrived. While these computers were only a year or two ahead of standard PCs in computing power, that was enough to encourage finding new, cutting-edge applications. Graphics, specifically very realistic graphics, were one use, and it wasn't long before the FX crowd realized they could quickly and easily create believable FX at the keyboard. All the fuss and expense of models, special cameras, and film processes were no more. Blockbuster movies like *Titanic* made it all seem worthwhile.

But in some respects it was not worth it, at least not to the CGI companies. Many were losing money or going out of business. They had plenty of business, but it was hard to stay *in* business. There were too many unknowns and too much rapidly changing technology. It was mainly a management problem; the studios were always hard on suppliers. Despite the spendthrift image of Hollywood, the people actually making the deals were very cost-conscious. The new CGI shops learned about this the hard way.

But there was a bright side to this, and you can see it in any software store. The computer games using the latest PC graphics are not far behind the hugely expensive stuff you see in the latest movies. This means that movie FX will get better and cheaper. Indeed, some FX producers are cutting costs by using the latest PCs instead of the more expensive workstations. TV stations were the first to do this in the late 1980s, because TV FX images could be less detailed than movie effects and get away with it.

Finally, for the twentieth century anyway, we will see, sometime around the turn of the century, CGIs that literally replace live action. The actors are not looking forward to this, for the Holy Grail of the CGI crew is first scenes, and eventually entire movies, that are all CGI but look like a conventional movie with live actors and indoor and outdoor photography. It's coming. It's almost here.

——The Curse of the Close-up——

Sometimes simple things, like the close-up shot in movies, can generate major changes throughout our culture.

The close-up shot is a staple of films, and has been from the beginning of moviemaking. The close-up shot was a unique feature; you couldn't do something like that in a live performance. Early directors were quick to make the most of this new tool, but in so doing the acting style of moviemaking nations was changed forever. Before the movie close-up, actors had to use a lot of body movement and hand waving to get their point across to a somewhat distant audience. The speaking style was also different, being louder and wordier than that of today, but this did not change until movies got sound in the 1930s.

The first movies were made by people with some experience in live theater, and many with no experience at all in entertainment. But everyone working on the early movies soon became aware that they could do things in a film that they could not do onstage. So before World War I, we had silent movies using special effects, close-ups, and all manner of new approaches to presenting entertainment to an audience.

But it was the close-up that changed acting styles for the rest of the century. Actors learned to use small gestures that could always be amplified by a close-up, rather than obvious, sweeping ones. When sound came in, many actors disappeared, because they did not have voices to match their looks. But those who remained had to use their voices in close-ups, as well as their faces and body parts. You can see this happening in movies made in the 1930s, '40s, and '50s. The earliest talkies had actors loudly delivering their lines as if they were onstage. Twenty years later, they were speaking in a conversational manner. You can even see the change with the same actors who appeared in movies throughout the period.

So what was the "curse" of the close-up? Simple. It made it possible to ignore anything else going on in a scene and eliminated a major incentive to develop acting techniques that used the entire body. Indeed, the use of a double for dangerous, or simply physically difficult, stunts became common. So you no longer had one actor playing a role, but frequently a team. It's hard to say if this was generally good or bad, but it was different, and thousands of years of acting techniques disappeared in the process. The close-up changed the acting profession more than anything else, ever.

——The Century of Celebrity——

We have always had celebrities. In times past, they were kings, warriors, and religious leaders. But in the twentieth century we found ourselves awash in celebrities. And the results were sometimes curious.

The mass media, appearing on the scene in the early 1800s, brought with them instant celebrities. One of the early quirks of the mass media was the tendency for a hot story to be picked up by many other papers. If certain people popped up in a story, they soon found themselves known far and wide, and very quickly. In the nineteenth century, this meant celebrities whom readers had to admire from afar, and the celebrity mania was much more subdued than in the twentieth century.

Few people who read about the newly minted celebrity knew anything beyond what was in the papers. There was no way to see or hear the celebrity in person and judge for yourself. But the newspaper editors noted that they had the power to create great heroes, or villains, and they exploited this power whenever circulation needed a boost.

In our century, we saw something new: mass media that brought personalities directly to the public. Recordings were now available to millions of families who owned record players. Movies caught on quickly and on a massive scale, reaching tens of millions weekly. Then came radio and talking pictures, to provide the next best thing to having the celebrities right in front of you. Mass-market celebrities could be compared to nothing we'd ever experienced before.

Like the nineteenth-century newspapers, the twentieth-century media quickly realized the advantages of being able to create celebrities. The movies were the first to make the most of this power. While there were celebrity actors in the past, they were few and were truly exceptional, as they had to prove themselves constantly in front of live audiences. But movie actors did not so much act but rather appeared in movies, under a clever director's expert guidance. The movie studios picked up on the value of celebrity power early and exploited it energetically. The hordes of attractive young men and women who wished to be movie stars had no problem with signing restrictive contracts with the studios. If an actor turned out to be a hit with the public, the contract made sure he was not able to run off and make movies for another studio. The actors were well paid, and they certainly enjoyed their celebrity status. But they could have made a lot more money if they could work for the highest bidder.

The "studio system" controlled not only the talent but also the distribution. It wasn't until after World War II, when the government forced the studios to sell off all their movie theaters, that the studios began to lose control. That signaled the end of the restrictive contracts. The major actors had begun freeing themselves from the studio contracts as early as the 1920s. It wasn't easy, and you had to be a really big star to get away with it. If you were a lesser celebrity, the other studios could afford to ignore you. And this is where the studios got into trouble. Despite the heavy use of studio publicists and adroit management of the actor's career, the newspapers and radio stations had their own agendas when it came to covering celebrities. Major stars hired their own publicists and tried to manage their celebrity status so that it was not so dependent on the studio they were under contract to. All this led to some fascinating battles in the media, as various factions used rumors, gossip, and press releases to enhance or defame reputations.

The 1930s and '40s were a golden age for show-business gossip reporters. The public loved this stuff, and rarely became aware of who was actually trying to hurt whom. The studios, stars, and media all wished to maintain the illusion that they were not simply playing games. The media, despite their eagerness for juicy tidbits, did show restraint. Stories about really embarrassing behavior (homosexuality, drugs, underage sex, and so on) were avoided. No one wanted to destroy the celebrities who were making everyone rich.

Most of the media celebrities were movie stars, and the reason for this was simple. Many people were impressed with the dramatic roles the stars played in the movies. Of course, everyone knew it was make-believe, but people enjoyed the realistic fantasy depicted in films, and the actors were closely identified with their roles. It was a unique situation in human history. Oh, there had been many stage actors in the past few thousand years who had achieved a similar form of celebrity. But with movies, millions could see even more impressive performances. In the past, only kings or mighty warriors had achieved such prominence in the public eye. Now it could happen to some youngster who looked good in front of a camera. The first movie stars didn't even need a fine voice, as movies had no soundtracks until the late 1920s. While many held movie celebrities in contempt because of the artificiality of their accomplishments, there were millions who didn't mind. It was glamorous and impressive.

There were other, non-show-business, celebrities who actually did something worth celebrating. When someone like this showed up, the media pulled out all the stops. Athletes got the star treatment, at least those who were outstanding and had a strong personality. Baseball player Babe Ruth was one of the first sports celebrities. But the first superstar of the century was Charles Lindbergh. His 1927 solo flight across the Atlantic was a truly heroic feat. Naturally, the newspapers and radio jumped all over it. But the movies now had a way to capitalize on news events in a big way. In 1927, newsreels began to appear with sound. Now nonactors could get the same big-screen treatment as movie stars. The dramatic voice-over, as well as interviews with the celebrity, had an enormous impact on the viewing public. Thereafter it became the custom for the media to pile onto anyone who did anything of note.

Events could also qualify for celebrity status. There were several highly publicized trials in the first half of the century. The Scopes "Monkey Trial" (over whether evolution could be taught in Tennessee) in 1925 sold a lot of newspapers. While crime was always a staple of the news, when J. Edgar Hoover became head of the newly formed FBI, also in 1925, he quickly realized that publicity and celebrity were to be among his most effective crime-fighting tools. Hoover did not allow his agents to become celebrities—he considered himself the only celebrity in the FBI—but he realized that the FBI's reputation was only as good as the crooks he pursued were notorious. One can thank Hoover for the constant stream of celebrity criminals in the 1920s and '30s. Naturally, most of them came to a bad end, dying in a hail of FBI machine-gun fire. Hoover liked it that way. So did the public. They ate it up.

World War II provided numerous genuine war heroes (and a few bogus ones), and the latter half of the twentieth century has taken all this celebrity business for granted. Others did more than take it for granted, for it was soon discovered that celebrity was a moneymaking proposition. Limited only by one's imagination, many ways were found to market celebrity. The most common one was the book contract. Publishers always had a hard time marketing books, but a celebrity solved that problem. It didn't make any difference if the celebrity couldn't write, a ghostwriter could be found (and was usually preferred, as these pros could be depended on to deliver on schedule). A book idea was no problem; whatever the celebrity was famous (or infamous) for would make a dandy subject. Book publishers began pushing the celebrity angle big time in the 1960s, and before long, the dark side of this approach became evident. Many of the books lost money. Celebrities don't come cheap, and when many publishers were bidding against each other for a particular deal, the price went up and up. It wasn't until the 1990s that publishers began to admit that they were taking a beating and began to back off. Celebrity books are still a publishing staple, but the bidding has become more subdued.

An obvious use of celebrity is making business contacts. Retired sports celebrities use this one to good effect. Normally out of work in their thirties, sports celebrities have a long life ahead of them, and before the multimillion-dollar contracts of the 1980s and '90s, sports stars had little but their name recognition to get them started in a postathletic career. Many did quite well, because people were willing to talk to them about something besides sports.

Television made celebrity a mass-market item. With hundreds of TV stations, plus many more cable channels, there was an ever larger amount of airtime to be filled. Old movies and TV reruns could fill only so much of it. Therefore, more and more shows brought on more and more people. Everyone who appeared became a bit of a celebrity, even if the appearance was via one of their unintentionally humorous home movies. By the end of the century, it's estimated that about 10 percent of the population has appeared on television. That's a lot of celebrities, but celebrities are one thing you can't have too many of.

——Visible Generations——

Another unique aspect of the twentieth century is the appearance of a real time machine. We can now see our past as none before us ever could.

For thousands of years, our picture of the generations before was largely a mental one, gleaned from the stories of our parents and grandparents and whatever printed, or painted, record that was passed on. That changed in the past 150 years. By 1900, photography was well established, and Thomas Edison's recording devices already had made some two decades of spoken records. The moving pictures were still getting started in 1900, and by the 1930s, sound and color were added. Thus, when television became common in the 1950s, the frequent showing of old (1930s) vintage movies gave viewers a very realistic look at a past generation. Now, over four decades later, kids can still catch some of those 1930s movies on cable. What these teenagers see is the world of their grandparents and great grandparents. At that distance, the differences between the generations seems pronounced. It is obvious that over two or three generations there are a lot of changes. People dress, move, talk and look quite different. In the past, we could, and many did, assume that there were not a lot of differences between generations at the same times in their lives. But via these old movies (and an increasing number of home movies), it is obvious that the teenagers of, for example, the 1930s, '40s, '50s, '60s, and so on *were* quite different. But so were people of all ages and social classes. Looking at old movies showing people several generations earlier, especially if it is a contemporary drama, provides a cornucopia of interesting differences between then and now—manners, gadgets, speech patterns, lifestyle, goals, and more. These old movies are a real time machine, and they really deliver the goods if you look at them that way.

——Recordings——

Recorded music was a hot new item in 1900, mainly because it had revolutionized personal entertainment, and did so throughout the twentieth century. We take the recordings for granted now, mainly because there is no one still alive who remembers life without them. Consider, then, where recordings came from and where they are going.

Invented and perfected by Thomas Edison in the late 1870s, by 1900 the phonograph was a common, if relatively expensive, feature in American life. Edison had introduced the phonograph using cylinders. Discs were also available, but Edison preferred the cylinders, and it wasn't until the first decade of this century that the discs began to push cylinders out of the marketplace. Cylinders were cheaper, however; a two-minute version cost about twelve dollars, while a four-minute, ten-inch disc sold for twice as much. Production of cylinders finally ceased in 1929.

The phonograph was a sensation in its day. It was the first high-tech entertainment toy to hit the market, and people loved it. The first models used no electricity, powered by cranking and the sound amplified via an acoustic horn. Even today, if you turn off the amplifier on a record turntable and put your ear down by the needle, you can still hear the sound. Trouble is, at the end of the century, there are few acoustic phonographs left. Oh, well, life goes on.

The earliest machines cost $200 or more. In 1913, suitcase-size portable phonographs were introduced, and in 1915 the electric loudspeaker arrived. The latter item was expensive, and it merely magnified the poor quality of the recordings made by the artist singing or playing into a horn device.

The phonograph was the first modern gadget people could tinker with, establishing a tradition that would be duplicated with the automobile, radio, television, and personal computers. Like the PC, the early phonographs were not standardized. There were several different formats, not just cylinders and discs, but many different disc formats. After World War I, there was a big shake-out in the phonograph business, but going into the 1920s there were still three different types of 78-rpm records in wide circulation. This experience is one reason there was so much more willingness to standardize recording formats after World War II.

In the mid-1920s, electricity finally caught up with the phonograph. Microphones, invented in 1917, were perfected, and this made recording much more realistic. Microphones also made it possible to record entire orchestras, instead of just one musician playing or singing into a recording horn. Electric motors drove the turntable, and amplifiers were also used for playback, and this provided a cleaner and louder sound. These innovations came just in time, as radio was beginning to cut into phonograph sales. Record sales peaked at a billion dollars in 1921, and would have declined even more had not the phonographs gone electric.

In 1927, more electronic innovations made high-fidelity sound possible, although the cost of the recording and playback equipment was so high that hi-fi did not become marketable for several decades. In the same year, the jukebox was perfected (an early version had been built in 1905). The new one was all electric, but again, cost and then the Great Depression slowed the spread of this technology. Wurlitzer introduced attractive multiple-selection jukeboxes in 1934, and by 1939 some 300,000 were in use. It cost sixty cents to play a tune, at a time when buying the record itself cost about four dollars.

The 1930s Great Depression stalled the marketing of new phonograph technologies, but not their development. Stereo sound was developed in the early 1930s, as was the more efficient 33⅓-rpm speed. But these innovations were not introduced on a wide scale until the 1950s.

One of the major recording innovations was developed not in the United States but in Germany. Magnetic recording tape was invented and perfected there in the mid-1930s. By today's standards, the tape equipment was bulky. To record twenty minutes of material, you needed 3,300 feet of half-inch tape. But much higher-fidelity recordings were obtained. This technology was largely unknown outside Germany until American army electronics experts came across the equipment during the conquest of Germany in 1945. Many of these recorders were sent back to the United States and demonstrated to engineers and recording-company personnel. The superiority of tape was immediately recognized, and by 1948, production began in America, mainly for recording studios to make master tapes. That was a fateful year for the American recording industry, for 33⅓-rpm high-fidelity records were introduced. Within a few years, the older 78-rpm discs were history. In 1949, the 45-rpm-single format was on the market. The "long-playing" 33⅓ disc made possible a collection of songs on one record. Thus was born the album. The smaller 45 was a replacement for most current records, which could play only a few minutes of music. But the 33⅓ made it possible to record all or large parts of longer (usually classical) pieces on one side of a record. By the 1960s, artists were not just putting many songs on one record but employing a theme for all the songs on a record. This encouraged fans to buy albums and not singles, and it led to the decline and eventual disappearance of the 45. The record companies encouraged this as much as they could, for more profit was made on the more expensive 33⅓ albums.

By 1954, reel-to-reel tape recorders were made available for the consumer market. The first models cost $80 to $90, a mass-market price.

And soon the tape units were selling very well, made possible by the introduction of stereo tape capability in 1955. But tape did not catch on big time until cassettes came in during the 1960s and '70s.

Tape was the hot new medium in the 1950s. In 1956, the first videotape recorder appeared. This was a revolutionary and much-needed device, for until then the only way to record a TV show was to film it off a TV screen. These were called kinescopes and, as you might expect, were quite crude. The first videotape recorders (VTRs) were expensive, costing $475,000 each. To record half an hour of material required 27,000 feet of tape. But 600 of these devices had been sold by 1960, mainly to the TV industry. By 1959, there was a mobile VTR, as well as ones that recorded in color. This tape technology made producing TV shows more efficient and cheaper (even with the cost of the VTR).

In 1963, the first consumer VTR was made available. Using the same technology as the professional units, these new recorders were expensive, at $6,000 each. Obviously not an impulse item. These were also reel-to-reel machines, and the tape was very expensive. It took over ten years of research and engineering to get the technology to the point where VTRs could be mass-produced. In 1975, Sony introduced its Betamax VCR (videocassette recorder). The recorder cost $7,300, and each half hour cassette was $50. Still not quite mass market, but the cassette made it much easier to use. The next year, the first VHS-format VCR was introduced, priced at $2,700. Sony responded later that year with a Betamax unit priced at $4,000. While Betamax produced superior picture quality, VHS was a lot cheaper and could put more material on a tape. VHS won eventually. It took another ten years before the VCRs became cheap enough to be mass-market items. In a common twentieth-century pattern, videotape recorders took about thirty years for a new technology to go from first functional prototype to a mass-market-priced model. For example, industrial-strength computers first appeared in the 1950s, and by the 1980s they were selling in the millions of units, even though no one had ever thought that computers would be a mass-market item. But VCRs were seen from the beginning as having mass appeal.

Some misjudged just what it was about VCRs that gave them mass appeal. In the late 1970s, laser-disc technology was introduced. These were playback-only devices that provided superb display quality. While they were popular among the hard-core movie fans, what most people wanted was the ability to record shows they wanted to see again. For this reason, tape won out. The film and TV companies knew this from the beginning and tried to outlaw VCRs that could record. They failed, but never lost their desire to prevent consumers from freely duplicating their video products.

There was one playback device introduced in the late 1970s that did go on to be a big hit. It was the Walkman portable tape player. This quickly became enormously popular, and seemed an obvious development. But in fact the idea was a brainstorm by the president of Sony (who wanted to listen to classical music while walking around). He suggested the notion to some Sony engineers, who, taking the hint, quickly turned out a prototype. One thing led to another, and once consumers got their hands on the Walkman in 1979, sales took off.

The audiocassette played in the Walkman had already been in use for two decades, but without major success. The Walkman changed that, and through the 1980s, audiocassette ate into sales of vinyl discs. But by the early 1980s, both these formats were in danger from a totally new format: digital sound.

One of the unforeseen side effects of the PC revolution was the growing use of digital media. All previous recording media had been analog (different-size bumps on a vinyl record's groove producing a different sound, etc.). Even some early computers used analog methods for keeping track of data. But computers really needed more precision, so digital (all data was numbers and as accurate as possible) became the computer standard. PCs also needed room for data, and technology was rapidly developed (like the floppy disk) or borrowed from the older mainframe computers (like the hard drive). Both of these devices used digital data, and musicians were already using digital data to record their music. Why? Because it was easier to manipulate the music. This was another aspect of the rock-and-roll revolution. All the new technology arriving in the 1960s led many musicians to experiment with the gadgets as well as with their musical instruments. The studio was no longer just a soundproof room for recording music; it was now also a laboratory full of electronic gear for making the recorded music into something more. Recording music digitally took a lot of storage space, and initially multitrack, reel-to-reel tape was used. This was not practical for a consumer product, but there were other ways of getting at large quantities of digital data in a hurry, and cheaply. The result was the CD (compact disc). This was introduced as a consumer product in 1982.

The key technology in the CD was one that originally had nothing to do with music or computers: the laser. This was a method of focusing light, and it was developed in the late 1950s. In 1962, a powerful laser beam was bounced off the moon. The popular perception of the laser was as something that would eventually become a death ray or a means to produce holographic 3-D images. Perhaps, but in the meantime it was found that the focused laser light was immediately useful for measuring things. This led to laser range finders and, in 1982, a small laser that read tiny pits on the surface of a 4.75-inch compact disc. This approach allowed the CD drive to rapidly read any of the 650 million characters of information (74 minutes of music) on each CD. The technology was, as it is with all new gadgets, expensive. But even with the first CD players costing over a thousand dollars and CDs themselves going for over thirty bucks, there was big demand. The CDs were touted as immune to wear and capable of much more realistic sound. Neither of these claims turned out to be true (CDs may start to degrade after five to ten years, and the sound does not have the "richness" of a good acoustic recording). But the claims were close enough to the hype to drive vinyl records out of the market within ten years.

But the PC was not done with the recording business. In the 1990s, with the widespread use of the Internet, much work was done to make it easier to send music and video over that medium. Without some kind of compression, it took too long to send sounds and pictures to Internet users. Computer manufacturers became obsessed with creating PCs with enough power to show real-time video and audio over the Internet. Much money was put into this effort through the late 1980s and early 1990s.

The result was a number of compression standards. One of these was MPEG-1 Audio Layer 3, or MP3, for compressing movie soundtracks. Whereas a CD needed 8 to 10 million bytes of data for one minute of music, MP3 needed only 1 million bytes. Few listeners could tell the difference between MP3 and CD sound, even though compression tends to distort the original a bit. It was now possible to copy a song off a CD onto a computer hard disk, compress it as an MP3 file, and play it or send it out over the Internet. Worse yet, for the record companies, these MP3 files were stored on the Internet, available for all to grab and use on their own PCs.

But it got worse.

There was nothing new in all this. When tape recorders first appeared, there was considerable copying of songs from records to tapes. There were lawsuits over this, but the courts decided that once you owned a record, you could make as many copies as you wanted as long as you didn't sell them. Many illegal copies were sold anyway, but the record companies were not put out of business. Yet record companies did lose a lot of sales and profits, especially outside the United States. As a result, the appearance of MP3 files on the Internet was viewed with horror. What was so scary was the new ease with which people could distribute their illegal copies of copyrighted music. Previously, people making tape copies of records or cassette tapes might hand a copy to a friend. Even those making a business of selling illegal copies had problems distributing their goods without attracting unwanted police attention. But the Internet changed everything. You could put your MP3 files in any of hundreds of locations on the Internet made available just for that purpose. Those Internet users with a bit more technical knowledge could set up their own download sites. Moreover, if the record-company lawyers sent a nasty letter to the company the computer an MP3 site was running on, it could be set up again somewhere else in a few hours. Sometimes the lawyers had a hard time finding out whom to send the nastygrams too, for MP3 sites could be set up outside the United States.

MP3 should not have been a surprise to the recording industry. The MP3 format was made a standard in the early 1990s. But at that time not many PC users had hardware capable of making the most of it. For example, fewer than a quarter of PCs had decent sound capability in 1995, although in the next few years, nearly all PCs had good audio, as well as much larger hard disks and faster processors. Independent software developers noticed, and the first dedicated MP3-player software (WinAmp) came out in early 1997. Within a year, over 5 million people had downloaded it. Nearly as many users downloaded similar programs from other developers. By 1999, there were over a quarter of a million different songs available on the Net. Most were copyright violations, but many were legal, and some were being sold. The recording industry scrambled to develop its own way of selling music via the Internet, while also trying to shut down the illegal MP3 file sites.

The recording business tried the legal approach. This had failed against VCRs in the 1970s, but it had succeeded against DAT (digital audio tape recorders) in the 1980s. By making it difficult to transfer CD music material to a DAT tape, the product failed in the marketplace. But software to move material from CDs to MP3 files has always been there, and by the mid-1990s, many companies were coming out with a lot more products that made the transfers even easier. The genie was out of the lamp, and there was no putting it back. When the recording industry tried to outlaw the RIO MP3 playback device in 1998, they were thrown out of court. As it becomes easier to play MP3 files, the temptation to illegally pass around the files will only increase.

The piracy won't stop. Many lawyers will be employed to search the Web, find MP3 sites full of copyrighted material, and shut them down. This is what the software and recording business has been doing, since the 1980s, to illegal reproductions of CDs and VCR tapes. In cases where large factories were tolerated overseas (via corrupt local politicians), even the State Department had to be called in. With the Internet, there will be a lot of person-to-person exchange of illegal copies of music that won't be stopped easily. But the music and software industries have survived this kind of theft before. It's another cost of doing business.

More worrisome is the piracy of digital movies. Even with MPEG compression, movies take up much more disk space than MP3 sound files. But at the end of the century, the average PC hard disk was over ten gigabytes, and the larger-capacity DVD drives were rapidly replacing the older (1980s era) CD-ROMs. Once the price of the read/write DVD drives falls under $500, there will be millions of potential movie pirates out there. Same thing happened with read/write CD-ROM drives in the 1990s. All of a sudden, many people were copying CD-ROM-based games and making their own music CDs.

The recording business has had a tough century. In 1900, recordings were a rapidly growing business. But first radio, then talking movies, television, and finally computers have cut into the recordings market. Rock and roll gave the business a big boost in the latter half of the century, as did the introduction of music CDs. But as the rock-and-roll generation got older, and after they had replaced a lot of their vinyl records with CDs, the recording business again fell upon hard times. Then MP3 came along.

The business won't disappear, but making money in recordings will not get any easier.

———Sex———

There's been a lot of sex in the twentieth century; otherwise the population would not have more than tripled between 1900 and 2000. But there was also a change in attitude toward sex in the twentieth century, partly as a result of science (better birth control) and partly as a result of publicity (mass media love steamy stories because more people will pay attention).

Sex is always there, but it has not always been indulged with the same enthusiasm throughout this century. Historians have noted that levels of sexual promiscuity tend to fluctuate from generation to generation. Looking at marriage and birth records going back several centuries, it is obvious when there was a lot of premarital sex (a lot of "premature" first children) and when there wasn't. After World War I and through the 1920s, we had one of those wild generations. Not for nothing was it called the Roaring Twenties, because a lot of the noise came from the bedroom and, more frequently, from the backseats of all those millions of new cars.

The Great Depression shut down the sexual adventures of the Roaring Twenties, and World War II then took most of the men off to distant battlefields through the mid-1940s. When everyone got back together, there were a lot of marriages and a lot of children. The Baby Boom was born.

Then came the 1960s, and two things happened to change the sexual landscape forever. First, all those Baby Boom children began to hit puberty. Given their enormous numbers, their adolescent interest in sex fed upon itself and became really, really big. What made it an enormous change was the gradual introduction, during the early 1960s, of the birth-control pill. There were already birth-control devices available, and there had been for most of the century. The commonest was the condom, but most men did not like this device for, as many commented after using it, "It don't feel right." IUDs and various spermicides were also available, but all made sex seem a bit premeditated. The birth-control pill was just taken daily and was actually more effective than all the other methods. It cost a woman about sixty dollars a month and first went on sale in 1960.

In retrospect, the 1960s may now seem like one big orgy. There was a lot more sex going on, and about half the people who were teenagers or under thirty during the 1960s thought they had taken part in the sexual revolution. Another quarter were not sure, but they were having a good time. Of course, the definition of "a lot of sex" varied depending on who you were. Drug users (everything from marijuana to heroin) reported that they had two to three times as much sex as those who did not get into drugs. Those who were politically active (protesting the Vietnam War or just out promoting a cause) were also nearly twice as likely to be more sexually active.

But the biggest promoters of sex in the sixties were the media. Whether just running a racy story to sell more ads or simply going along with a hot trend, the media paid a lot of attention to the sexual antics of the population.

The good times continued into the 1970s, leveled off a bit as many Baby Boomers got married and had kids of their own. Things really hit the wall in the 1980s, when AIDS and genital herpes became more common. Both were incurable. But while AIDS could kill you, it was, and is, largely confined to male homosexuals and needle drug users. Herpes was more worrisome, as it came back periodically in the form of painful genital sores and rapidly spread to a victim's sexual partners. There were a number of other venereal afflictions showing up that could be cured but still caused discomfort and, for some women, brought infertility.

Thus it was that for about three decades in this century, the sex was really outrageous. The rest of the time, the activity was more restrained. And during the sixties a new generation of birth control came along that forever changed the ground rules for sexual relations. With the birth-control pill, women had more say over contraception than they had ever had in the past. Another one of those twentieth-century revolutions whose reverberations are still rattling around.

——Drugs——

One of the more dubious distinctions of the twentieth century was the massive distribution of recreational (as opposed to medical) drugs. It was the century of getting high. It was also a problem that existed for the entire century, despite strenuous efforts to stamp it out. We go into the twenty-first century facing a drug problem, just as we did the twentieth century.

Most of these drugs have been around for a long time, thousands of years in many cases. Marijuana grows wild in many parts of the world and has been eaten or smoked for as long as humans have been around it. Opium has long been extracted from poppy plants. Throughout the nineteenth century, chemists derived several new, and more powerful, drugs from opium (morphine, heroin, etc.). At first, the painkilling and sedative features of these drugs were seen as very good, and the addictive aspects were either not known, played down, or ignored. But by 1900, the addictive properties of the "opiates" was getting out of hand. At that time, women could buy heroin (for oral ingestion, not injection) as a cure for menstrual cramps and such.

Cocaine, first derived from the South American coca plant in the nineteenth century, was less addicting than the opiates. The coca leaf itself was for many centuries, and still is, chewed to provide a minor buzz, much as a cup of coffee does. A century ago, opiates and cocaine were commonly dispensed for those who were feeling anxious or otherwise mentally upset.

By 1900, there was a formidable movement to outlaw and/or regulate many of the opiates then freely bought and sold. Laws were passed and implemented in 1914, which not only outlawed (except for medicinal use) opiates, but also marijuana and other recreational drugs. At the same time, an even older movement was gathering support to outlaw alcohol. This would take place in 1919.

Up until 1900, drug addiction had never been a catastrophic problem in America. At the turn of the century, few were addicted. Take away the marijuana users, and the percentage goes down even further. Marijuana, being easily grown or growing wild, was not only more freely (literally, at least in rural areas) available, but was addictive only in its concentrated form: hashish. What really worried the public was the hard stuff—opium, heroin, and cocaine. These drugs were scary and had long been known to be capable of wrecking addicts physically and psychologically.

In 1925, there was an international treaty to restrict the trade in marijuana and hashish. Some of the most potent hemp plants (from which marijuana was derived) came from tropical Asian countries. This merely increased efforts by users in other nations to breed more potent strains of hemp plants.

There was less addiction in the Great Depression, mainly because there was much less money flying around compared to the Roaring Twenties. Marijuana was more widely used, but it wasn't as addictive as the hard drugs and was considered by most users to be in the same category as beer or wine. Public opinion did not agree, and publicity campaigns continued against "reefer."

After World War II, prosperity returned, and so did drug use. But there were some new drugs available. During the 1930s, amphetamines ("speed" or "uppers") were developed. First as a medical treatment, but since this stuff was pretty easy to make, it soon became another illicit drug. This set the tone for the rest of the century. While drugs that required crops (poppy, coca, or hemp plants) continued to be consumed, the drugs that could be made in a lab, especially a lab set up in a garage or basement, rapidly caught on in popularity.

Drugs were still a fringe thing until the 1960s. Bikers, beatniks, gangsters, and any group likely to indulge themselves in mind-altering substances and exotic behavior were the principal users. The police kept the pressure on, but the drug users were not seen as a major menace. And they weren't. But in the 1950s, what would seem today as no problem at all was perceived as a threat to the very fabric of society. Or at least this was how it was played in the mass media. As always during the twentieth century, the mass media played a crucial role in putting a magnifying glass on issues that would otherwise be seen as a minor matter.

Then came the 1960s, and the largest generation of adolescents in United States history discovered drugs and jumped right in. All of a sudden, recreational drugs were showing up in a lot more families. Drugs were no longer a small problem.

Initially, the kids confined themselves to marijuana. But usage quickly escalated as the sixties generation discovered the large and, it turned out, growing array of recreational drugs. One of the more popular, and dangerous, new drugs was LSD. This caused industrial-strength hallucinations that often led to harmful, and sometimes lethal, side effects. But the prolific use of amphetamines, opiates, cocaine, and even more exotic concoctions went on unabated until the Boomers outgrew their youthful sense of excess.

But then there was an obvious development as the greater number of drug users was noticed by a new generation of criminals. Well, maybe not all that new. Noting that after the sixties there was a mass market for illegal drugs, the organized-crime wave of the 1920s repeated itself. In the 1920s, prohibition of alcohol presented criminals the opportunity to set up large-scale illegal enterprises to supply a mass market for illegal substances. In the 1980s, it was drugs. But the eighties gangsters had two advantages. First, most of the illegal drugs were more addictive than alcohol. Second, the drug barons developed an even more addictive and cheaper (per "hit") version of cocaine: crack cocaine. The cocaine boom of the 1980s increased the number of users enormously, especially the hard-core group that comprised about 20 percent of all users but consumed (and committed a lot of crimes to pay for) some three quarters of the drugs.

Unlike during Prohibition, when a lot of the illegal alcohol was produced locally in hidden stills and breweries, the popular cocaine and opiates had to be imported. Other illegal drugs were produced locally. Highly potent marijuana could be grown indoors using artificial light. In remote rural areas, small patches of high-potency marijuana was grown. Amphetamines continued to be produced in home laboratories. And chemists with a taste for recreational drugs developed new varieties. Many were so unique that the Federal Drug Administration (FDA) had to constantly amend the drug statutes to outlaw the new concoctions.

By the 1980s, for the first time since the turn of the century, recreational drugs became big business, and an illegal one at that. The same problems encountered during the alcohol prohibition of 1919–34 reappeared. This included a call for the legalization of recreational drugs. It became, and continues to be, a highly contentious issue. Some European nations have, in effect, legalized these drugs. This approach has not eliminated drug use; indeed, usage has gone up. The Netherlands legalized drugs and saw use of marijuana among adolescents go up 250 percent. The number of registered users of hard drugs went up 22 percent. Illegal use of hard drugs, often by underage adolescents, also went up considerably. Into the 1990s, a movement to outlaw drugs in the Netherlands developed.

In America, Alaska legalized marijuana and saw use of marijuana and cocaine increase to the highest rates in the nation. Alaskans again outlawed marijuana in 1990.

As with alcohol users, new drug users tended to recruit from one to six new users during the first year of addiction, if the new user was in an area that did not already contain a large number of drug users. This is why drug use spread so quickly in areas where there had previously been little or no drug use. Even without a strong dealer network, the most common drug, marijuana, was at least tried by 10 percent or more of high-school students. Most did not go on to use it regularly, but 20 percent of those who used marijuana from three to ten times would then go on to use the more potent cocaine. For heavy users of marijuana, those who used it a hundred times, some 75 percent went on to cocaine.

Heavy users often realized that their drug use was life-threatening and eventually sought treatment, but this normally took about four years to happen. Even then, there was only about a 25-percent cure rate. Not for want of trying, for most users eventually became desperate to leave their addiction behind. About half of all users managed to stop after six or seven years of heavy use. Many users kept going at lower levels of use. But it appears that this did shorten life span from ten to twenty years or more (depending on intensity and length of drug use).

Recreational drug use in America peaked at about 25 million users in 1979. The increase began in the early 1960s, and it was at that time that police in most parts of the nation began to ignore a lot of drug use. The main problem was not the widespread youthful enthusiasm for these drugs but rather the unwillingness to build more jails and courtrooms to deal with all the additional arrests. As a result, between 1960 and 1980, drug arrests fell from 90 per 1,000 arrests to 19 per 1,000. Crime rates more than doubled, and the majority of the criminals were drug users. Drug use in general went way up, especially among teenagers. Heroin use, by 1980, went up nine times what it was in 1960.

Felling that the "don't arrest the druggies" approach was not working, the policy was changed, and the drug arrest rate began to go up. As a result, both drug use and crime rates went down, both by over 50 percent in many urban areas (including New York City).

By the end of the century, the number of drug users in the United States was down to about 12 million, of which about half were hard-core addicts. The number of new teenage users was way down.

But recreational drug users are not going to disappear. It's still a multibillion-dollar-a-year illegal business. The most successful programs to reduce drug use concentrated on going after the dealers. As a result, by the late 1990s, about 7 percent of state convicts are in on drug charges, and most of these are dealers. Even more dealers are in federal prisons, as most dealers are caught operating across state and international borders. By the end of the century, only about 8 percent of all arrests were for drugs, mostly dealing. The public has supported this in a way they never supported the prosecution of illegal-alcohol dealers in the 1920s. We tend to forget that, despite all the additional crime during Prohibition, there was a decrease in alcohol use and a decrease in the health and social problems present when alcohol could be freely purchased. The problem was that such a large portion of the population liked alcohol, and the general feeling was that whatever the problems with alcohol were, people would prefer to have their booze and deal with them. The 1919 prohibition of alcohol was repealed in 1934. The turn-of-the-century prohibition against addictive drugs has not been repealed but has actually been beefed up over the years. Most people show no interest in repealing this prohibition. So the recreational drug problems will follow us into the next century.

——Rock and Roll——

Rock and roll changed American, and world, culture in a way that no previous form of music had. Music, like science, underwent unprecedented change in the twentieth century. The cause was mass media more than anything else, because the wide availability of films, radio, and phonographs made it possible to rapidly spread new forms of music. These same media also made it possible, once a new song or musical style had caught on, to churn out a lot more of the new stuff on short notice. Musicians had never had that capability before, and it took some getting used to.

Before mass media, there were two musical cultures. For most people, there was what we today call "folk music." For those with more money and musical knowledge, there was "court music." We call this classical music today, but for centuries this more refined music was subsidized by aristocrats and the wealthy in general, and heard by relatively few people, for until the late-nineteenth-century invention of the phonograph, all music was live. A popular feature of any king or prince's court was the latest music his "choirmaster" had thought up. Most of the classical music we enjoy today was composed while the artist was working for some aristocrat.

This began to change in the nineteenth century, as the industrial revolution produced more wealth and a larger segment of the population had the money to buy things like sheet music of new tunes. There was still a lot of locally produced folk music, but even these musicians saw that if you could write your tune down properly and interest one of the many music publishers in selling it, you could make a nice bit of money from the royalties. You can still go this route, but when recorded music came along at the end of the nineteenth century, everyone immediately saw how much more efficient, and profitable, it was to sell the performance. Moreover, recordings provided additional income for musicians as well as composers. Of course, it wasn't quite that simple, or easy. It took most of the first half of the century to build the kind of music business we now take for granted.

Then along came rock and roll.

It all started in the early 1950s, as the "pop(ular) music" business kept growing with the unprecedented post–World War II economic growth. More people had radios and phonographs. Moreover, in 1949, the modern vinyl records ($33^1/_3$ and 45 rpm) came into use. These new formats could put a lot more music on a single disc, making recorded music cheaper. It took a few years for this format to displace the earlier 78-rpm records, but when the new formats took hold, they provided the opportunity to provide more music at less cost than ever before.

Until the 1950s, popular music had grown from the musical theater, which had been the biggest source of tunes that would sell. This, plus blues and jazz, had given birth to the hugely popular big-band (twelve to sixteen pieces) swing music of the 1930s and '40s.

Record producers noted that there was now an enormous demand for new music. There was also a new generation of kids, born during and after World War II, who had a whole different attitude from their parents'. These kids, and a lot of the adults, would listen to and buy just about anything.

Meanwhile, other musical forms were slowly becoming popular, largely unnoticed by most of the population. There were many distinct types of folk music found in America, from the Appalachian reels to the New England chanteys back to the well-established forms now known as "country music." And then there were the African musical forms that had been slowly spreading from their Southern roots. Sustained and further developed by the descendants of slaves, what was then known as "race music" had not yet broken out as a distinct musical form of its own. The blues, boogie-woogie, swing, and jazz were all

African-American-influenced musical forms that tended to hide their roots.

Right after World War II, it began to happen. Up-tempo forms of Western or "hillbilly" music began to adopt a fast-paced version of blues music to create what would sound like, to modern ears, rock and roll. But it wasn't; it was "rhythm and blues" and was seen as a strictly black form of music. But, as with jazz and the original blues, white musicians were attracted to the new music. In the early 1950s, record producers began to notice that if you had white musicians singing black, you had some very popular music. Elvis Presley was not the only new white artist who got his start because he could "sing black," but he was certainly the most successful.

America was still largely, although not completely, segregated racially, in the 1950s. This meant that black musicians could rarely be booked to perform for a white audience. There were not many places this could be done, and thus not a lot of money in that approach. In the fifties, musicians had to get out and perform live to promote their recordings. It was only several decades later that we saw the development of the studio musician, who rarely performed live and got rich just off recordings. Thus it was hard for a black musician to make a dent in the majority white market.

It turned out that there was tremendous pent-up demand among white teenagers for the kind of music many black rhythm-and-blues musicians were playing. Most radio stations dared not play (too much) black music for white audiences. Sponsors might get nervous, and sponsors were paying the bills. But some stations did play rhythm and blues for white audiences, and white musicians began playing the music for white (and sometimes black) audiences.

By the early 1950s, astute record producers were signing white artists to cut records of their "black" music. Most of these musicians came from down South, where whites and blacks, despite slavery and segregation, had been sharing music for generations. Often called "rockabilly," this music merged elements of Celtic folk music (that formed the foundation of much country music) with rhythms and vocal styles from Africa.

But rock and roll was not so simple. Many different styles of music were called rock and roll. This was one reason for the success of rock; it appeared in many different forms and was able to appeal to many different audiences. No matter how eclectic people's taste in music, they would probably find some form of rock to their liking. And the record producers loved it, signing up groups as fast as they appeared. Unlike past forms of popular music, it was easy to play rock. The key musical elements were the rhythm instruments, mainly drums and bass. Even the electric guitarist could spend most of his time strumming chords. Many successful rock groups got by with minimal instrumental skills. The singing was not always prime quality, but in a way rock also drew from its gospel-music roots, where enthusiasm often made up for shortcomings in technique. There was also a lot of a cappella music, more popularly known as doo-wop. Again, this came from ancient Celtic and African forms of singing, but the rock version put greater emphasis on the beat.

"Rhythm-oriented" applied to much of the popular music that has been invented ever since humans began to create tunes. Rock was unique because the rhythm and beat were pervasive and the lyrics often uninhibited. This could describe songs sung for centuries when people got together for a few drinks and a good time. But this kind of music had rarely been the officially sanctioned entertainment. That honor went to more solemn religious or "classical" music. But in the latter part of the twentieth century, the popular music of the heart became the music of the land. Mass media met popular music, and the will of the people won out.

At the end of the century, rhythm music still rules the entertainment world. But this is not rock of the 1950s, but rap. Originally a minor form of music in the island of Jamaica (although much more ancient as a way to tell rhyming stories), it caught on in the black and Hispanic neighborhoods of New York City in the 1970s. First called hip-hop, it was thought to be a spin-off of the then popular disco music. But rap had more legs than disco. While disco required musicians and elaborate production facilities, rap was simplicity itself. The lyrics were more spoken than sung, and the musical accompaniment was purely rhythm, usually just drums (or other rappers singing a cappella). There were usually other singers in a rap group to provide call-and-response interplay, a direct take from West African styles. A major attraction of rap for adolescents was that just about any kid could perform it. All that was needed was a decent speaking voice and some rhythm backup. The rhythm could be provided, as with the pros, by a drum machine. These had been around since the 1950s, but became wildly popular when disco broke big in the 1970s. By the 1990s, you could get a decent drum machine for a few hundred dollars. Another appealing, and initially illegal, aspect of rap was "sampling." This was the inclusion of snippets of older (often rock-and-roll or rhythm-and-blues) songs. Using his own voice, a drum machine, and a tape recorder, any kid could turn out a passable rap track. The more talented kids created impressive stuff, which earned them a local following or, if they were really good and ambitious, a recording contract. Rap, like all earlier rock music, moved from the bottom up to achieve mass-media reach. About three quarters of rap recordings sell to nonblack buyers, mostly white suburban kids.

Rap also created its own forms of promotion. While the early rock-and-roll musicians hustled their music with months of one-night stands in any venue that would have them, rappers saw that the buzz for a hot new group began within urban neighborhoods where rap was the main form of music. The folks downtown and in the suburbs took their cues from that buzz. So the rappers formed their own promotion teams that put up posters everywhere. This included places where posters were prohibited, as in railroad tunnels, freeway entrances, and anywhere else where potential listeners might see them. Rappers would sometimes personally distribute tapes and CDs to small (but influential) urban record shops. The Internet was also used, via Web sites and newsgroups. Once the buzz got going, it took off, and another hit rap artist got picked up by the major recording distributors and radio stations.

Rappers were not the only ones with unique record-promotion techniques in the 1980s. There was also MTV (Music TV), which recognized that members of the rock-and-roll generation spent at least as much time watching television as they did listening to music. Thus, in 1981, MTV first appeared on cable television. Before the 1980s were out, it was a major force in music promotion. The concept was simplicity itself. Musicians made short (the length of their current hit) videos, adding catchy visuals to their music. The musicians paid for the videos and submitted them to MTV, which selected the ones they thought would attract the audience. It was a natural fit, and the "MTV approach" soon spread to movies and other TV programs. The music videos presented dramatic images that changed as quickly as the lyrics and tempo of the songs being performed. By the end of the century, rock and roll had conquered not only ears but eyes and brains as well. Filmmakers and publishers soon noticed that young Americans had shorter attention spans, or at least that they responded more enthusiastically to material presented in the manner of an MTV video.

Rock influenced other forms of entertainment in large part because it was a form of music that could, and did, draw from all others. This included classical, jazz, folk, and the prerock pop music. Not only was rock big, it was all-inclusive. The popularity and inclusiveness of rock were complementary characteristics that defined popular music at the end of the twentieth century. And with that widespread popularity, rock changed many other things that were not considered music.

Rock itself was more than just the music, and the ultimate impact of rock was still unclear at the end of the twentieth century.

——Shopping as Entertainment——

"Going to the market" has always been a fun thing for people to do. This is one reason markets were first set up thousands of years ago. What we lose sight of is that the twentieth century was a time when shopping became a major form of entertainment. Not the sort of thing that gets much attention in polite conversation and public discourse, but there it is.

Humans have long enjoyed wandering around "looking for stuff." Children will bring home animals, flowers, and sundry junk that they have picked up. It was long thought that most people eventually grew out of this. The shopping that adults did was a necessity, not an entertainment. Oh, much was made about how women liked to shop, and some women of means did seem to go at it with remarkable gusto. But it wasn't until the 1970s, when several market-research surveys showed that shopping was considered a major form of entertainment, that the truth was revealed. The survey questions were not asked deliberately, but simply because the survey authors were looking for new categories of entertainment. Few of the experts thought that shopping would turn out to be seen as an entertainment. But the people who put together opinion surveys long ago learned that you never know what the missing questions are, so you just keep throwing out new questions.

The survey results showing that shopping was one of the leading forms of entertainment, for men and women, were not that much of a surprise once the researchers thought about it. Ever since the 1960s, when the modern shopping mall was introduced, it was obvious that hordes of people were being drawn to the malls by more than convenient shopping. By the 1980s, teenagers hanging out at the malls was becoming common. While a lot of the kids were there to shop (if not buy), many others were there to act like . . . teenagers. What was obvious was that these citadels of shopping opportunities were a favorite leisure-time activity. When finally asked in surveys, people were up-front in admitting that they simply enjoyed the act of shopping.

Retailers had long known that there were pleasure buttons one could push once a customer got inside, or even within eyeshot, of their business. Shopkeepers learned by trial and error that attractive displays of merchandise increased sales. Once the larger department stores came into being during the nineteenth century, working out what to put where started to become a science. This process took off in the twentieth century. By the 1970s, the science of store layout was fully established. Research, plus a lot of trail and error, developed very effective techniques. For example, supermarkets (another twentieth-century innovation) put the most popular items (usually meats) at the far end of the store, so you have to pass the maximum number of other items to get to and from the goodies. These and other items are displayed as attractively as possible, and because trail and error is used to determine which pitches work best, don't feel too bad if you end up with a few extra items in your cart after going to the back of the store just to get some franks and chicken.

Malls are equally calculating. Mall owners don't take just anyone when they are renting space. They want a few large, well-known stores in their mall as "anchors." These stores will bring in the traffic, and this enables relatively higher rents to be charged to the smaller stores. But it is the customer who ultimately pays for all this fun and games. Mall prices are relatively high, which provides an opening for the discount stores. And so it goes.

The sociologists and anthropologists promptly got into the act by pointing out that men and women in more primitive cultures took pleasure in the act of gathering food. For women, it was a matter of foraging around the village for edible plants and insects. Women often did this in groups, as well as teaching the younger girls what was useful and what was not. For most of these foragers, this was a pleasurable activity. Sort of like a treasure hunt, for you never knew what you would find. But what you did find you could eat, and eating has also long scored high on the list of pleasurable activities. Men generally had a different approach to shopping; they called it hunting. Men went after edible animals that could not just be picked up. The animals had to be chased down and killed. This was often difficult, and twentieth-century scientists measuring the effort used by male hunters and female gatherers often found that the women's technique was a more efficient way of obtaining food. But the men were bigger and louder and had weapons, so the male version of "what form of food-gathering was more valuable" became the standard for thousands of years. The women knew better, and now everyone else does. But, one must remember, for a long time, who was going to argue with a big guy carrying a nasty spear?

When it comes to shopping, women still forage and men still hunt. The women cannot understand how men can go into a store, go right for what they want, buy it, and be done. No comparison-shopping? No wandering around to see what else is available? Men are equally baffled by the hours women spend in stores, seemingly wandering around fingering merchandise with no purpose. Malls make it more obvious what is going on. Take a good look and you will see mostly women wandering about handling the goods. In the open areas and outside the mall, you will find numerous men, waiting for the women's shopping to be done. The women are enjoying themselves, while the men would rather be home playing with the TV remote. But that's another story.

Shopping became such a popular activity in the last few decades of the century that people went freelance. Flea markets developed into a major form of commerce during the 1980s and '90s. Every weekend, thousands of flea markets spring up in parking lots and empty lots. Millions of shoppers descend on these collections of secondhand goods and, well, shop. No one anticipated this; it was basically an outgrowth of garage and apartment sales. While most people like to shop, a lot of folks love to sell. The flea markets are basically the ancient bazaars updated as pure fun, and not simply a means of getting life's necessities (or luxuries).

Once the World Wide Web was established, auction and flea-market sites began to appear. By the end of the century, millions of people were buying and selling via the Web.

People love to shop, and you can't stop them.

——Radio——

Radio changed the world early in the twentieth century. It was a technological and media revolution unlike any experienced before or since.

The fundamental theory of radio was developed in the nineteenth century—1860, to be precise. Physicist James Maxwell worked out on paper the existence of electromagnetic (radio) waves. But like much else that scientists have discovered in theory, it took some diligent engineering to make the theoretical a reality. This is an important point to remember the next time you hear about some new scientific breakthrough. Eventually those engineers make it more than neat new stuff; they make it work.

By the 1890s, another physicist, Heinrich Hertz, actually created radio waves. But by 1898, a more practical engineer, Guglielmo Marconi, actually built and patented a working radio. It could only send code (Morse code, as used in the telegraph). But this was an enormous breakthrough, for now ships at sea could maintain contact with each other and with people on land. By 1900, such "wireless telegraphs" were being installed on ships, and in 1912, the sinking of the *Titanic* provided a vivid demonstration of how useful the wireless telegraph could be. Without the wireless, no one would have lived through the sinking of the *Titanic*, for no one would have known about it until the survivors had frozen to death in their lifeboats.

The wireless was also useful on land, for now it was possible to establish telegraph stations in remote areas where it was not economical to string telegraph wire. Remember that much of rural America did not get electricity until the 1930s, and wireless telegraphs were a practical way to keep in touch out there. The military promptly saw the usefulness of wireless and has been in the forefront of developing new radio technology throughout the century.

Between 1900 and 1906, inventors in Britain and America developed key components that made it possible to broadcast speech. In 1906, the experimental radio stations were broadcasting short but clear voice messages that were picked up by receivers on land and at sea. Existing wireless telegraph equipment could receive these voice messages. It was the broadcasting equipment that was different. By 1915, an experimental broadcast from North America to Britain got through.

During the 1920s, hundreds of commercial stations were set up. There was a period of chaos before governments intervened and regulated the use of frequencies, so that two or more stations would not broadcast on the same frequency. The engineers were not idle, coming up with more effective broadcasting and receiving equipment.

What really made radio work, however, was advertising. The first radio stations were set up by universities to distribute news and educational material, or by newspapers to promote the papers themselves. These all quickly went broke, for radio broadcasting was expensive, and an ongoing way to pay for it had to be found. Early radio faced problems similar to those of the Internet in the 1990s; it's neat, and everyone likes to use it, but how do you make it pay for itself? Well, if you want to see how the Internet "broadcasters" are going to pay their way, look at what happened in radio during the 1920s.

Businesses began asking to buy time on the radio stations to advertise. Adept radio broadcasters realized that this was how they could run radio stations at a profit, and mass advertising found another outlet. Movies had always been able to make money by just charging admission. But since anyone with a receiver could listen to radio broadcasts, and since there was no easy way to charge them for it, advertising was an efficient way to make radio broadcasting pay. Some nations, like Britain, did charge a license fee for owning a radio set and thus paid for the government-owned radio stations. But even in Britain, radio advertising soon appeared as a superior economic model.

America was in the lead in introducing radio on a wide scale. But through most of the 1920s, all was chaos, as there were no firm rules about who could use what frequency where. Moreover, AT&T, which had a monopoly on long-distance telephone lines, refused to let any radio station use its lines for transmitting programs unless that station joined AT&T's network. This slowed the development of networks, until AT&T was persuaded to get out of the radio business in 1926. But in the meantime, the power of network radio was demonstrated. In 1925, a twenty-four-station hookup reached 30 million listeners with the presidential inauguration.

In 1927, the Federal Radio Commission (FRC) began issuing radio-broadcast licenses. This promptly eliminated some 150 of the existing 782 radio stations. The broadcasters taken off the air lacked either the money or the ethics to run their stations according to the new regulations. But this regulation also made it possible for large investments to be made in radio, which quickly resulted in the first radio networks. With AT&T out of the way and the legal situation cleared up, the NBC and CBS networks formed and began expanding before 1930.

In less than ten years, radio came out of nowhere to become a major political, cultural, and economic force. This was an unprecedented development, although it was to be repeated in the 1950s with television and the 1990s with the Internet. But radio was the first of these electronic mass media, and once a society was exposed to radio, it was changed forever.

In the 1930s, most of the now standard radio—and later television—formats were developed. Situation comedies, soap operas, talk shows, and "you are there" news. President Franklin Roosevelt pioneered the use of network radio to reach the entire nation with important announcements or simply reassurances during the Great Depression. Indeed, radio was one of those things that made the economically disastrous 1930s more tolerable.

The Federal Communications Commission (FCC) was established in 1934, as a beefed-up, and renamed, version of the earlier FRC, which had brought order out of the chaos during commercial radio's first decade. The FCC promptly attended to some more of radio's growing pains. The two most troublesome involved freedom of speech and fraudulent advertising. The speech problem arose from the tendency of many radio-station owners to consider their powers equal to those of a newspaper publisher. This was not the case, for the mandatory FCC license to use a particular frequency had to be renewed periodically. And one of the requirements of the license was to provide public service via programming. This was then, and continues to be today, a contentious issue. Basically a station had to avoid upsetting too many people in its broadcast area; otherwise someone else might be able to grab the license when it came up for renewal. Even with this hanging over their heads, many station owners behaved in a high-handed manner, and the FCC brought these folks up short before some broadcasters were to become local dictators of what could and could not be said on their stations. This did not eliminate biases on the part of many station owners, but it did prevent the broadcasts from being completely one-sided.

The problem with fraudulent advertising was a legacy of what was still going on in print advertising. Newspapers and magazines regularly accepted ads that made false claims or were used to sell questionable merchandise. This problem continued throughout the century, but to a lesser degree. In the 1920s and '30s, however, shady advertising was rampant. It was difficult to go after print media, as they were unregulated and had First Amendment—freedom of speech—protection. People had to sue to get print media to clean up their act, and the concept of class-action lawsuits had not yet developed enough for that. But the radio ads, which did additional damage by virtue of their ability to reach the illiterate, who could not read the print ads, were subject to government sanctions for fraud. The FCC was not able to eliminate the problem completely, but the threat of losing one's license cleaned up most of the shady advertising.

When World War II came along, radio was considered so important that men working for stations could be exempted from the draft. On the downside, the government froze all licenses, not allowing any new stations to start up for the rest of the war. Moreover, all radio stations were placed under tighter government control for the duration. The one bit of good news was that just before the war began, the FCC authorized the construction of FM stations (a straight-line signal, rather than longer-range AM signals that bounced off the upper atmosphere), which provided a higher-quality sound from the radio. But the war, and the introduction of television right after the war, meant that it would be over twenty years before FM became a formidable broadcast medium.

In 1940, only 73 percent of United States households had radios, and few radios could be bought during the war. But by 1946, as the electronics industry quickly switched from military to civilian production, 93 percent of households had radio. People saw clearly how important radio was, during the war, for information and entertainment.

But just as radio stood poised to become even more pervasive in American life, along came television. TV was actually ready to roll out in 1941, when the FCC authorized the first broadcasting licenses and manufacturers were gearing up to produce receivers. But then World War II came along, and everything was put on hold until the fighting ended. As soon as the war was over, the electronics and broadcasting companies went forward with TV. It took off beyond anyone's expectations. In 1953, annual radio advertising revenue peaked at $3 billion. The next year, TV advertising revenue passed radio's. It was not the end for radio, but TV was now the principal mass medium. While TV revenues raced ahead ($7.3 billion in 1960, and over $10 billion by 1966), it wasn't until the late 1960s that radio revenues got back to where they were in the early 1950s.

Radio had to redefine itself, and it did. The major radio stations were not hurt as badly as you might think, for the people who grabbed most of the first television-broadcast licenses were the same firms that owned the local radio stations. This made sense, as who else had that much experience in broadcasting? There wasn't much difference between broadcasting radio and TV signals (which were basically FM). What the coming of TV did do was turn radio into a small business. When radio was the only broadcast show in town, it was a big business, and a few stations tended to get most of the advertising revenue. But after television arrived, radio broadcasting specialized. The number of stations increased from 3,300 in 1955 to over 7,000 in 1975. FM stations went from 800 in 1955 to 3,000 in 1975. Instead of a few music formats, dozens were developed. There were all-news and all-talk stations and listener-supported public radio stations. Radio broadcasters learned to position themselves to complement TV. "Drive time," the morning and afternoon rush-hour periods when millions of people were in their cars, became mainly a radio market. You could not drive and watch TV at the same time. Decades of experimentation in formats and development of advertisements that worked well on radio returned radio to profitability and growth.

At the end of the century, radio was the most profitable of the mass media. The United States alone had 10,000 radio stations. It was not just the low overhead of radio that made these stations so popular; there were also economies of scale available to radio that the other media could not match. A radio-station manager didn't have to own anything except his license to transmit on a certain frequency in a specific area. Everything else could be outsourced. Numerous programming services can provide whatever kind of music, talk, or other "content" you want to carry on your station. Accounting, ad sales, and even news broadcasts can be obtained from firms that specialize in providing those services to radio stations. Most stations have some on-air staff, but many have fewer and fewer of their own people on the air, or working in station administration. It's no wonder radio is so profitable, and often the listeners don't realize, or don't care, that they are listening to a robostation. The same trend is appearing in television.

It's the future.

Send in the droids.

——Television——

At the end of the century, television is the top media dog. Bursting on the scene right after World War II, television was rapidly adopted by an increasingly affluent population. Television changed everything, often in ways we do not yet fully understand.

Television was invented, as a practical device, in the 1920s. Work continued into the 1930s, and the first broadcasting license was actually issued in 1941. But World War II intervened, and no television sets could be produced until the war ended in mid-1945. The electronics industry gained a lot of experience designing and manufacturing electronic equipment for the military during the war. This included many TV-like displays for radar sets and a multitude of FM-band (which TV uses) broadcasting equipment.

By 1946, there were 8,000 TV sets in homes and 30 TV stations. In 1948, there were 172,000 homes with TV and 108 stations. The business took off like a rocket. TV was hot, and everyone wanted to have it. Initially, TV sets cost several thousand dollars, but the price began dropping quickly and continued to drop until the end of the century. By 1951, there were 10 million TV homes but the same number of stations as in 1948.

At first, TV was still restricted to the major cities. By 1955, this had changed, with 458 stations serving 30 million TV homes. This meant that most of the population was covered by a TV signal. In 1975, there were 60 million TV households. At the end of the century, over 95 percent of American households had television, serviced by over a thousand TV stations and nearly as many cable channels.

TV was a shocking development. Consider that in the 1950s, there were many people born at the turn of the century who grew up without even radio. They never imagined having something like television in their own homes. They had seen silent movies when they were young, but that was perceived as cut-rate live theater. Then radio came along, and all of a sudden people could hear all this information and entertainment at home. Amazing. Then, thirty years later, their grandchildren are growing up with television. There had never been such lightning improvements in media before.

But while the rapid appearance and spread of TV might have been impressive to the viewers, it was devastating to all other forms of mass media. Radio, newspaper, and film saw their revenues slow, and in many cases shrink. People started staying home to a degree never experienced before. The phrase "glued to the set" entered the vocabulary. Before long, most people were spending about a fifth of their time in front of the TV.

The generation that grew up after World War II grew up on TV. Much of the early programming consisted of films from the previous twenty years. By the 1960s most of the material was created expressly for television and had much greater appeal and impact. A generation had become addicted to the tube and was dependent on it for much of its entertainment, information, and direction.

Before long, heavy users of TV were seen developing an epicurean approach and becoming picky. The widespread introduction of cable TV and VCRs came along to feed this. Soon the average person was spending far more time viewing than reading, and the trend continued throughout the century. A more ominous development noted in the late 1990s was that a quarter of the population was spending more time watching the tube than talking to other people. That was a situation that did not exist in 1900.

VCRs led to the development of tapes that emulated most popular print categories, including "how-to" and inspirational subjects (both sacred and profane). These tapes used ever more carefully crafted production values that shared a symbiotic relationship with an increasingly video-literate audience. In effect, print was being replaced, for many people, with video editions.

Televised material was called, not literature, but programming, which was one of the few candid terms used in the business. New users required no training to appreciate it; even animals and infants could be entertained by having a TV placed in front of them. The simplicity of TV material can be, and usually is, misleading. Simplification is required to get points across. The passive nature of the medium does not allow for too much exposition, lest you lose your audience. To hold a viewer's attention programmers need to dole out a lot of short, self-contained, and striking visual and sound elements. This approach is used for all forms of video. Advertising, propaganda, public relations, and broadcast news all use their striking visual presentations to influence the hopes, fears, lifestyles, desires, and consumption patterns of viewers. This is an unavoidable result of TV viewing. We have been conditioned to react a certain way to certain video images. Calling it brainwashing might be too strong a term, but conditioning is very close to the mark.

Television quickly became the preferred advertising medium. TV was the easiest way to reach the greatest number of people. Heavy doses of TV appealed particularly well to the illiterate, less educated, inattentive, and semicomatose. Because television is such a direct and visual way to present material, there developed constant competition to create programs that appeared different. This wasn't easy. It had to be outrageous without being too offensive. Selling hysteria and fear is a generally unplanned by-product of TV news. Print was guilty of this also, but TV does it better and faster.

Advertising, and TV programming in general, also manages to push a feeling of inadequacy if the proffered products are not, or cannot be, bought. This causes social unrest and increased consumption, as people try to match the lifestyle portrayed as "average" in numerous television programs.

What made American TV so effective was its impressive production values. Other nations, particularly dictatorships, looked on in envy. For propaganda, as pioneered by the fascists and communists, was useful for keeping strongmen in power. Propaganda tends to take a rather uptempo approach, although the results are less than expected because the governments that use it the most have the least resources for quality work, and a lot of cynical citizens. Late in the twentieth century, dictators learned from their democratic colleagues that public-relations professionals did a better job. Public-relations activities influence all aspects of media and unleash a lot of talent for the express purpose of getting someone or something on the tube.

Theatricality is to be expected by performers, but the pervasive presence of TV increases the impact of the sensational and often frivolous material. Print operates on the mind differently than video. While words can be compelling, they can never reach the impact of pictures. If you want to convince someone, use print; if you want to overwhelm someone's emotions, use video.

Information is also obtained largely from video in a TV culture. Increasingly, people get most of their news from TV and radio and consider it superior to print sources. This process is often more a matter of entertainment than information. A minority of the population reads books, and even among this group, as many prefer the TV version as rely on print. "How-to" VCR tapes and video education are growing in importance, to a large degree because students cannot be gotten to read printed materials. Corporations maintain their own closed-circuit networks with live and recorded material. The favored means of transmitting information in business and government is "the presentation." This is basically a narrated slide show and revival meeting.

Voice mail and fax also show up increasingly. Much of this replaces print. A picture is literally worth a thousand words, as the same amount of data is required on a computer for a thousand words as for a picture. It is becoming easier to use less print.

Print eventually adopted visual techniques. Illustrated novels, instructional manuals in comic-book form, and many other trends show the heavy influence of video on print. This has been for the better, as complex concepts are difficult to present quickly and clearly in print. The primary problem is showing restraint; one is easily led to go heavy on the sizzle at the expense of the steak. Visual entertainment has so overtaken print that the illustrated novel has become a major source of entertainment. In Japan and Latin American nations, the fully illustrated novel form outsells the traditional text version by a wide margin. Comic books are a major source of reading material in highly educated and industrialized Japan. Part of this is due to their underdeveloped video industry. But even in the United States, comics are a growing source of entertainment, and the illustrated approach is becoming more pervasive.

Videotape recorders, rather than decimating the movie business, revitalized it. Revenues from theater showings of films now make up the minority of the income. Showings on broadcast TV and VCR not only grow at an outstanding rate, but the release of VCR versions has not markedly decreased theater attendance. This arises largely out of the part a large screen plays in the spectacle effect of a film, as well as the shared experience of an audience, which becomes part of the performance. The need for this is shown by the persistent use of laugh and applause tracks on TV shows. However, the growth of VCRs has led film to become a more personal experience. Sales of movie-theater tickets and VCRs exceed sales of nontextbook books. The move away from print is understated by this, as most of the tapes sold are actually rented out several times and then sold.

One thing that led to the decline in theater attendance and network-TV viewing was the erosion of generalist films. Pictures were increasingly targeted at specific demographic groups, thus making attendance by mixed groups of people with different interests less likely. This was a response to the inroads of TV and inadvertently created libraries of films that appealed to VCR users.

Television, initially heavily influenced by movies, eventually turned the tables and forced movies to look more like television. Film uses different techniques than TV. Television developed unique styles for presenting visual material, partly because of the need to accommodate frequent commercial breaks. Creating TV programming requires a much larger bag of tricks than filmmaking. Indeed, what chiefly distinguishes TV films from conventional ones is that the TV version is shot with the smaller screen and shorter attention span of the viewer in mind. The smaller screen, and the need to break frequently for commercials, forced directors to come up with new tricks and techniques to keep people looking at their show. Plot lines were kept simple, and this eventually developed into a show's having multiple plot lines, the better to hook more viewers. If one plot line didn't work, another would. Eventually news shows followed the same pattern, with newsworthy items being those that could be presented in a minute or less. More important for the news was the need to show things that people *wanted* to see, not, as one would imagine, items that people *should* see. News became entertainment. Longer news-magazine shows were little different, with a soap-opera form being used. For example, a preferred (and frequently used) angle was that of the little guy battling big government, big business, or some other "big but evil" entity.

Perhaps the most obvious example of uniquely television-oriented programming is found in the commercials and, later on, in the MTV-type music videos. The latter were derived from the former. Commercials were made for maximum impact and, second for second, are the most expensive forms of video made. Many of the music videos were made by directors of commercials. This type of work became the training ground of those who went on to direct television and movie features. And it shows. But it also works. For a generation mesmerized by television programming and commercials, the quick cuts and sharp production values were familiar and popular. It's not for nothing we soon heard the phrase "MTV generation." Short attention spans, abetted by the TV remote control, made it essential for any creator of video programming to produce product that could hold its own against short attention spans.

Heavy viewers of TV come to expect the same style of film when they go to the movies, and to get these heavy TV viewers back into movie theaters, the movies have changed. Books, newspapers, and all other media have also changed. Television changed everything.

And it isn't over yet.

In 1998, high-definition television (HDTV) was first available to the public. This consists of a larger-screen television (similar to the shape of most movie screens) with greater detail. New broadcast frequencies and techniques are needed to get the HDTV signal out, so it will be a while before use of HDTV is widespread. Will HDTV change anything? It will make television more pleasant to look at. Some of the advantages movie theaters still retain will be lost when HDTV arrives in force. Going into the twenty-first century, TV will be the media format to beat.

So what?

Well, after fifty years of television, some trends have been noted. Kids, and adults, who grew up with TV, tend to be overweight and in poor health because of all that TV viewing and the lack of exercise. Moreover, as TV was introduced into other nations, it was noticed that within ten to fifteen years, there was a precipitous rise in juvenile delinquency and crime in general. A coincidence? Probably not.

What TV did that movies did not was to present, powerfully and often, a different view of what an acceptable lifestyle should be like. Real life is not nearly as luxurious or exciting as portrayed on television. But many people, especially the younger folks, don't realize that. It's not only the advertising that is promoting stuff. The shows themselves—and the most popular ones overseas are American-made—push a lifestyle and attitude that has an effect on the viewers. It's subtle at first, but soon becomes obvious. It's largely because of television that American culture has become so popular everywhere.

The casual portrayal of so many consumer goods has been good for manufacturers of those goods, for many more people see what used to be luxuries as necessities. It took several decades for this effect to be noticed. But there it is.

You didn't really think all those hours of TV viewing would leave all those people unaffected, did you?

——Cable TV——

Cable television is the future of television. But it didn't start out that way, and at the end of the century, it's unclear exactly what that future will be.

Cable television came about because of two problems: poor TV signals and not enough channels. The concept was that, as with telephone service, people would pay to have another wire attached to their home, this one bringing in television broadcasts.

The idea for such cable systems is not new. They first began to show up in the 1920s to provide better radio reception. Although radio signals have much longer ranges than TV (or other FM) broadcasts, there were still places in America where it was hard to get good radio reception. And so in the early 1920s, large reception towers that caught distant signals were built and then provided those signals over cable much as cable TV is provided today. The cost was about thirty dollars a month. Some of these systems still exist, although now they concentrate on carrying TV programming. When television came to the rural areas in the 1950s, there were even more people, and communities, who were too far away, or too surrounded by mountains, to get decent reception. So there were more cable operations set up, all for the purpose of getting better reception. The technology had to be a little different, as the TV signals were more complex than those of the older AM radio. Not surprisingly, some of the first people to set up cable-TV operations were rural appliance dealers. In the late 1940s, televisions were a hot new item, but dealers could sell them only if potential buyers could get a good TV signal. So one rural appliance dealer after another set up cable-TV operations so they could get local folks to buy the new TVs.

In big cities, there were also cable-TV operations early on, partly to get a better signal from one good antenna, but also to use one "master antenna" for large apartment buildings and eliminate the forest of individual TV antennas that were beginning to sprout on these buildings.

By the late 1950s, microwave towers were being used to pass TV signals to remote locations and to the local cable-TV company. Always looking for a new angle, in the 1960s some cable operators tried to set up pay-TV operations that would offer premium content (new movies, sports events) for a small fee. It took some ten years to work through all the legal and logistical problems for doing this, but in 1972, Home Box Office (HBO) made its debut. While HBO appears a brilliant idea at the end of the century, in the early 1970s it was seen as a major folly.

Through the 1970s, cable grew slowly, until HBO began transmitting its signals by satellite. This made it much easier to get the programming to every cable network that wanted it. Commercial satellites were just getting started in the 1970s, and cable television turned out to be a major customer. In 1980, another seemingly rash venture, Cable News Network (CNN), began broadcasting. The idea of a lot of people wanting a twenty-four-hour cable news show seemed a bit over the top at the time. But before too long the idea caught on. The 1980s brought more and more specialized cable channels, each seemingly stranger than the last. At least at first. But most of these ventures succeeded. In 1987, half of all United States households had cable access, and this proved a kind of critical mass to allow over a hundred new cable channels to appear and flourish.

Cable also had a major influence on traditional, network-oriented programming. Through the 1980s, increasing numbers of people watched cable channels more and network programming less. By the end of the century, the networks had less than half the TV audience. The networks knew they had to change or go broke, as their business was based on having a larger portion of the viewing public watching their stuff. By 2000, the networks were still there, but it was obvious that the future would see many smaller cable (and noncable) networks offering programming to more specialized audiences. Thus, in half a century, television had gone from being the most massive of mass media to the most highly fragmented of media.

All because of cable TV.

Now you know.

——World Wide Web——

The World Wide Web is the first interactive mass medium, and it didn't come from nowhere. It came from nearby, with some strange baggage in tow, and some unexpected results.

First there were the movies. But this was just theater on a grander, cheaper, and more frequently visited scale. Then came radio. Now we had a mass medium that was always there. Television muscled its way past radio and film to become the major leisure activity of most people because it provided sound and pictures in the home.

But then the personal computer appeared, and those who had PCs spent less time watching TV. But in the early 1990s, the Internet became widely available, and suddenly television had a really serious rival. The World Wide Web provided a new, if initially crude, form of television that was interactive, and there was a lot more than just viewing. Not bad for a system assembled, like Dr. Frankenstein's monster, from odd parts and whose main purpose was originally to provide communication after a nuclear war.

The Internet is simplicity itself. No one owns it, for the Internet is just a bunch of agreed-on technical rules that enable different computers to send messages to each other. Data is sent in electronic bursts (or "packets"), each one with a unique identity and information on where it is going and where it is coming from. The Internet just delivers the packets or, if it can't do that, reports to the sender that there is a problem. The Internet uses private long-distance phone lines to move all this stuff to local telephone exchanges, where the data proceeds as a local phone call. The company from which you get Internet access pays a telephone company a hefty monthly fee for the right to connect to the main Internet "backbone" lines. That's why you have to pay the monthly fee to be connected. Those with Internet access from school or work have their access paid for them by the school or company. But everyone pays. In effect, the Internet is a huge private telephone company using what are called "leased lines" (direct, twenty-four-hour-a-day telephone connections of a certain capacity between two places, "leased" from a communications company). When too many people try to send stuff through some parts of the Internet at the same time, everything slows down. But most of the time it works fine. And because it is so unstructured, the Internet (much of it) will work even after a catastrophe. Well, at least that's what it was designed to do.

Communications between computers over telephone lines is nothing new. By the 1960s, it had become common, but only in large corporations, some universities, and the like using their massive mainframe computers. When personal computers came along in the late 1970s, many of the first PC users were techies who worked on the mainframe data networks and saw no reason PCs could not do the same thing. By 1979, the first BBSs (bulletin-board systems) were up and running. These systems used PCs to run a BBS program, which allowed other PC users to call in to the BBS with telecommunication (telcom) programs to leave, and read, messages (the bulletin board) as well as send and get files (programs, data, pictures of naked women, whatever). The only other piece of equipment needed was a modem, which enabled the PC to send and receive data over a phone line. At first these modems were very expensive, as the only ones available were sturdy models used by corporations. But the modem manufacturers saw a large new consumer market, and soon under-$500 modems came out. The early models were slow (300 baud, or about 30 characters a second, versus 56,000 baud in the late 1990s), but they brought people together.

Within a few years, there were thousands of BBSs in operation, and some of the more popular ones had multiple phone lines and were charging monthly fees for use. By 1990, there were some 30,000 BBSs, mostly in the United States. The vast majority were run as hobbies by their operators. This was in the spirit that had early arisen among many computer professionals and hobbyists, an attitude of sharing and public service. This attitude would be carried over to the World Wide Web, for that's where most of the BBS operators and users ended up.

But even as the BBSs were being invented, the commercial data-communications systems saw an opportunity to cash in. The first of these was CompuServe, which grew rapidly in the 1970s by providing computer-to-computer access for businesses. CompuServe's main-frames provided data and other resources that businesses could use via a modem, phone line, and a data terminal (keyboard and TV-like CRT). It seemed an obvious idea to make the system available at night and on weekends, when business users were off-line, so BBS-type activities could be conducted. Great idea. It worked. Even though initially the cost was over ten dollars an hour. CompuServe, and the other data networks that did this (like GE), had national (and international) links for their business customers, and these local phone numbers meant that the BBS-type customers avoided long-distance charges. One of the disadvantages of the BBSs was that if you wanted to call one out of your local area, it was a long-distance call. That could get expensive really fast. So the data networks became popular despite their hourly charges.

But by the early 1990s, there were only a million or so people on-line, on many different networks and generally unable to contact other nets directly.

Meanwhile, the Internet was being invented on college campuses and military laboratories. The Department of Defense needed a communications system that would survive a nuclear attack. Many of the defense researchers in labs and universities across the nation wanted a more convenient way to keep in touch. Since the late 1950s, research on how to set up such a network had been going on. By the late 1960s, ARPANET was in operation, at least for research purposes. ARPA (the Advanced Research Projects Agency), by the way, was one of those rare government organizations that actually did what it set out to do. Basically, ARPA had a pile of money and a mandate to find seemingly off-the-wall ideas and turn them into something useful. This ARPA has done time and again. The Internet was merely one of the better-known ARPA projects.

But by the early 1970s, over a dozen campuses and major government research centers were linked. The first e-mail message was sent in 1972. Everyone who saw ARPANET in operation wanted it. Year by year, more sites were linked. In 1979, USENET (bulletin boards) was established on the Internet.

But in 1980, the Internet was still small. There were 400 computers connected and about 10,000 users. The BBS and commercial systems had more users, and these folks saw the Internet as nothing more than the Pentagon's form of telecommunication. True enough, but the Internet proved to be much more. In 1983, the military users of ARPANET split off to form MILNET. ARPANET was reorganized as a purely civilian service, and in 1989 it got a new name: the Internet. Now that it was separated from military and government control, the Internet could reach out and connect with all the other networks out there.

In 1989, the Internet was still just one of many networks, but it had developed one major advantage. It had a set of standards that enabled many different types of computers and software systems to talk to one another. That was the main point of developing ARPANET in the first place. But until 1990, the Internet was noncommercial. However, after years of agitation by users and potential users, the Internet became a commercial operation during the early 1990s. Corporations quickly established links, and companies began offering access to anyone willing to pay a monthly fee. This spotlights another generally unknown aspect of the Internet. Its most energetic users, from the beginning, were businesses. Not so much for marketing but for communication with other businesses (suppliers and customers). Naturally, most people don't see this, but there it is.

In the 1980s and '90s, a growing number of students had been coming out of Internet-equipped universities and were eager to use it again. Even though most people knew nothing about the Internet in the early 1990s, a lot of people in the computer business, and most recent college grads, had already used it. In 1992, the first of the commercial nets (Delphi) linked its system to the Internet. In the next two years, most of the other commercial nets established Internet links.

By 1983, there were 10 million PCs in the United States; by 1986, it was 30 million; and in 1989, 50 million. The number of computer users, especially those who had modems, was also growing at a rapid clip during the early 1990s. At the beginning of the decade, only about 10 percent of households had PCs, by the end of the decade, it was over half. And those households that did not have an Internet connection at home often had one at work. The world was getting wired, but it wasn't until the World Wide Web came along that most people were willing to try out the Net.

In the early 1990s, several groups of scientists were looking for a quick and convenient way to exchange technical documents and graphics over the Internet. What evolved from these discussions was the World Wide Web, which was nothing more than documents stored on Internet computers that required a special viewing program to be looked at. The viewing program was called a browser. It was simple to use (much like the 1980s Macintosh PC and the 1990s Windows PCs), so that more people could easily get information off the Web, and it caught on like wildfire. Not only did this bring "point and click" to the Internet, but also the concept of hypertext (documents within documents, much like footnotes, but a lot easier to use). In mid-1993, there were only 130 World Wide Web sites. By 1995, there were 30,000; by 1996, over 600,000; and in the spring of 1997, the number of Web sites (not URLs; each URL is a separate page) exceeded a million. Not only was the Web easy to use, but it was almost as easy to create Web pages. A Web page was nothing more than a document in a hard-disk directory on a computer connected to the Internet. A Web address (URL, or Universal Resource Locator) was simply the name of an HTM (Hypertext Markup Language) file on that hard disk. If URLs look like locations of files on a hard disk, it is because they are. The Internet was always based on simplicity and standards, and the Web took that one step further.

By late 1995, some 9 million people were regularly using the Web, twice as many men as women, and twice as many users as six months earlier. Most users were getting access from their workplace, a quarter of all users from company nets, and another quarter via the Internet's original access point, universities. By the end of 1997, there were over 40 million Internet users in the United States. That came out to about 27 percent of all male adults and 17 percent of all adult females. By the end of the century, over two thirds of Americans had access to the Web, nearly half men and half women. Web users were spending over an hour a day on the Web, and more and more were watching television and taped movies and listening to distant radio stations via their increasingly powerful PCs, often with an assist from the Web.

How did this happen? Some of the reasons were obvious. The Web made the Internet extremely easy to use. This was really important, for while many of the first few million PC users were an adventurous and technically adept lot, most of the later users were not. The complexity and unpredictable performance of PC software did not slow down the first users all that much. But as the number of users mushroomed going into the 1990s, ease of use became more of an issue. The Internet would have remained small and populated by the PC elite had not the Web came along. But there was more going on than ease of use, for just having a browser was not enough. You had to get connected via your phone, and telecommunications were never as "plug and play" as advocates preached (or simply wished). Salvation came from one of the older on-line services: America Online (AOL).

AOL took five years to reach 300,000 users in early 1993. AOL grew to 1.5 million by 1994, 5 million at the end of 1995, and over 18 million in 2000. They did it the same way the Web did, via an easier-to-use interface. AOL had been around (under a different name) since the mid-1980s. Early on, AOL went for ease of use. All on-line services had started out providing really basic access, much like looking at a DOS prompt (the "c:\" rarely seen these days). Users were expected to climb a steep learning curve in order to do anything useful. "Front end" programs were created (often by users) to make things easier, but until the late 1980s, no one really went all out to make it easy to get on-line. The first attempt was Prodigy, in the late 1980s. But they made several mistakes (like charging extra for e-mail) and didn't quite get the interface right.

Meanwhile, Microsoft was desperately trying to create an easier-to-use interface for all those DOS PCs out there. Apple's Macintosh had a much easier interface, but the DOS PCs were up to a third cheaper, and this premium kept the Mac a minority player in the marketplace. But in 1990, Microsoft released its Windows 3.0 program. This version of Windows worked where the earlier versions, 1.0 and 2.0, did not.

Microsoft had labored through most of the 1980s to make Windows a useful user interface for people who saw the PC as a means toward an end, not an end in itself. Microsoft encouraged software developers to create programs for the new, improved (and finally usable) Windows. AOL went after creating a Windows front end for their service with vigor. And it showed. Windows 3.1, the definitive Windows (it worked well enough to convince a lot of users), came out in 1992, and AOL began to promote their new, easy-to-use interface in a big way. Between 1994 and 1996, AOL established a clear lead among the commercial on-line services. This, and the appearance of the World Wide Web, caused explosive growth among the on-line community, and much of it came from AOL. The first year of explosive growth in the number of Web users came in 1994, and AOL was there to take advantage of it.

While more and more businesses were going on-line (and linking into the Internet because it was a cheap way to get on-line for e-mail), it was AOL that was driving increased Internet access at home.

Prodigy's non-Windows front end, while easy to use, was pushed aside by the even easier and more mainline AOL Windows approach. AOL also had a better-organized service and a more aggressive promotion policy, based on sending out over 100 million free diskettes containing their software and a free month (or more) of service. In 1996, AOL switched from the hourly charges long customary for commercial services and adopted the flat monthly fee offered by Internet providers.

The Web appeared and grew so fast that it was difficult for users, and the society at large, to comprehend what had happened. Not only was the Web easy to use, but it offered so many new things to do. Publishing, for example, changed in ways no one had ever anticipated. Anyone could "publish" a Web page, and just about everyone did. Businesses found the Web a much easier way to communicate with their customers and suppliers. Individuals found new ways to shop, locate information, or simply "surf the Web." E-mail, chat, bulletin boards, games, promotion, and exchanging information in ways unheard of— all these sprang to life as the Web mushroomed. Media businesses, the traditional ones as well as ones established just for the Web, sought ways to make money on the Web. The comparison most often used

HOMES WITH ON-LINE ACCESS (as a Percentage of PC Households)				
SERVICE PROVIDER	JULY 1994	JAN. 1995	JULY 1995	JAN. 1996
America Online	4	5	13	14
CompuServe	5	4	6	6
Prodigy	10	8	7	5
Microsoft Network	—	—	—	1

was cable TV, which started out free (except for the monthly access fee, which is also paid to get onto the Internet) and eventually became profitable through advertising. This is the direction in which the Web is going, with the major difference being that much of the Web will remain ad-free. No one knows exactly how this will work out, which is part of the charm the Web holds for its millions of users. One interesting angle about advertising on the Web is that the ads can be truly interactive. This makes some of the more adventurous advertising sites an entertainment in themselves.

All of this media and material flowing through the Internet has provided the theoretical possibility of free long-distance phone calls and free video and audio files. But in practice, the Web is like a huge water pipe. When too many people try to get water at the same time, many get less than they expected and some get none at all. Sound and video files are big offenders. But throughout the 1990s, the telecommunications industry managed to create more carrying capacity almost as fast as Web users could find ways to use it up. Lurking in the shadows, though, is the replacement of the existing telephone service with a new one. The phone companies were caught by surprise when millions of people began to use modems. These users would get on-line for hours of time and grab a lot of line capacity with files being downloaded and messages going back and forth. Normal phone calls take up much fewer resources, since the phone company sends only the sounds and not the 50 percent of conversations that is silence. The average phone call takes only a few minutes, while the average session with a modem is at least five times longer. Since most people get onto the Internet with a local phone call, the phone company makes only the dime or less they charge for a local call, then see that line tied up big time for as much as an hour or more. In effect, every phone user supports the heavy-duty Web users. While the phone companies have asked the government to allow new fees to reflect the reality of Web users' load on the lines, the non–Web users have not complained. Meanwhile, in most of the rest of the world, local phone calls cost a penny or two a minute, and Web users have an incentive not to tie up a line for hours on end. All this line-use stuff has not become a crisis because line capacity has gotten cheaper and cheaper in the last few decades of the twentieth century. But as most PCs become powerful enough to show full-screen video as it is downloaded from the Web (and if this feature becomes popular enough) there could be some memorable traffic jams on the information superhighway.

In a century of media, the World Wide Web was a fitting medium to show up just when people thought they had seen all the new media that could possibly exist.

——What PCs Are Really Used For——

The personal computer turned out to be more personal than its inventors ever imagined. But what people actually used the machines for most of the time came as a shock to many, and a dirty little secret that deserves to have a little light shed on it.

I'll bet you didn't know that the single most compelling reason to buy a new computer is to better play the latest games. It's true. And most game publishers didn't know it either until the early 1990s, when user surveys revealed this dirty little secret. Turned out that a small segment of the computer users was buying most of the games. Nothing new here, but these same people demonstrated a breathtaking willingness to get the latest, most powerful PC available if that would make a new game play demonstrably better. Thus, through the 1990s, the minimum hardware needed to play new games escalated as never before.

Meanwhile, back at the office, many managers fought a guerrilla war with their employees over the amount of games played on company PCs. It took the suits a while to catch on; not so the players and publishers. In the early 1980s, games were being sold with the popular "boss screen." Hit a particular key while playing the game, and up pops what looks like a spreadsheet program. The players knew, the publishers knew, and eventually the boss figured it out. By the 1990s, most office PCs were on a network, which provided the opportunity for staff to play networked games like "DOOM." Great fun. Many folks stayed late at the office for this. Then the empire struck back. Several vendors brought out "sniffer" programs that looked for games on the network and removed them. A report was sent to the boss, who sometimes removed a player or two from the payroll. But this did not put an end to the work-time gaming. Players simply installed and uninstalled their games so there was nothing for the sniffer to uncover.

In the 1980s, most of the PCs bought were for business use. The "home PC" did not arrive in a big way until the 1990s, especially after the price fell below $1,000, then $500. Besides price, the other obstacle to greater home ownership of PCs was the success of the game console. Nintendo, Sega, and a few others sold tens of millions of these dedicated game computers. Cost for these "game consoles" was usually below $200, and the games came on cartridges. So there was very little illegal copying or problems getting them to run. You put the cartridge in and started playing. Console manufacturers also tightly controlled the quality of their games, further reducing problems with using them. It should be no surprise that software for these game machines outsold PC game software at the rate of 20 or 30 to 1 throughout the 1990s. Even though the console games were more expensive (often costing twice as much as PC games), they were easy to get into, and players rarely had any problems operating the console. People liked to play games on a computer more than anything else.

The rivalry between game consoles and PCs goes back to the very beginning. A year before the first PCs became available, Atari released the first game console, the Atari 2600. This 1976 bit of technology was basically a stripped-down PC, using an 8-bit microprocessor. It had no additional memory; that was in the cartridges. The 2600 didn't have a keyboard either, just a connector for a joystick and other simple game-control devices. The 2600 did have more powerful graphic routines than most PCs, because graphics were what these early arcade games were all about. The "arcade game" market grew enormously until 1981, with games like Pac-Man enormously popular. In that year, Commodore came out with its very inexpensive PC, the C-64. The C-64 could play Pac-Man as well as a console. Atari came out with an upgraded game console, the Atari 5200, in 1981. But gamers weaned on the 2600 opted for PCs, and the C-64 outsold every other PC for the next few years. It wasn't until 1985, with the introduction of Nintendo, that the console-game market recovered. Nintendo had better graphics and strict quality control over its software. The recovery took several years, and the PCs found themselves losing a lot of potential customers to the flashy graphics of the consoles. The 16-bit game consoles introduced in 1990 were even capable of running versions of some of the more popular PC-based games.

The PC manufacturers were aware of what was happening with the consoles, and constantly sought to upgrade PC power and ease of use. The ability to run more popular games on PCs was seen as a key element in beating the game consoles. What is most interesting about all this is how little attention this rivalry got in the press. Part of the reason for this is the idea, fostered by the console manufacturers, that the consoles are not computers. But they *are* computers, and because PCs in particular and computers in general have such a reputation for being hard to use, there was good reason to portray the consoles as something other than computers. Moreover, the consoles have been getting more like PCs, with the addition of CD drives, keyboards, and modems to some models. But another reason why this rivalry got downplayed is that few on the PC side are happy about talking up the large role games play in what people actually do with PCs.

The sad fact is that while people respond to surveys with a list of worthy PC activities, closer examination shows that games are the major PC activity. Even the games that come bundled with Windows (especially Solitaire) are major diversions. Some companies remove these games every time they install Windows in their PCs.

A pattern of home-PC use emerged in the late 1980s that did not appreciably change in the 1990s. Software sales for home PCs consisted of about half games, a quarter general home software (graphics, word processing, personal finance), and a quarter educational (mostly for the kids). Actual use patterns were different. Games were used more and educational software used less.

A major change in the 1990s was the growing use of the Internet. By the end of the century, over a third of American households were on-line. This was a big jump in one decade, for at the end of the 1980s, only about 3 percent of households had a modem-equipped PC. Even in the 1980s, when the only on-line activity was hard-to-use commercial services and BBSs, the most popular on-line activity was simply communicating with other people. There was e-mail and chatting, and the latter was quite popular, even though users were paying up to ten dollars an hour so they could type to others on-line at the same time. With the Internet, people could chat away for practically nothing, and they did. Hours spent on-line soared, at the expense of television and other computer activities. Easy access to chat came along with the introduction of the World Wide Web. Just wandering around the Web ("surfing") became a popular pastime. There was much to do on the Web. Shopping, information, games, and just seeing what the next Web page would bring. It was something of a game, and it suddenly gave PCs an edge over the game consoles. Although the game consoles could, and some did, get themselves equipped to use the Web, PCs were better at it. The Web was dynamic; there were always new software gadgets being put on PCs to make the Web experience better. Game consoles had to add a hard disk to deal with this angle, and doing that made game consoles PCs. Not very good PCs, thus the Web advantage for personal computers.

Throughout the short history of PCs, the main promotion angle has been the educational and home-management aspects. But these two items were seen as work by most PC owners, and were a hard sell. Given a choice, people preferred to play. This was especially the case at home, even though everyone admitted that it was a good thing to pay some attention to the education and home-management items. So software publishers worked on turning out educational software that was more fun and home-management stuff that was easier to use (and even fun).

Radio's initial appearance was touted as an opportunity to provide more education and public-service programming, but what made radio work was entertainment. It should be no surprise that at the end of the century, most PCs were still being bought to provide entertainment.

——On-line All the Time——

You may have heard of Internet junkies, people who spend hour after hour on-line. They exist, and the disease may spread. Read on and be warned.

You know a new technology has caught on and is changing the culture when you discover that a lot of people have become addicted to it. But there are addictions and there are addictions. There have been many new gadgets in this century that people got hooked on. Radio, film, TV—but nothing like on-line computer networks. The difference with on-line addiction is that it is interactive. The other electronic media are passive; you just watch, or listen. With on-line activities, you are involved, and way before the Internet came along, there were primitive (by current standards) on-line activities to hook the unwary. Naturally, the first on-line addiction was games. As soon as multi-user computer systems began to appear in the 1960s, restless programmers were creating games everyone could play. And play they did, for hours and hours. Since it was the programmers creating these diversions, it was difficult for management to stamp them out.

These early games were crude, at least in terms of graphics. There weren't any. They were what are now called "text-based adventures." The most famous of these was Zork. These games were, in effect, the current adventure games without the graphics. Zork eventually came out in a graphic version.

There were also strategy games, where a grid was created and the players searched out each other and valuable items. The most famous of these was Empire, whose premise was searching out a vast hidden world, gathering resources to build weapons and then, when players came across other players, trying to destroy them. And expand their empire.

Then came the MUDs (Multi-User Dungeons). These arose first among university-student users of the Internet. As with the earlier games, student programmers had access to programming tools on their local networks and proceeded to create games. The model they used was not so much the old adventure-type games (Zork) but rather computerized versions of the popular (in the seventies and eighties) fantasy role-playing games (like Dungeons & Dragons). These games were played in a "dungeon" created by one of the players (the Games Master), who generally supervised the proceedings. Thus the name of these new games—Multi-User Dungeons. The MUDs were basically mazes, with monsters, treasures, and tools scattered about for the players to interact with. What made the MUDs different was the ability to handle a lot more players and a greater emphasis on role-playing (acting out the characters in the game). The role-playing angle became a major draw, as those players not terribly interested in the complexities of play could simply talk. This led to a proliferation of variations on the basic MUD theme where the emphasis was almost solely on role-playing. Everyone was happy. The programmers built and tinkered with their MUDs, and the players happily explored and interacted. The MUDs also became a tremendous time sink. In some schools, a marked decline in grades was noted among those who were spending the most time on-line. Some schools tried to crack down on what the administration called "system abuse." But it was difficult to pull the plug on all those bright, and obsessed, computer-science students. Fortunately, never more than 5 or 10 percent of the students got hooked, and the worst offenders removed themselves from their obsession by flunking out (or breaking themselves of the habit). The MUD phenomenon spotlighted another on-line addiction: chat, just talking to a bunch of other people on-line in real time. This was a very popular feature of the commercial networks throughout the 1980s. Some 5 to 10 percent of users would spend thirty or more hours a week chatting. On AOL, about a third of the time used was for chat.

The attraction of chat went beyond just talking to strangers. The anonymity of the Net meant you could partake in a little role-playing, and many people did. Unfortunately, this capability brought out the creeps, and some interesting law-enforcement situations developed. Not to mention proposed legislation to "protect the children." Amazing what trouble people can get into when they have too much time on their hands.

The Internet added IRC (Internet Relay Chat) in the 1980s, and when the World Wide Web took off in the mid-1990s, so did use of the IRC. Since this chat service was essentially free, the addicts had nothing to restrain them. Fortunately, there was a bright side to this, as a lot of the people getting into IRC were retired, disabled, or otherwise unemployed. IRC was a nice way to pass the time in an interactive fashion. The IRC, however, was where most of the chat-related problems began with child molesters and creeps in general using the anonymity of the net to mask their dirty deeds. On the commercial networks, bad actors could be identified and punished. Not so on the Internet.

The commercial networks pioneered on-line games in the 1980s, but with an hourly charge of up to ten dollars an hour. The hourly charges fell throughout the 1980s, but never got below three bucks an hour. Pretty steep, and hundreds of players who couldn't help themselves suffered credit-card meltdown. Many players spent thousands of dollars a month playing these games. Some could afford it, most could not, and the player turnover was high.

The commercial networks, because of their hourly charges, never had more than 5 or 10 percent of their users turn into addicts. The Internet was another matter. The flat-rate plan allowed people to pay twenty dollars a month and stay on all they wanted. The ISPs (Internet-service providers) noted that this could cost them a lot of money. Most ISPs had one modem line for every ten to thirty customers. If too many people logged on and stayed on too long, others could not get on. Busy signals were bad for business. Some of the line hogs just logged on and left the connection going without doing anything. These were easy to deal with, as the ISPs simply had programs that monitored each active line and disconnected anyone idle for, say, fifteen minutes. But what to do about the true addicts who were on-line all the time actually doing something? The solution was to modify the flat-rate agreement, providing, say, 150 hours a month for the flat fee and charging a dollar or two per hour beyond the 150 hours. This caused a bit of a stink at first, but most users realized they used nowhere near 150 hours a month. That was about five hours a day, when average Internet usage was growing from less than half an hour per day per user in the early 1990s to an hour a day at the end of the century. The addicts either paid up or throttled back. Some simply opened a second ISP account, giving themselves ten hours a day on-line. Few addicts went beyond that, but some did.

As more things appear on the Net, more people will have reason to get an on-line jones. One example of this is instant messaging. This was pioneered by many on-line services, and the best implementation was on AOL. By the mid-1990s, there was an Internet version called ICQ. AOL bought that, and by the end of the century there were over 30 million confirmed instant-messaging users, chatting away on the spur of the moment with friends and strangers. It's a sign of the times, and you'll be seeing more stuff like this in the future.

THREE

MAKING A LIVING

ONE of the really outstanding developments in this century is the growing wealth among all people. At least in the industrialized countries, and particularly the United States. While Americans like to think that so many foreigners want to come to the United States because we are a free country, what propels most immigrants is the ability to make money. Even before the twentieth century, many immigrants left their homeland because they felt that in America the "streets were paved with gold." Well, not literally, but to the average immigrant, America was a place where you could make something of yourself. Economic opportunity was a big draw.

And generally the immigrants were correct. As more than one American politician has observed, "The business of America is business."

Note: All dollar amounts are given in terms of year-2000 dollars. That is, they are adjusted for inflation and represent the dollar value at the end of the twentieth century. If you want to see what the actual money values were for a year, see the Appendix.

——What We Earned Then and Now——

We tend to think of folks earlier in the century as being quite poor compared to the current generation. That is an illusion created by inflation and different lifestyles. Americans have actually been quite well off throughout the century.

In 1900, the average American had a lot less money to live on than we do today. Not that the average worker was poverty-stricken back then. Most workers thought they were doing pretty well. Up through World War II, the average family income was about $20,000 a year. This was for the middle 40 percent of the population. The top 20 percent of families averaged a little over twice that. The bottom 20 percent averaged about a quarter of that, and the second from the bottom 20 percent about half that.

In 1900, the average industrial worker was making about nine bucks (in 1900 dollars) a week. This was about $10,000 a year in today's money. Yet most households were making twice that. While wives rarely went out to work back then, there were often other adult family members living in the house, and they often had jobs. Children back then rarely got more than eight years of schooling and were out working as soon as they were out of school. Adult children lived at home longer and contributed their earnings to the household income. More so in the past, even married children still lived with their parents for a time. Actually, this is an ancient tradition that only went out of style in a big way during this century.

Another source of income that does not show up in the statistics is that of the housewife, children, and other family members staying at home. There was a lot more to "housekeeping" in 1900 than there is today. Many mothers (and grandmothers) made clothes for the adults and children in the household. It was common even in suburbs for family gardens to supply much of the fruit and vegetables consumed, and it was also common to preserve food for use over the winter. In many parts of the country, wood was still widely used as a fuel, and women would often do a lot of the chopping. All of these goods and services had a cost. Converting this to cash, you can see how the actual

Dirty Little Secrets of the Twentieth Century

family income was 10 to 30 percent higher than the cash amount showing up in the statistics.

At the end of the century, few households make their own clothes
or grow their own food. But there are even more abundant sources of
income that don't show up in the official statistics. Not just working
off the books, but things like food stamps, Medicaid, and public housing. In America, you are officially poor if you are a family of four and
have a household income of less than $16,000 a year. But when you
look at different sets of official statistics on what is bought, sold, and
given to people, you find that most poor Americans are not poor. Indeed, some 40 percent of the official poor own their own homes. While
some of these are rural hovels, two thirds have air-conditioning, and
90 percent have color TV. The average poor American has a third more
living space than the average Japanese (rich or poor). In an effort to
stamp out poverty, so many benefits have been made available that for
many people, it often does not pay to go to work. In such a situation,
anyone going to work would actually suffer a decline in living standards.
If you spend any time living in a poor neighborhood and getting to
know the people, you quickly see how all this works. Most of the people
in those neighborhoods are looking to get out, because there is a small
percentage who are criminals, antisocial, or both. That's why they are
"rough neighborhoods." Many people in those areas are simply inept,
and they are stuck there. But for everyone, there are ample opportunities
to get by. Over two thirds of poor households have cars, and a quarter
have two or more. There is plenty of work available off the books, and
someone who has access to food stamps, public housing, and welfare
can do quite well. There are always plenty of really sad cases, of people
who cannot cope, for the media and welfare bureaucrats to spotlight as
needed. But in the meantime, most of the officially poor spend substantially beyond the official $16,000 a year per household. The gov-
ernment's own statistics show that, as will some time spent living among
the poor. Just because the government declares you poor doesn't mean
you are stupid. And the people who are unable to form families or
function with other people in general tend to comprise most of the
poor. The two-earner household is one of the major factors for higher
household incomes, which is one reason why the poorest 20 percent of

the population has gotten poorer. Too many unmarried, socially inept individuals just scraping by.

There are several other things going on here. Per capita gross domestic product (GDP) has actually gone up five times from 1900 to 2000, while household income has increased only 2.6 times. What happened was that the average household got smaller. In 1900, the average household consisted of 4.75 people. By the end of the century, the average household was 2.6 people. As a lot more wages became available, a lot more people chose to live alone. In 1900, only 5 percent of households consisted of one person, while a century later this rose to over a quarter of households. Moreover, in 1900, 41 percent of households contained six or more people; a century later, only 4 percent of households were that large.

After World War II, the economy really took off. By 1950, the average household income was about $32,000. By 1960, it was $38,000; and by 1970, $48,000. Then came the aftereffects of the Vietnam War, and income stagnated and actually fell a bit over the next fifteen years. But by 1990, things had gotten better; the average was now $53,000, and there it pretty much stayed through the end of the century. In addition to having more money to spend, the worker at the end of the century had more time to spend it. The average workweek was seventy hours in 1900, and about forty a century later.

One of the major factors contributing to the end of income growth in the 1970s was the end of America's post–World War II dominance of the world economy. In 1945, the United States, untouched by the devastation of the war, had its industry intact. Already the planet's largest economy when the war started, and with much of Europe now in rubble, the end of the war found the United States with half the world's productive capacity. It took three decades for Western Europe and Japan to rebuild their economies, and, coming from behind, they were more competitive than most American firms. Competition ran into lazy management and entrenched unions. The management problems were generally easier to fix than the union ones. American management has always been quick to reshape itself, a generally unrecognized characteristic that has played a major role in keeping the American economy on top. Unions, however, were basically a twentieth-century development that had not aged well. Unions came along when many of the major U.S. companies implemented their new twentieth-century technologies without much regard for the workers. Not all companies were so thick-headed, but the new automobile companies were. It wasn't until late in the century that the companies found ways to make the automobile assembly line less grueling. Meanwhile, unions were organized and obtained higher and higher wages for the workers, as well as a growing number of work rules (which worker could do what and when). Union management got fat and happy too, right along with their adversaries in company management. While the stockholders could, and often did, get rid of less capable management, it was more difficult for the labor unions. There, the "stockholders" were the workers, and it was easier to sell "more" than "less." But as foreign competitors took more and more automotive and steelmaking jobs away with better and cheaper products, the unions had no choice but to cooperate. Management also continued improving the way they treated their workers. Thus the portion of American workers in unions fell from a peak of a third in the 1960s to less than half of that by the end of the century. The proportion would be even lower were it not for the increasing numbers of government employees who join unions. Of course, government employees do not have much foreign competition, and notably inept management. But in the private sector, management found that keeping the staff in a good mood was an excellent investment. It was also cheaper than trying to placate unhappy workers with more money than companies could afford to pay them.

One of the more successful management changes to improve labor morale was the move toward more fringe benefits. Pensions and health insurance are the two most popular, and most common. As workers made more money, they noted they were paying a lot more taxes. Actually, the big increases in worker pay coincided with a much higher percentage of national income's going to state and local taxes. So the workers liked the idea of fringe benefits that were either not taxed or taxed at a lower rate. This created a rather odd situation between the 1970s and the end of the century. Although most people were living better and better, their pay, after adjusting for inflation, declined 15 percent. But adding in the value of fringe benefits, income went up 17 percent. It was a confusing time.

Oddly enough, "are you happy?" surveys taken throughout the century do not show much change. In other words, money doesn't buy happiness. We can see this today when the same "are you happy?" surveys are conducted around the world. They find that people in the wealthiest nation in the world, America, are only a few percentage points happier than poverty-stricken (by U.S. standards) inhabitants of nonindustrialized nations. The main things that will depress the happiness level are war and other anxiety-producing events (like the Great Depression or any major economic downturn). Even there, it's mostly a matter of perception. The American unemployment rate during the Great Depression was about the same as it is in many nations today, including some in Europe. Yet these other nations did not take it nearly as hard psychologically. Americans expected better, and the Great Depression was as much an assault on American pride as it was on the family income.

Another aspect of American family income and expectations are several surveys taken since World War II asking "how much more than you are making now" would "make a difference in your life?" Across the board, no matter what the income level, it was always 25 percent more income.

Americans have a lot of traits that explain their attitudes toward income and happiness. Americans work hard and party hard. U.S. workers are the most productive in the world and have been throughout this century. For that reason, Americans have been the best paid in the world throughout this century. That is a major reason for all those people's willingness to leave their homelands and go to America.

America is not only the land of the free, it's the land of the rich.

——Inflation——

Inflation has clouded our view of what things cost in the past. When Thomas Riley Marshall said, early in the century, "What this country needs is a really good five-cent cigar," he was really talking about a stogie costing a dollar or so. Here we will clear the air—about inflation, anyway.

Inflation is what happens when there are too many people, with too much money, trying to buy scarce items. The prices of those items go up as the sellers realize that people are willing to pay more for scarce goods. A little inflation does no harm, but too much inflation can do serious damage to the economy. For one thing, it destroys people's savings, for too much inflation makes money worth less, and when there's too much of it, banks are unable to increase their interest rates on savings fast enough to prevent the savings from losing much of their original value. Seeing this, people are less prone to save, thus providing less money for investment in new economic endeavors. Inflation damages banks by causing loans paid out to be repaid with money worth much less. Many times this century, in many countries, inflation has trashed economies and ruined lives. It's not for nothing that most people fear inflation.

The twentieth century has been the century of inflation, for one dollar in 1900 is worth twenty-five at the end of the century. Wars were the most common cause of inflation, as they have always been. Wars give governments the opportunity to borrow a lot of money for weapons. Building all those arms means you cannot produce as many civilian goodies as usual. Yet the workers are getting even more money because they are paid a lot to build armaments. When the workers look for something nonlethal to buy, they find a shortage, and many are willing to pay more. So prices go up. When the war is over, the prices don't come down much. Inflation tends to be permanent.

The rate of inflation is calculated by measuring the prices of a variety of consumer goods from year to year. This is not a perfect measurement, as there are always new items that simply did not exist earlier (like radio and TV sets), and the quality of many goods goes up substantially (foods are more wholesome, overall, than they were a century ago, and housing is of higher quality). But as a rough measurement, it's perfectly usable.

Another item related to inflation should also be taken into account, and that's the cost of living. The same goods do not cost the same in different places in the same year. This is a form of inflation at work.

Cities tend to be more expensive to live in than suburbs or rural areas. Mainly because more people are living on less land in the cities and, because so many more people are trying to buy the same piece of land, the land is much more expensive. It's more expensive to provide government services in those crowded conditions, so the taxes are higher. Everything costs more, thus the term, "cost of living." You also have vast cost-of-living differences between regions and countries. If the local economy has too few jobs and too many people, wages will be lower, and everything will be cheaper. That is why you can go to some poor countries and live very cheaply if you go native. But if you expect the same housing and other goodies you had back home, you will pay a lot more, because a lot of this stuff has to be imported. Supply and demand.

To put inflation in perspective, imagine you made $20 a week in 1900. That was actually a decent wage back then. But because of inflation, to have the same purchasing power today, you would have to make $500 a week. Still a living wage, depending on what part of the country you live in.

To get a better look at it, let's use snapshots of what a dollar's worth of goods would cost in 1900, then 1910, and so on. In 1900, grocery prices were much lower than today. Chicken was thirteen cents a pound, pork chops about the same. Five pounds of flour would cost you thirteen cents, ten pounds of potatoes fourteen cents. A pound of sugar was six cents, a quart of milk, seven cents, and a dozen eggs twenty-one cents. A pound of butter was twenty-six cents. Taking these prices to your local supermarket would show that food prices have not gone up twenty-five times, but that is because other items, like medical care and housing, have gone up much more. Transportation is higher, partly because we do more moving around and we tend to use automobiles rather than a trolley or train as we did back then.

The table on page 132 shows what the dollar bag of groceries would have cost in the years indicated.

Inflation is usually gradual, so gradual that most people don't really notice it. For most of this century, inflation moved slowly. It took seventeen years (and World War I) for inflation to double prices. It took another thirty-nine years for inflation to do it again. And in the meantime, there was the Great Depression of the 1930s, when deflation

YEAR	GROCERY BAG COST ($)
1900	1.00
1910	1.35
1920	2.94
1930	2.45
1940	2.06
1950	3.53
1960	4.35
1970	5.70
1980	12.10
1990	19.18
2000	25.24

brought prices down 25 percent from the 1920s high to the Great Depression low in 1933. World War II got inflation going again, but it never got out of control and just grew gradually and did not double again until 1956. But another war, the Vietnam War, really got inflation going. It took only twenty more years for inflation to double again in 1976. The last forty years of this century saw a torrent of inflation, doubling again by 1987. The damage was done, the lesson was learned, and inflation was tamed by the late 1980s. Going into the twenty-first century, it looks as if it will take thirty or forty years for inflation to double once more.

Inflation distorts our perceptions of the past. But if you are aware that inflation has always existed, do a little simple math and put it all into perspective.

——Unemployment——

Unemployment is a hot issue in America, as it is everywhere else. But Americans managed to turn unemployment into an economic weapon where other nations have found it to be a political liability.

As robust as the American economy has been this century, most workers nervously keep an eye on the national unemployment rate. Oddly enough, the unemployment rate in 1900, 5 percent, is the same as at the end of the century. The average for the century was a little over 5 percent. But there was a lot of variation, which reflected the booms and busts of the economy. Unemployment went up to 6 percent or higher when the economy stalled. This happened in 1908, 1914–15 (as a result of World War I's cutting off a lot of trade with Europe), 1921–22 (the aftereffect of the end of World War I), 1930–41 (the Great Depression), 1958 and 1961 (the first post–World War II "recessions"), 1975–78 (aftereffect of the Vietnam War), 1981-83 (more post–Vietnam War–related stuff), 1986 (a recession), and 1991–94 (a mild recession).

When the economy stalls and the unemployment rate goes up, it is big news. Losing their job, even just seeing an increasing chance of losing it, is something that gets people's attention. All the news that "downsizing" got in the 1980s was not followed by similar media attention to the declining unemployment rate. This constant unemployment and reemployment is called the "churn" and has come to be considered the sign of a healthy economy. Too little unemployment can actually be bad for the economy, as this causes wages to go up, without an increase in productivity. This, in turn, causes more inflation, which eventually does the economy no good. At the end of the century, the American economy went through another evolution and found out how to keep unemployment down without causing inflation.

As serious as unemployment has been, it has never resulted in large-scale social upheaval. As has been the case for thousands of years, most people maintain a network of family and friends to sustain them through rough economic times. The problem most people have had in the twentieth century is that many forget how they coped in the recent past, when what was normal economically is now considered a catastrophe. The Great Depression was a good example. Although the unemployment rate was in double digits for most of the decade, a larger proportion of the population was looking for work. But the tremendous economic growth of the 1920s made people forget that, economically, the population was still better off in the 1930s than it was in 1900.

TWENTIETH-CENTURY UNEMPLOYMENT

YEAR	WORKFORCE	RATE (%)	UNEMPLOYED
1900	29	5	1.45
1910	38	6	2.24
1920	42	5	2.18
1930	49	9	4.26
1940	53	15	7.74
1950	60	5	3.18
1960	70	6	3.85
1970	82	5	4.02
1980	109	5	5.45
1990	126	4	5.54
2000	141	5	7.05

"Workforce" is the total American labor force, in millions. "Rate" is the unemployment rate for that year. "Unemployed" is the number of workers unemployed, in millions.

Unlike the rest of the world, Americans believe in progress and take any setbacks as a personal affront and a great disaster. On the positive side, the traumatic experience of the Great Depression left the American population and its leaders obsessed with the unemployment rate for the rest of the century.

America is unique among industrialized nations in the way it deals with unemployment. Most industrialized nations fear social unrest as a result of unemployment. Americans see unemployment as a natural part of the economic landscape. In America, there is social unrest as a result of unemployment, but it generally takes the form of spurring workers to work harder and to look more diligently for work when they are unemployed. Other nations prefer to pay generous unemployment benefits and play down the possibility of unemployment as much as possible. At the end of the century, it was becoming pretty obvious, especially in Europe and Japan, that the American way was more efficient in creating jobs. Britain, in the 1980s, changed its labor and employment regulations, and unemployment became the lowest in Europe. Britons complained that while they were employed, they felt a lot more pressure on the job. Few, however, wanted to go back to the old ways.

Job pressure is one thing; unemployment pressure is worse.

——The World's Greatest Job Machine——

For most of the century, America was the most prolific creator of jobs in the world. That's the main reason so many people wanted to come here. But it's a little more complicated than that.

The U.S. economy created over 100 million new jobs in the twentieth century. Moreover, so many jobs were created, especially after World War II, that there was always a labor shortage, or threat of one. This drew an increasing number of people into the labor force, especially housewives and the elderly, as well as millions of legal and illegal immigrants. Most Americans got used to this; after all, a constant torrent of new jobs became the norm. But the rest of the world noticed, and America became a magnet for foreign researchers and job seekers.

How did we do it? Several ways. The United States is a huge market undivided by national borders. People were free to go where they wished, and often did. Starting a new business was, unlike in the rest of the world, unencumbered by a lot of bureaucratic obstacles. The American economy has always been large, in 1900 it was taking the position as the world's largest industrial economy. Americans are obsessed with a free market and individual initiative. Worldwide, it was not generally accepted that this was the best way to go, but the results of the last century make it obvious that if you want a dynamic economy, you need a free market and a lot of eager entrepreneurs.

There are other reasons. As Americans became wealthier, they had fewer children and lived longer and healthier lives. This provided more adults for the workforce. Housewives had an easier time entering the workforce. With fewer, or no, children at home, women could devote more time to a full- or part-time job. All adults were more productive because of less disease and more efficient medical care. More money meant that more kids went to school and stayed there longer. Adult education took off after World War II, providing not just a better-educated workforce but one that could keep up with the latest developments in technology and management practice.

The presence of more, and better-educated, workers led to a higher employed percentage of the population. This produced more wealth and the ability to buy more things. This in turn led to more jobs, and so it went. Moreover, American workers became the most productive in the world, even more so than the industrious Japanese and Germans. This kept a lot of jobs in the United States, while many other industrialized nations exported work to nations where the wages were much lower. But American infrastructure was so efficient, and American workers so productive, that many jobs either never left or did so and came back a few years later, when the manufacturers realized that lower wages aren't everything. Lack of infrastructure (roads, utilities, security) and high corruption (meaning the lack of a good legal system) can increase costs enormously.

The other side of this reveals much about why there is still poverty in America. The poor are generally those who do not encourage (I mean really, really encourage) their kids to do well in school. Look at the poor families who move out of poverty (and many do), as well as the increasing number of "downwardly mobile" middle-class kids sliding into poverty, and you will find that the most important element is education. The kid coming out of poverty has gotten an education, the middle-class kid heading for hard times has neglected his (and it's usually a him; women tend to pay more attention to education). There are many temptations in America, and the most devastating one is to skimp on your education.

America also gave birth to the concept of a "consumer society." As automobile manufacturer Henry Ford noted early in the century, when he gave all his workers a substantial raise, he did it to make them work harder and to be able to afford the cars they were producing. While all manufacturers and retailers wanted to sell more product, only in America did the entire nation subscribe to "consumerism" as a means of keeping the economy growing and everyone prospering. This is not to

TWENTIETH-CENTURY JOBS CREATED			
YEAR	POPULATION	WORKERS	% OF POPULATION
1900	76	27.6	36
1910	92	35.8	39
1920	106	39.8	38
1930	123	44.7	36
1940	132	45.3	34
1950	151	56.8	38
1960	181	66.2	37
1970	205	78.0	38
1980	228	103.6	45
1990	249	120.5	48
2000	277	134.0	48

"Population" is the American population for that year, in millions. "Workers" is the number of employed workers, in millions. "% of Population" is employed workers as a percentage of the population.

be underestimated, for most other nations have a significantly different attitude toward consumerism. In the 1990s, Japan entered a long recession, and attempts to spur consumer activity to get things going again failed. The Japanese people never bought into the concept of consumerism. Japan has long followed the older precept of exporting goods to grow the national economy, while the Japanese people continued to make sacrifices to support this philosophy.

Through most of human history, buying more than you needed was seen as wasteful and counterproductive. Surpluses were hoarded, and when this applied to currency, as it often did, economic activity went into a decline because so much cash was buried in the ground behind the family dwelling. Great for coin collectors and archaeologists who later dig up some of these coins, but devastating for those ancient economies.

Other nations have been slow to adopt the American model, but many are doing so, and the unemployment rates drop as a result. Many nations have resisted the American model for ideological or religious reasons. During the Cold War, communist governments regularly criticized American economic practices even while envying American economic success. Muslim clerics condemn American consumerism for religious reasons, the main one being that Muslims tend to become less religious the more they become consumers.

Meanwhile, the Great American Job Machine chugs on into the twenty-first century.

——Down on the Farm——

American farmers don't get no respect. They are the most productive farmers on the planet, which is why fewer than 3 percent of Americans are farmers. Most of the planet's population is still farming, and not very efficiently. A comparison is in order, to spotlight how far agriculture has come in this country.

The main reason there are more people on the planet is that humans have developed much better ways to grow food, and food is the foundation of any economy. The more food you can get, by either growing it or buying it, the larger your population will be. In the last three centuries, there has been, alongside the industrial revolution, an even more important agricultural revolution. To understand what this means, consider how all societies functioned for most of the last six thousand years since the discovery of agriculture. Throughout that period, 80 to 90 percent of the population struggled to coax a living, and perhaps a surplus, out of the soil. It wasn't easy, but by using a wide variety of techniques it was done, and often with marked success. Crops varied somewhat depending on the climate and soil quality. Europe, during the last few thousand years, saw crops of mostly wheat, barley, peas, and oats, along with vegetables and the products of vineyards and fruit orchards.

This form of agriculture, like that still practiced in many Third World areas today, got by without machines, hybrid seeds, or chemical fertilizers. A horse, an ox, or a wife was used to pull the plow. Harvesting was done by hand. Crops available for export went a short distance by oxcart, and thence by river barge or seagoing ship to market. For local consumption there were vegetable gardens and fruit trees. Fruit, however, was often turned into cider for export or winter use. Berries, nuts, and anything else edible was also gathered when available. These subsidiary crops kept the farmers busy most of the time, for the main crops required only a few weeks' intense labor at planting and harvesting time.

To compensate for the lack of modern fertilizer, the farmland was treated with animal (and sometimes human) manure and allowed to remain fallow (idle) every second or third year. When fallow, the field was sometimes planted with legumes (peas, beans) that restored the lost nitrogen in the soil. Medieval peasants didn't understand the chemistry of this, but they had learned by trial and error over the centuries that it worked. The normal practice was to leave a field fallow every other year, and the more adept farmers would plant legumes in the fallow year, which increased the nitrogen content of the soil. But if the land was particularly good, the climate right, and the farmer particularly skillful, that farmer could get away with fallowing a field every third year. Normally, however, farmers would switch between the two methods. Too many every-third-year cycles would reduce the yields noticeably, at which point the farmer would have no choice but to use every-other-year fallowing in order to rebuild the fertility of the land.

Small changes in agricultural methods could have a huge impact on food production. For example, there were two major agricultural innovations that appeared about twelve hundred years ago. One was the moldboard plow. This elaborate metal-and-wood device was developed by Slavic tribes and spread west from the sixth century on. Its design allowed six or more oxen to pull a plow and break up virgin ground or the heavy, clay-laden soils typical of Northern Europe. As an example of the impact of this new plow, consider the huge population growth that occurred after its introduction. The area including France, Germany, Switzerland, Austria, and the Low Countries had a population that fluctuated between 10 and 15 million from A.D. 1 to 600. In came the new plow, and during the next six centuries, the population grew to about 36 million (from a low of 10 million, as a result of all the invasions and civil strife). These areas now support a population of over 250 million, which gives you an idea of how sparsely populated the area was way back then.

The second innovation was the horse collar. Previous horse tackle was rather inefficient, resulting in an underutilization of an animal's full strength. The horse collar allowed horses to be used for pulling a plow, or heavy loads in general. This created a big increase in the horse population, as the horse was more versatile a beast of burden than the ox.

Farming was a matter of numbers. While most peasant farmers might have been illiterate, they knew how to count. They knew that wheat would yield 250 to 300 liters of grain per acre (modern farming methods, on the same land, yield over 1,500 liters of grain per acre). Barley would bring 700 to 720 liters per acre. The higher yield for barley was partially the nature of the plant, plus the fact that farmers put 72 liters of seed into each acre of wheat and 144 liters per acre of barley. Oats yielded 360 to 400 liters an acre, for 108 liters of seed. Peas, an important diet supplement and protein source, gave 300 to 340 liters per acre, for 108 liters of seed.

One reason China was so much more populous than the rest of the world during the last two thousand years was rice farming. This is a complicated process, and it took the Chinese centuries to work it all out. But primitive rice cultivation yields more grain per acre than growing wheat or barley. Rice growing also requires extensive irrigation and a lot of teamwork. This need for discipline and local organization, plus the denser population, is a major reason Chinese culture developed differently from others, particularly European culture. This pattern still applies in most of the world.

Grain yields of slightly under four times seed grain sown were the norm until the eighteenth century. There, another burst of innovation brought productivity to ten times seed sown. In the twentieth century, this rose to twenty times. It was this enormous swell in agricultural productivity that created the rapid population increases over the past few centuries and especially in the twentieth century. American farmers led the way in producing these more efficient farming methods.

Agricultural experimentation did take place in ancient and medieval times. The Romans had a keen eye for innovation and constantly tried new things. In the medieval period, the research was often done at abbeys under the supervision of monks (who were the medieval scholars and scientists). Consistent yields of eight times seed sown were reported. But the medieval period was one of poor communications and strong traditions. The new techniques were not broadcast far and wide, and even if they were, most farmers would be reluctant to change their ancient (and reliable) methods. Moreover, some of the methods, such as using much higher doses of animal manure, were not always possible because there would not have been enough domestic animals available to produce the amount needed. But some of the new techniques, such as denser planting to crowd out weeds, would have worked widely. One could say that the agricultural "reforms" of the eighteenth century were basically a side effect of the "Age of Enlightenment," whereby the new was given equal opportunity with the traditional. The rapid increase in European and American farm productivity from the 1700s on was largely a result of just using the better techniques the old monks had developed over the centuries and systematically coming up with new techniques. As the food supply grew, so did the population. While it is often difficult to convince Third World farmers to change their ways, once new methods do take hold, the farmers find their lives changed forever.

Third World farmers survive using traditional methods that provide an adequate living. These farmers are using techniques that are thousands of years old.

With adequate land, primitive farmers were able to work their land efficiently enough to feed themselves and produce a surplus for sale. Wheat grain could be sold for about $40 a bushel. Barley went for $25 to $30 a bushel, and peas for $15 to $20 a bushel. In a good year, crops could generate grain for sale that would bring $1,500 to $2,000. Another $1,000 could be obtained by selling off cheese, wool, honey, sheep, eggs, fruits, and vegetables. Some of this profit was saved, some was spent on repairing or replacing farm equipment, and some went for household necessities (utensils, salt, furnishings) or luxuries. And some went to pay taxes and fees. There was, and is, often a lot of this.

Primitive farmers did more than just grow grain or rice. Most farmers had one or more horses or oxen, two or more milk cows, a few pigs, several dozen sheep or goats, beehives, and some chickens. Many farmers kept geese as well. The horses and/or oxen pulled the plow and did other heavy work. The cows supplied milk, most of which was turned into cheese. The pigs were fattened to supply the main course for major feasts. The sheep supplied wool, which was spun into cloth for the family's clothes. The chickens supplied eggs and meat to liven up the diet of peas and porridge. The "peasant" or "subsistence" farmer you often read about is actually running a pretty complex operation. American farms followed this model until the late nineteenth century, when research into more productive seeds and the development of new planting and harvesting machinery created the "industrial farming" that became the American style in the twentieth century.

For the majority of farmers with small holdings, life was hardly secure. An acre of barley could, in an average year, produce about five hundred liters of grain (after making allowances for taxes and seed for the next crop). This was enough to feed one adult for a year at a very basic level. A farmer with a wife and two children could get along with five acres. Everyone would have to work, especially on other sources of food like tending the vegetable garden and rummaging in the woods for mushrooms, nuts, and berries. But a five-acre holding left little margin for bad weather. Several bad years in succession could lead to widespread famine.

American farmers in this century developed a quite different problem: chronic overproduction that depressed prices and caused bankruptcy. American farms in this century have become big business. The land and equipment of farms at the end of the century typically cost over a million dollars. Farmers must take out loans to buy the seed, fertilizer, and fuel needed. A bad crop or two or, more likely, too low prices for the crop, and the farmer is out of money and credit.

Farming has always been a complicated business, even before the twentieth century. But the most striking thing about twentieth-century farming is that most of the world is still just getting by with centuries-old techniques, while in America, farmers are the victims of their own success. It's tough being a farmer.

──The Green Revolution──

One reason the huge population increase in this century did not lead to mass starvation was that America did manage to export some of its superior farming methods.

In the 1950s and '60s, American agricultural scientists turned their attention to the types of crops grown in the Third World and developed new strains of wheat, barley, and rice that eventually more than doubled the yields per acre of these crops.

The world's farmers currently produce about 1.7 billion metric tons of wheat, rice, and similar grain a year altogether. A ton of grain will feed four or five people a year. So we are producing enough food for over 6 billion people. Other crops are grown to feed livestock, for meat and diary products.

The new grains had been bred to produce more food per acre as well as to be more resistant to insect pests, plant diseases, and climate extremes. At the same time, the new strains had to taste like the older ones, or at least not too different. Most of the farmers for whom the new seed was intended are very conservative. Just getting them to eat the new grains can require some effort. Getting the farmers to grow the new grain is often more difficult. It's not enough for the foreigners to come in and buy some local land for growing a demonstration crop.

GRAIN PRODUCTION (in Million Metric Tons)				
GRAIN	**1992–93**	**1993–94**	**1994–95**	**1995–96**
Wheat	562	559	522	533
Coarse grains	865	790	863	787
Rice (milled)	352	353	361	359
Total	1,779	1,702	1,746	1,679

The locals will just attribute any success to something special the foreigners did. Those foreigners always have some new gadget or technique, as the locals tend to view it. What does work is to convince one local farmer to try the new seed. This is often quite difficult, as the locals have visions of the new seed "poisoning their land." So, often the farmer growing the demonstration crop is paid for his efforts.

Once the farmers accept the new seed and begin taking advantage of the larger yields, they have to cope with new farming methods. New seeds often require pesticides, fertilizer, or more water. Sometimes it must be planted and/or harvested differently. But the biggest change for many very poor farmers is the need to buy additional materials (pesticide, fertilizer, special tools) to get the better yields. Often, these farmers just live from year to year, putting aside a portion of each harvest to provide seed for the next. Having to buy additional stuff is a new experience, and some have problems managing their money and new "inputs" (as things such as fertilizer and pesticides are known to American farmers).

Despite the problems of getting farmers to use the new seeds, and then to manage continued use, the green revolution has transformed both farming and the standard of living in many poor countries. As poor farmers saw neighbors getting better crop yields out of the new seeds, they got on the bandwagon, and soon entire regions had switched over. Even newer seeds continue to come out of the agricultural laboratories, although the biggest gains in yields are in the past.

China and India can still grow all their own food because of the green-revolution programs, and many poor nations have eliminated chronic starvation with the new seeds. But there are still some ancient problems. For one thing, population continues to expand and contract with crop yields. In centuries past, too much population growth was taken care of by starvation and disease. But in the late twentieth century, food and medicine are customarily sent into areas suffering from famine and pestilence. The population continues to grow, and more people need more food. The usual chorus of doomsayers proclaims that there will inevitably be a great population die-off because of inadequate food. This doesn't happen, and in many of the newly prosperous farming areas, the population growth rate is beginning to slow down. As people get richer, not just better fed, they have fewer children. In the twentieth century, bigger crops provide other economic opportunities. So newly prosperous farming villages in India and China now contain new schools and factories. Farmers are building themselves better homes and buying tractors to replace the children who will go to the new schools and then work in the factories or go to the cities.

The green revolution was revolutionary in ways more than just agricultural.

——The Educational Advantage——

The American economy grew so rapidly in the twentieth century largely because of the increased level of education in the workforce. This happened somewhat by accident. A fortunate accident, one of the unlikely side effects of World War II.

In 1900, only 95,000 students graduated from high school, and only 29,000 received college degrees. Most degrees went to males, and most of the graduates went on to the traditional careers of law, medicine, the ministry, and teaching. Most went on to teaching. Even high-school graduates were used as teachers. As the century wore on, more people graduated from high school and college each year.

YEAR	HIGH-SCHOOL GRADUATES	COLLEGE GRADUATES
1910	156,000	40,000
1920	311,000	54,000
1930	667,000	140,000
1940	1,221,000	217,000
1950	1,200,000	497,000
1960	1,864,000	477,000
1970	2,906,000	1,065,000
1980	2,748,000	1,731,000

One of the many reasons for America's rapid economic growth in the past two centuries has been the tradition of education. From the earliest colonial days, Americans had a higher literacy rate than any other part of the world. At the beginning of the nineteenth century, most Americans were literate, and during that century, free schools for all children became the norm. The major thing holding back more children from getting more education was the need for many children to get jobs in order to help sustain their families. With increasing prosperity in the twentieth century, it became easier to send the kids to school rather than to work. That's what Americans did, and it paid off big time. As more and more technology was developed in the twentieth century, it became obvious that you could use this new knowledge only if you had a well-educated workforce. While America did not have the best-educated workforce in the world (some European nations had higher education levels), America had the *largest* well-educated work-force.

Moreover, the United States did something no one had tried before: college education for the masses. For centuries, a college education was seen as something for a small elite. Lawyers, doctors, clergy, and teachers were the main products of universities. But in the twentieth century, college graduates with more technical skills, like engineering and science, became more common.

And then came the American G.I. Bill. One of many laws passed during World War II to reward the veterans of that conflict, it subsidized a college education for the former soldiers. This was a novel idea at the time, for providing a university education for "just anyone" had never been tried before. The decision to reward the civilian soldiers of World War II turned out to be one of the most fortunate events of the twentieth century.

The universities braced themselves for the hordes of former G.I.'s and were pleasantly surprised to find their new students older, more mature, and eager to get the most out of this opportunity. In a word, excellent students. Most of these men were the first in their families to get a college education. For many, the war had taken them overseas and exposed them to different ways of doing things. Perhaps most important, these men grew up during the Great Depression. They were anxious to improve their, and the nation's, economic situation so that they would never know the fear and uncertainty of the 1930s again. No one knew that this mass college-education experiment would work. Many denounced it as a boondoggle. The naysayers were wrong.

By 1950, the annual number of college graduates had more than doubled since 1940 (which was itself seven times more than 1900). The number of high-school graduates actually declined from 1940 to 1950 because of the very low birthrate of the 1930s Great Depression. But the success of the G.I. Bill college program instantly made millions of families aware of how they could and should send their children to college. It took the rest of the world several decades to catch on to this approach. At the time, many educators outside the United States thought this "college for the masses" thing was just another example of American exuberance. When the U.S. economy continued growing rapidly through the 1950s and '60s, the rest of the world began to pay closer attention and soon realized that all those newly minted college grads were a key reason for American economic juggernaut.

——Every Man a Scholar——

One of the major differences between Americans in 1900 and those a century later was education. More learning was better, in a big way that is not fully appreciated at the end of the century.

Through most of mankind's history, few people were literate. Rarely more than 10 percent of the population, and usually closer to 5 percent. That began changing in the last two centuries, as the industrial revolution got under way. With the number of factories and the advances in technology and knowledge growing at a rapid pace, more people were needed to record things and be able to use what was written down. By the nineteenth century, literacy rates in industrialized nations moved quickly past 50 percent and on to 90 percent and more. But in 1900, most people were only getting enough years of education to make them literate. In the 1930s, a smaller percentage of the population went to high school than attends college in 2000.

After World War II, the United States showed how valuable a

college education could be by offering generous college scholarships to millions of veterans. The explosive growth in the number of college-educated people was one of the key elements in the sustained growth of the U.S. economy after World War II.

By the 1970s, it became commonly accepted that everyone who could go to college should. Historically, it was a trend that sought nothing less than at least trying to turn everyone into a scholar. By the end of the century, over two thirds of high-school graduates went off to college.

But there were problems. While many students did benefit from a higher education, it eventually became apparent that not everyone was gaining something. Moreover, the drive to get everyone through high school (so as to prepare them for college) was also running into problems. As any statistician could have pointed out (and some did, but few people bothered to listen), ability, like everything else, is not equally distributed. Rather, a chart of people capable of finishing high school, or college, would show up as a bell curve. Most would have an average chance of success, with smaller groups being less able or more able.

Many European countries took this distribution of ability into account and structured their educational programs to match it. There were different types of colleges, from the more elite for the smartest, down the scale to those barely able to do the work but still able to gain, and make something of, some higher education (community colleges, often providing technical training).

In America, such pragmatism was often lacking. The general idea was to get everyone (or nearly everyone) into college, and that meant getting all these youngsters through a college-prep high-school education. The foolishness of this became apparent when it was discovered that school scores were being inflated (or ignored) in order to obtain the highest possible graduation rates. Teachers at the high-school and college level often found it easier just to give inflated grades and pass the kids they could not, or would not, teach on to another teacher. It took a decade or so before everyone paid attention to employers' complaints that many of the high-school and college graduates were incompetent, holding degrees that were more fiction than fact. Even though everyone began to realize that empty high-school and college degrees were counterproductive, there was less agreement on what to do about it.

Simply enforcing graduation standards doesn't always work, because the teachers are under a lot of pressure not to fail anyone and corners are often cut to ensure that everyone comes out looking good, until the kids graduate and find themselves unqualified for the better jobs.

The problem is that kids, parents, and teachers are all working at cross purposes. Many of the kids will look for an easy way out, and without strenuous efforts on the part of teachers, will not get much done. While some children, especially those of immigrants, see education as a means to a prosperous future, many kids need some adult supervision in the education and career-planning department. Often they don't get it.

In the United States, two large groups of parents, with quite different attitudes toward their children's education, have had a noticeable impact on public-school practices. On one extreme, there are many parents who appear to be uninterested in how their kids are doing at school and who react with indifference or hostility if the teachers bring the child's lack of effort and/or disruptive behavior to the parents' attention. As a result, disruptive children are increasingly tolerated, to the detriment of classroom discipline and the learning of all the kids.

At the other extreme are parents who have a keen interest in their children's education. These parents pressure the schools, either individually or as part of very activist parent organizations, for "gifted child programs." The schools often give in and designate any child with a loud parent as "gifted" and put the kid in "gifted" programs along with similar children. Too many parents want results more than performance, and seeing their child in a gifted program and getting good marks keeps the parents happy.

All of this carried over to colleges. Under tremendous market pressure (there were more college places than potential students), it was found prudent from an economic point of view to gradually increase the grades. This also cut down on the lawsuits, as colleges that graded students according to what they were actually learning found themselves sued by students and parents for "fraud" (not imparting the education a college was supposed to, forgetting that the students' failure was usually self-inflicted).

The unwillingness, or inability, of students to do college work also manifested itself in what subjects kids majored in. Fewer and fewer went after scientific and technical degrees. These required more work, and kids couldn't talk their way out of an aversion to studying math. By the end of the century, a third to over half the students majoring in engineering and scientific subjects were from abroad.

A lot of this has to do with the rapid increase, after World War II, in the proportion of children expected to get high-school and college educations. Until World War II, most of the children who went to high school were those who were eager to do so and qualified. High school was not mandatory in most places, although it was generally free. Initially, the new schools took a no-nonsense attitude toward disruptive and reluctant students. In some cities, special schools or programs were set up for the unruly, and most of these kids were kicked out as soon as legally possible. Many states now had laws requiring school attendance until age sixteen, and after that age, attrition was heavy among those who were not willing to bear down and apply themselves to their studies. But in the 1960s, there arose the attitude that all children were capable of being taught enough to get them into and through college. This seems absurd in hindsight, but at the time this approach had the votes, and discipline and academic performance went out the window in many school systems. Sanity did not begin to return until twenty or thirty years later.

At the same time, parents, and the public in general, were beginning to bewail the educational mess we had gotten ourselves into. They noted that the Japanese, a rapidly growing economic superpower from the 1960s to the '80s, had a school system that stressed discipline and diligent study. What was generally missed was that Japanese education underwent many reforms after World War II, and the current system in Japan owes much to the way America was educating its students in the late 1940s. It was during that time that many Japanese investigation commissions visited American schools and took back to Japan what they saw. Japanese schools didn't change much in the succeeding decades, while American schools did.

One difference in the Japanese system, and in most other school systems outside the United States, was the recognition that different children required different types of education. Some kids were suitable for college; others benefited more from a practical, technical education. Germany, for example, takes many students at age sixteen and puts them into a work-study apprenticeship program that trains them to be skilled craftsmen. These are very well paying jobs, and there are never enough qualified applicants to fill them in the United States.

But even families who are energetic about getting their kids educated run up against a school bureaucracy more interested in self-preservation than in student performance. This leads to unwillingness to discipline or remove incompetent teachers. The unionization of public-school teachers since World War II created an "us versus them" attitude on the part of many teachers. Union politics, in which different factions battle each other by promising the members more and more (often outrageous) contract demands, is all too common. Many of the most onerous contract provisions obtained cover dealing with incompetent or misbehaving teachers. It's customary for unions, whether of laborers or teachers, to defend members accused of misbehavior even after guilt is proven.

Everything happened so fast. The movement to provide high-school education for all children got going early in this century but was slowed down by the Great Depression in many areas. After World War II, high-school education rapidly spread, so that by the 1960s, nearly every American teenager had access to a high school. By the end of the century, over three quarters of high-school students at least tried to get a college education.

Despite all the problems, America does have the most educated population in the world. Not the best educated, but the most educated. The emphasis on quantity of instruction over quality of instruction has left a lot of people with meaningless college and high-school degrees. To America's credit, when failure is noted, new approaches are attempted.

For example, one thing that made the shortcomings of the public schools' problems obvious was the continued success of less well funded private, particularly parochial, schools. At first, parochial schools were dismissed as selective and thus not comparable. This was true; the parochial schools did not tolerate disruptive or reluctant students. But rather than summarily expelling such students, parochial schools often insisted on parent involvement, and when they got it, they solved more problems than public-school advocates cared to admit. Moreover, it was painfully obvious that parochial schools in poor neighborhoods—the same areas containing the worst public schools—were not only very popular but very successful, and with a fraction of the budget used by the public school down the street.

Also, looking at the education statistics nationwide, interesting differences arose. Areas with much lower per-student spending had much higher student performance. Again, the difference was parental involvement and a proeducation attitude among kids and students. One really dirty little secret of poor inner-city neighborhoods is the "street attitude" that paying attention to your school studies is uncool. Black kids will accuse the studious of "acting white" and often deliver a beating upon the hapless scholar. Other ethnic groups in these schools have a similar bad attitude toward academics. Many teachers eventually stop trying to change this attitude. Other teachers guide their studious kids as if they were running a guerrilla war. But most of the schools involved just give up, and it shows. Parents are aware of the problem, and try to get their kids into parochial or other private schools or send them to relatives living outside the city. In some cities, the public schools have responded by setting up small schools open only to kids who can pass an admission test. Thus these schools get the kids who want to learn, and not the young thugs.

Teacher quality is another major problem that developed through the century. Teacher training became a big issue in the 1800s. By 1900, there were dozens of colleges devoted to producing elementary and high-school teachers. That was the good news. As the century wore on, and especially after World War II, the bad news emerged. Initially, the "normal schools" (as the teaching colleges were originally called) simply provided a college education, with the future teachers studying the subjects they would teach. There were also some courses on the techniques of teaching. These "teaching courses" increased as the century went on and soon became the principal thing teaching colleges taught. These schools also added graduate departments offering doctorates in education. By the 1960s, these education experts and their teaching courses were becoming increasingly detached from what was going on in the classroom. Teachers who were really teaching came to consider the teaching-school crowd a bad joke at best and a major obstacle to effective teaching at worst. But the teaching schools had the attention of school administrators and politicians. The education-school professionals were skillful at the use of public relations and delayed the public backlash for several decades. By the end of the century, the education schools were on the defensive. School districts were no longer insisting that new teachers have the "education courses." The education schools also took a major hit when competency-test laws got passed in many states. It turned out that those who had gone to teaching colleges did no better, and often a lot worse, than those who had gone to non-teaching colleges.

Another debilitating side effect of the teacher colleges was the successful campaign of the educational professionals to get all schoolteachers tenure. The supposed intent was to prevent teachers from getting fired for holding unpopular opinions. But this was rarely an issue; more often, tenure was used to make it impossible to fire teachers who were incompetent or even many who had committed criminal acts.

But teaching colleges were not the only reason for the decline of teacher quality. Part of the decline can be blamed on the Vietnam War. During that time, getting a teaching job was one way to obtain a draft deferment. So you had thousands of young men becoming teachers not because they wanted to teach but because they wanted to avoid going into the army. Many of these stayed in teaching because they found that once they had tenure they could make minimal effort and still get paid, plus there were the short hours and the long summer vacations.

The other part of the teacher decline came from a more robust post–World War II economy. There were now more, and often better, opportunities for bright young college grads. This actually provided an opportunity for the teaching colleges, who advocated the substitution of more effective teaching methods for the steadily lower talent level of new students entering teaching colleges. This didn't work, and as many former students can tell you, what counted was the quality of the person doing the teaching, not so much the particular methods being used. While the declining quality of new teachers was something schools soon became aware of, they also noted that whenever there was an economic slowdown, they got higher-quality applicants from non-teaching colleges. If the school was on the ball, they would give the new teacher a challenging and interesting job and the new teacher would stay. Many did in the post–World War II years.

Education is becoming a larger and larger segment of the economy, growing as the body of human knowledge does. The twentieth century will likely be seen as a time when a lot of mistakes were made in the way teachers and curriculum should be developed.

The solutions will apparently have to wait for the twenty-first century.

——Marketing——

Improved marketing has been one of the principal economic benefits of the twentieth century. Without better marketing, we would not be as wealthy as we are. But the downside is that marketing tends to make you buy things you otherwise would not.

Nothing is perfect.

Marketing is a twentieth-century technique for selling goods, or even ideas, using as many different techniques as will work. Or not. Marketing is not as much of a science as many of its practitioners would like it to be. But marketing did become more visible in the twentieth century, and perhaps the invention of neon lights in 1910, promptly used to create gaudy promotional signs, was a very visible symptom of what was to come.

People have always sold things to each other, but never was there so much stuff to sell until the twentieth century. And never was there as much money to spend as in the twentieth century. Before that, only a small percentage of the population were "consumers." As is still the case in many Third World nations today, most of the population just gets by, and if they acquire anything besides necessities, it is often done via barter ("I'll give you some rice for some of your homemade cloth"). But as nations industrialized over the last few centuries, much of the new wealth showed up in the form of cash. Before that, there was not always a lot of cash in circulation. Nor was there so much wealth that people could just buy things on impulse. For customers among the nobility and rich commoners, purveyors of luxuries would often travel from town to castle with their goods. Marketing was up close and personal.

Manufacturers and store owners began to realize that there were many ways they could move the goods (from the factory to the consumer). Again, the very complexity that developed in twentieth-century promoting and selling became an opportunity. This new way of moving the goods was called marketing. The marketing expert considered everything. The design of the product and pricing. The advertising and the display of the item in stores. And as a follow-up, there were the questions asked of people who had already bought the product. Marketing was eventually applied, successfully, to intangible products like political candidacies or government policies.

Marketing, like so many other twentieth-century innovations, is more engineering and management than science. Basic statistics propelled most successful marketing campaigns. Marketers became very good at collecting information. Not just from potential customers regarding what they want but also from the culture as a whole. There are always new methods of promoting stuff, and the able marketer is always on the lookout for these new opportunities. Early in the century, successful marketing often had to do with who was first to use radio advertising. TV also revolutionized marketing, and the World Wide Web appears to be moving in the same direction.

Nearly all of the marketing techniques now used are creations of the twentieth century. Advertising has been around for centuries, but mass advertising is new. Radio networks made it possible for major products, like soap and automobiles, to be easily promoted nationwide. Public relations is also a new technique, at least in the way it is practiced in this century. Putting out the word via press releases, planted stories, and whatever else the PR expert can come up with proved to be a very economical way to promote a product by taking advantage of the mass media's increasingly insatiable appetite for "news." At first, movies did not get in on the advertising game, but by the 1970s, movie producers were selling "product-placement fees" to manufacturers who were willing to pay for their products to be seen in a film. About the same time, even major retailers got on the bandwagon by selling better placement for products ("slotting fees").

Marketers developed a new way of looking at selling products. It was not enough just to sell more products. Market research revealed that having a larger share of your market (for types of clothing, cars, or appliances) enabled you to advertise more cheaply and made it harder for competitors to come after you.

Not all products were marketed the same way or with the same vigor. Some products do not sell better because of lower prices. Strange as it may seem, it is true. Cosmetics are one of the best examples. Attempts to grab more market share, or simply increase sales, by lowering the price actually lowered unit sales. Cosmetics are the classic "image" product. People will pay more because they feel the more they pay, the better the product they are getting. Manufacturers took advantage of this by spending a higher percentage of their revenue on marketing. Some of these image products spend more than half their sales revenue on marketing. Most is advertising, mainly to position their inexpensively manufactured lipstick as a high-quality product. They are selling mostly image, and marketers love to sell this. But as with many products, cosmetics manufacturers will spend some of their marketing dollars on free samples or special sales. Actually, many manufacturers of relatively inexpensive items will use the "samples and sales" technique.

Supermarkets and other retailers "design" sales by allocating a dollar amount for a "sale." The marketers (often just the store manager or staff trained in how to do it) will cut prices on items they feel will bring in additional customers. The store staff knows that the design of the store presents anyone coming in with ample compelling opportunities to buy additional, nonsale, items. And the customers usually do just that. A well-designed "sale" will increase overall sales and profits. So the next time you see a sale, remember that it's being done not in the spirit of charity but to put you in a position where you will spend even more money.

Marketing, you might say, is less a technique and more a way of thinking. A philosophy, if you will. The marketers takes it for granted that if they are given enough control over the design, pricing, and promotion of a product, they can do wonders with it. In theory that is true, but in practice there are a lot of marketers. And not all of them are equally skilled. Nor are all their products equally marketable. Most new products fail.

Marketing has become more and more pervasive and, as a result, has acquired a rather distasteful reputation. What probably pushed it over the top is unsolicited e-mail messages ("spam") and telemarketing.

There is no end in sight.

——A New Product for Everyone——

There have always been new products, usually minor variations on existing ones. Until this century, people tended to be very conservative when it came to innovation. So really new products were rare. It was different in the twentieth century, a time when more new products were introduced than ever before. It took some getting used to.

As more people acquired more money and a greater appetite for new products, manufacturers discovered that they could increase sales simply by introducing new products. Lots of new products, hundreds of thousands of new products. There had never been anything like this before. It all got going after World War II, fueled by the increased advertising opportunities of television and the improved distribution provided by the new supermarkets and malls.

Much of the effort turned out to be wasted, as the market-research tools were not accurate enough to spot products that would fail before a lot of them had been sent to the stores. But enough of the new products were successful enough to encourage more. Many of the new products were safe bets, merely being variants of existing goods. It was discovered that a product's sales could be easily increased by providing the goods in a variety of sizes. Thus the many different quantities in which you can buy cereal, soap, cleaning liquids, and beer.

The automobile manufacturers were the first major companies to push the "new product" angle in a large way. In the 1920s, General Motors gave then market leader Ford Motors a beating by selling many new models.

Alfred P. Sloan replaced William Durant as president of General Motors in 1920 and developed new marketing techniques that had a huge effect on the way all other products were produced and sold. Sloan pushed the use of the annual model change. The new car designs were not much different from each other, except in appearance. Most buyers did not realize that the many different brands of General Motors cars often used the same body, the same engine, and many other common components. The price differences, which were always significant between, say, Chevrolet and Cadillac, were mostly related to the weight of the car and the perceived prestige of the model. So buyers were paying by the pound, plus a surcharge for those luxury models at the top of the line. General Motors managed to convince people that heavier cars were better. Well, they were to the extent that people were safer in an accident. Plus, the extra weight made the "luxury" cars roomier and filled with more gadgets. But mostly this was marketing. The car ads stressed the fact that the Cadillac was one of the largest and most expensive cars available. Marketers had discovered that consumers always wanted something a little better, and General Motors provided a ladder of brands from Chevrolet to Cadillac to provide something for everyone to aspire to. While Cadillac owners could aspire to the superluxury brands like Rolls-Royce, General Motors helpfully provided gradations of luxury within their Cadillac line. Plus—and this was also a big selling point—"new" models each year. For some car buyers, luxury was buying a new car every year or two.

The annual car models were usually different from each other in superficial ways, particularly in the sheet steel that formed the body. This metal was stamped into new shapes each year, an inexpensive process if done right (and General Motors mastered that technique). And there were always new features, sold as options in the cheaper models and "standard" (built into the basic price) of the more luxurious models.

While not quite a scam, the annual model change was a bit of a hustle. Non-American cars generally did not have annual model changes, although they did add new features regularly. These items—such as new transmissions, brakes, tires, radios, air-conditioners, and the like—could often be fitted to existing models, although it was much cheaper to install them at the factory while the car was being built.

It wasn't until the 1970s that General Motors got brought up short. The Japanese came in with cars that did not change as much but were of higher quality. General Motors, a paragon of high quality in the two decades after World War II, had gotten sloppy. When higher-quality Japanese and European cars showed up in the 1970s, buyers voted with their wallets.

Other manufacturers were quick to pick up on Alfred Sloan's marketing innovations at General Motors. The concept of the "annual model change" caught on in as many product areas as the marketers could get away with. If not a new model, than an annual change in packaging. The basic idea was that if you could make an existing product look new, without going to the expense of actually creating something new, you would increase sales. And it often works, often enough to encourage more and more new products.

The latest example is computer software. This manuscript was typed using Word 97, which itself was running on Windows 98. Well, you get the idea. The concept of an annual model change was a little slow to arrive in the software industry. This was mainly because there were so many other opportunities to bring out improved models. When PCs first arrived on the market in the late 1970s, new products came fast because more powerful hardware became available sooner and sooner, and more and more cheaply. As PCs capable of doing more came out, the software developers hustled to get out new software versions to take advantage of new possibilities. Also, because the PC software business was still young, no one was quite sure what users wanted, or what was possible with the increasingly powerful machines. So there was a lot of experimentation, not only in developing products, but in adding features to existing software.

By the late 1980s, things had settled down a bit. Many PC users had found software they were quite content with. Software publishers saw their profits shrinking and looked around for another gambit. The marketing folks came up with several ideas. One of the most successful was the "buy-in/upgrade" technique. This approach solved two problems while making software publishing more profitable. First, publishers provided two versions of their programs. One was for users who had no software. They paid full price (perhaps $300) for, say, a word processor. A similar "competitive upgrade" version was made available for $100 or less. The competitive-upgrade version looked for a competing program on the user's hard disk. Once it found such a program, it proceeded to install the new program. A user who liked the new one would eventually delete the older program and just use the new one. Then came the kicker. Periodic (once a year or so) "upgrades" of the program were made available to existing users at about the same price as the original competitive upgrade. Increasingly, much was spent on advertising what a great deal the new version was (and often it wasn't, but it was *new*). The sales of the upgrade were very profitable, for if the competitive upgrade had worked and increased the number of users, the publisher was basically selling an upgraded version of the older program. They could also sell a lot of the upgrades directly to the customer, rather than selling them at half the list price to stores, which then sold them at the list price. In this way, the software manufacturers have done the same thing that General Motors began doing, very profitably, in the 1920s.

What goes around comes around.

Marketers have conditioned most Americans to accept annual model changes as a good thing. Sometimes they are, but often this is just a marketing angle to convince people to buy something they don't really need. Marketers have not rested on their laurels. Fresh variations of the "new models" idea are constantly being dreamed up and tested. And as long as enough of those ideas work, we can expect more of the continual pounding we get from exhortations to abandon useful products we already have for "new, improved" models that will definitely cost us money, but may or may not add anything useful to our lives.

Then again, this *is* the fourth *Dirty Little Secrets* book.

——The Consumer Society——

Another unique aspect of twentieth-century culture is the emergence of consumerism. There is so much to buy that "consuming" is seen as a major activity. It is, and it has made us quite different from any of our ancestors.

People have always liked to get new stuff. The first human cultures were based on hunting and gathering (fruits, nuts, whatever). We never lost our joy for going out and getting things. The industrial revolution brought people to cities, where there was little opportunity for hunting or gathering. But if they had money, they could shop; there were lots and lots of places to shop in the city. Before this century, many people didn't have much money. But in the twentieth century, money came to the masses—and the masses went shopping.

The 1920s were a time of exuberant economic growth and cultural change. One new wrinkle was shopping as entertainment. Well, it wasn't entirely new, but now more people could do it, and the concept of shopping as a fun activity took root in popular culture. The Great Depression and World War II took some of the fun out of shopping. In the 1930s, there was constant fear of unemployment at any moment, and during World War II there wasn't much to buy. But after the war, and especially after a population made quite tight-fisted by two decades of economic disaster and world conflict, people began to power-shop again.

In 1952, the first bank credit card was issued. The idea caught on in a big way. It was now easier to buy things you couldn't afford. Actually, buying this way was nothing new. From early in the century, stores would extend credit and allow customers to pay for purchases over time. Credit cards made "buying on time" even easier by simplifying the paperwork.

In the 1960s, the shopping malls began to appear all over. The big-city department stores expanded, manufacturers produced more new products, and the joy of shopping swept the land. The more companies sold, the more they had to manufacture, and that put more people to work. This had been recognized for most of this century as an economic fact of life. But with the post–World War II good times just going and going, the idea arose that what was keeping this unprecedented economic boom going was "consumerism."

This was a somewhat radical thought, for Americans had always been frugal. And the 1930s and '40s had shown such frugality to be necessary. But now, being tight-fisted was becoming passé. If people wanted a strong economy, they had to spend. In the 1960s, Americans had a lot more to spend, over three times as much as their turn-of-the-century grandparents. People bought cars, homes, vacations, clothes, records, gadgets—everything. Whether they needed it or not.

By the end of the century, Americans owned twice as many cars and drove them 2.5 times as much as their parents had in 1950. The automobile was becoming a way of life, with the average 1990s American spending nine hours a week behind the wheel. But when Americans weren't driving to the mall, they were watching television. Viewing increased 39 percent since the 1960s. We were doing less of some things, like being with our children. Parents in the 1990s spent 40 percent less time with their kids than parents in the 1960s had. People were also working more, spending about three more hours a week at work in the 1990s versus the 1960s. We were also spending a lot more time consuming.

Members of the generation that grew up during these three decades of heavy-duty consumerism are different from their parents. For one thing, the kids have seen nearly 400,000 ads by the time they graduate from high school. This changes attitudes. In 1967, 44 percent of college freshmen thought it was essential to be well off financially. By 1987, 76 percent thought so. In 1967, 83 percent of freshmen thought it necessary to develop a philosophy of life. By 1987, only 39 percent were interested in such things. Well, that's not exactly true. For many, consumerism had become a philosophy of life. It was so natural, so easy. Don't believe me? Go spend an afternoon at the mall and think about it there.

In 1987, the number of shopping centers exceeded the number of high schools. With 32,563 shopping centers, that's one for every 7,400 of population. Americans were spending six hours a week shopping and forty minutes a week playing with their kids. Not that the kids weren't being entertained as well. Some 93 percent of teenage girls reported that shopping was their favorite activity.

The people running the stores knew that only about a quarter of the people in stores were looking for specific items. The rest could be tempted, because it was also known that some 53 percent of grocery-store and 47 percent of hardware-store purchases are impulse sales. Tempt the buyers and many will bite.

Stores were carefully designed, along with advertising campaigns, to sell. But the most powerful means of obtaining sales was television. Not the ads on television, but the programming. The lifestyle portrayed on television was described as "average," but it was actually quite upscale. All of a sudden, most of the population got the feeling that they were not living as well as they should. Producers didn't do this on purpose; it was simply a long-standing theatrical convention to show things as they were, but a little nicer, a little larger, a little more expensive. By the 1980s, the television and movie producers became fully aware of what they were doing and began to see placement of products in their shows. Such "product placement" deals became quite lucrative, and many of the products were upscale, being used by what were supposed to be "ordinary folks."

At the end of the century, awash with more income and consumer goods than anyone in 1900 could have imagined, fatigue was setting in. Surveys indicated that more and more people would be willing to work less, for more free time. Of course, it was easier to admit this to a poll taker than it was to convince everyone in the family that this was the way to go. But, like any other trend, it began to grow. In the early 1990s, over two thirds of those earning average or better salaries ($30,000 and up) said they were willing to give up a day's pay for that much extra free time. A third of all workers were willing to forgo raises and promotions in order to have more time with their families.

Many college grads moved back in with their parents so they could take a lower-paying, more satisfying, and less stressful job. Or just to save their money for some future opportunity. It became increasingly common for college and high-school grads to bum around for several years.

Temporary-employee agencies were soon doing a booming business providing skilled "temps" to firms. "Temping" was not as lucrative, or as stable, as full-time employment, but a new generation was learning to live on less and like it. Actually, many of the sixties generation grew older practicing a decidedly unconsumer attitude. The strains of the two-paycheck household were convincing many women (and some men) to stay home with the children.

Consumerism was an accidental phenomenon. Manufacturers and retailers were always eager to sell their products. But it was the fortuitous collision of sustained prosperity, the introduction of television and more effective advertising and merchandising, and easy credit that produced an apparent mania for buying everything in sight.

It couldn't last, and apparently it won't.

——One Step, Two Step——

Everyone likes low prices, especially Americans. And we have the lowest prices of any industrialized nation. It's no accident. Americans came up with some very interesting new angles that the rest of the world is slowly catching on to.

One reason retail prices in the United States are the lowest in the world is the efficient method by which American manufacturers get their products to consumers. At the end of the twentieth century, many U.S.-made products go straight from the factory to a large store. There is no middleman or "distributor" in the middle. At the beginning of the century, the use of one or more levels of distributors was common. If you had one level of distributors, you had a two-step system (products were shipped to the distributor's warehouse, and then from there to the retail outlet). If you shipped directly to a store, you had a one-step system. Of course, now we are seeing more and more "no-step" distribution arrangements, where the manufacturer does its own selling and ships direct to the customer. This form of distribution became particularly popular among PC manufacturers. Dell is the most prominent and successful user of this system, and their consistently high profits demonstrate how well this works. Each level in the distribution of goods is expensive. For example, in a two-step system, the distributor buys the goods from the manufacturer at about 60 percent of list price (if an item had a list price of $100, the distributor would get it for $40). The distributor then sells the item to stores at 50 percent to 80 percent of list price. The store owner will sell the product for full list price, if he can, or at varying discounts if he wants to move it out of the store.

With a one-step system, the manufacturer can sell to the stores at the same discount off list price that distributors do (50 percent to 80 percent). This enables chain stores (or "chains") like Wal-Mart and Toys R Us to offer the lowest price and still make a good profit. This, as many consumers have figured out, has been death to a lot of smaller local stores.

But it gets worse. For the small stores, that is.

The chains, including the recent book "superstores," go further than just taking advantage of a one-step distribution system. Knowing that they can buy (or not buy) large enough quantities of goods to make or break manufacturers, the chains go to some of their suppliers and ask some point-blank questions about what it costs to manufacture the goods. The chains then propose a rock-bottom price for the goods, a price that will result in even lower selling prices and even bigger profits. This angle did not make the chains popular with manufacturers, especially since the chain could later drop a company's product after the manufacturer had invested a lot of money into extensive production facilities. Maybe the chain found that the product was not selling, maybe they found another supplier—maybe any number of reasons. But the supplier suddenly losing its biggest customer could be driven into bankruptcy.

The chains found that this approach with suppliers was more efficient than an earlier (in the century) approach by supermarket chains and automobile companies (especially General Motors), who sought such efficiencies by setting up their own factories to supply goods or automobile parts. At first this worked, but eventually it was discovered that executives from the chain running these plants were not as efficient as independents. A company hireling, in general, would not hustle as much as an owner. An independent supplier could move faster, not being required to wait for some distant vice president or board of directors to size up the situation and make a decision.

This problem with internal suppliers is fairly recent, mainly because the general prosperity throughout the American economy after World War II and lack of any real foreign competition hid the inefficiencies.

General Motors–owned plants still make a lot of parts for their cars and are in big trouble because other American car companies (as well as most of the foreign ones) buy cheaper (and often higher-quality) parts from independent suppliers. For most of this century, GM was the biggest car company on the planet and had so much market share that it could hide a lot of inefficiencies. GM's competitors had to be more efficient to stay in the running. Dealing with independent suppliers, who could be forced to raise quality and lower prices (or lose their contracts), resulted in superior automobiles. The Japanese were the first to do this in a big way, and by the 1980s, American car companies, except for GM, responded by adopting the use of independent suppliers in the "Japanese style." This meant not just muscling the suppliers to provide better parts at lower prices but also getting the parts delivered just when they were needed. This "just in time" system was a Japanese innovation (learned from American manufacturers like Henry Ford earlier in the century) that eliminated the need to stockpile parts (bought and paid for by the car company and stored at the car company's expense).

Ironically, although the Japanese dreamed up "just in time" and the way to squeeze suppliers, their own distribution systems are much less efficient than the American. In many ways the Japanese, and the Europeans, are much more traditional when it comes to business practices. In other countries, the small businesses are also well organized politically. This political muscle, plus a riot or two as needed, has slowed down the growth of chains outside of the United States. In Japan, the distribution systems are often three- or four-step, with multiple layers of distributors providing jobs (and their employees becoming concerned voters) to keep prices high and chains out. This is finally changing as more Japanese tourists come to America and figure out why prices (even for Japanese goods) are so much cheaper in the United States. So much cheaper that Japanese ready to do a lot of shopping find it cheaper to fly to America, buy the stuff, and fly back at less cost than buying the goods at home.

Worldwide, the distribution system is moving toward the American model. But slowly, for America is unique on the planet for its willingness to change things. Most other nations are resistant to any number of changes that just move right ahead in the United States. Although the cost and convenience advantages are obvious with larger stores, most non-Americans also look to the displacement of small store owners and the closing of their shops. American society has re-formed itself around suburban living since World War II, and this has included malls and large stores. But most non-Americans still live in older cities or older (or newly built or rebuilt) villages. They prefer the smaller stores, even if it costs more. Only in America has there been such an enthusiasm for the suburban/mall lifestyle. These cultural and economic differences explain why not all U.S. innovations spread equally quickly overseas.

——Packaging——

For as long as there have been goods, things to get and take somewhere else, you have needed a container to put them in. Until the twentieth century, these containers were quite utilitarian. A sack, a bowl, some palm fonds, or just your hands. But in the twentieth century, it was discovered that packaging could be an important part of a marketing campaign.

Things eventually got out of control.

A common twentieth-century phenomenon.

In 1900, most goods were carried in a cloth bag or a brown paper sack (invented in the previous century). In 1912, cellophane was invented, but it wasn't until 1924 that the DuPont company developed a way to manufacture it economically and began selling it as a packaging material. Plastics became the hot new packaging material of the twentieth century. After World War II, the use of plastic packaging took off because of the advantages it brought to the marketing and, to a lesser extent, the usability of goods. In stores, goods packaged in plastic were more visible and attractive. So, more such goods were sold. Plastic packaging was also used to cut down on theft, for the package could be made larger than the goods and thus harder to sneak out of the store.

Fast-food companies found the plastic packaging attractive to look at and useful in keeping hot food warm. Many supermarkets, especially in cities, eventually replaced the century-old paper sack with plastic bags. The latter were more expensive, but they had handles.

The expensive (okay, a few pennies each) plastic bags were primarily an American development. In the rest of the world, shoppers continued the thrifty habit of bringing their own bags. In Europe, this tended to be the popular string bag. But this sense of economy never caught on in the United States. America had plenty of money, and Americans saw nothing wrong with spending it on minor conveniences like plastic bags. Convenience was largely what packaging was all about.

But going into the 1970s, especially after the OPEC oil cartel managed to jack up the price of oil (used to make most plastics), extravagant use of plastic in packaging became less popular. There was some reduction in such use of plastics, and in Europe, laws were passed to force manufacturers to be more prudent with their packaging. There was some similar commotion in America, but not much came of it. Americans could afford to pay for the additional packaging and paid no attention to the situation.

Sometimes plastic packaging was applied in a very clever and unique manner. In 1938, the ballpoint pen was invented. At first, the pens were made to receive refills, but after World War II they were made as refills packaged in plastic, the first of many disposable products made largely from plastic. Before the end of the century, there were several widely used disposable products, such as lighters and razors.

Plastic wasn't the only innovative packaging material. In the 1930s, beer became available in cans. You needed a special (albeit simple) tool to punch one or two triangular-shaped holes in the top of the can so you could get at the beer. Even the tool ("church key") became passé in 1962, as pop-top cans (currently in use) became available. The canned beer became so popular, and the litter of empty beer cans so extensive, that many states passed laws requiring a nickel deposit be added to the price of all canned beverages. As expected, the nickel bounty brought out enough people eager for the small change to clear all the cans from gutters, roadsides, and vacant lots. But there was still a lot of litter from packaging that did not have a bounty on it.

In 1900, packaging was seen as a wasteful extravagance. A century later, a necessity. In some areas, it is illegal to sell foodstuffs loose, as they were sold in 1900. But sanitary considerations were not the only, or even the primary, consideration in the spread of packaging during the last century. Convenience, for the manufacturer, retailer, and consumer, has always been touted as the main reason for the proliferation of packaging. And to a large extent, convenience was a valid reason for a lot of packaging. Goods were often shipped long distances, and sellers either used sufficient packaging or risked taking a big loss from damage. Packaging made it easier to keep track of and display goods in stores. And consumers found it easier to locate specific products they were after when easily seen packaging was used. By the middle of the century, Americans entering the armed forces got a bit of culture shock when they came across the plain, utilitarian packaging used elsewhere in the world. Later attempts to introduce this plain but sufficient packaging in the civilian market failed.

Thus it was no surprise that marketing, merchandising, and selling soon became an even more important reason for packaging, and these considerations are what carried packaging as far as it has gotten by the end of the century. Too far, according to many consumers, but until customers vote with their wallets, the proliferation of packaging will continue.

——Women at Work——

Throughout history, women have generally had to work harder than men. The men were in charge, and it was a man's world. The introduction of laborsaving devices for the home (washing machine, vacuum cleaner, etc.) early in this century began to lessen the workload of the hard-pressed housewife. More household income meant that more women could buy bread instead of baking their own. There was a golden age for the housewife in the 1950s, as family size decreased, household automation and income increased, and being a housewife became a lot less work.

It didn't last.

I leave it to you to figure out why.

It wasn't until after World War II that it became common for married women to work outside the home, especially when they still had school-age children. When these women did go to work, they added considerably to the household income, even though households have become much smaller. The vast increase in the economy after World War II created a labor shortage, providing wives with job opportunities they had recently seen, and taken advantage of, during World War II, when millions of men were in uniform.

Women had always been in the workforce, but usually as part of a family business. Farm wives had, for thousands of years, been instrumental in the success of the family farm. Some archaeologists believe it was women who invented farming, as women had always taken care of the home and children, supplying much food by foraging. And it is thought that this led to their deliberately growing plants, closer to home, for which they had long foraged. From here the early women farmers cross-bred and selected the most nutritious plants and, it is believed, invented the baking of bread. As towns developed, the wives of shopkeepers and craftsmen continued to play a crucial role in the family enterprise. We have numerous centuries-old records showing how widows would step in and run the family business all by themselves. When the industrial revolution began in the eighteenth century, women (mostly unmarried) became factory workers. As the industrial economy created more jobs, there developed a growing labor shortage, especially for skilled workers. Women were prominent in the teaching professions, especially in grades one to eight. But few of the higher-paying industrial jobs were open to women, and service-sector jobs, while more attractive to women, paid even less. Eventually, however, it would be education that would provide women with the kind of employment opportunities they always wanted.

It wasn't until after World War II that women began graduating from college in significant numbers. In 1900, women got some 17 percent of all college degrees awarded. This proportion rose steadily until, by 1940, women were getting a third of the degrees. But most of these women went into teaching or nursing, the only two careers considered suitable for women college grads. Actually, many nurses were still female high-school grads who had gone to two-year nursing schools.

In the early 1980s, women college grads began to outnumber male graduates. This was not just the continuation of a trend but the realization by many women that their career prospects were greatly enhanced with a college degree. Women also had different work objectives from those of men. While some women tried to have and raise children while still working, most interrupted their careers to deal with the kids. And when these women reentered the workforce, they preferred to do it with part-time jobs. There are about twice as many women as men working part-time. Women also prefer to work indoors at jobs that don't deal with a lot of heavy lifting. This extends even to the growing number of women in the military. While there are highly publicized incidents of women construction and heavy-equipment operators, most women avoid these jobs. In order to attract more women to factory jobs, the formerly utilitarian and sometimes dreary plants were spruced up considerably. Women responded by turning out when these jobs were offered.

There has always been a wage disparity between men and women. At the end of the century, women were getting about 60 percent of what men made. In 1900, it was less than 50 percent. But this is deceiving. When you adjust for such things as part-time versus full-time, years in the job, rank in the workplace, and educational requirements, most of the difference disappears. It's also not fashionable to point out that men are simply more aggressive in going after raises. Men are more aggressive in doing practically anything. Men are also much more likely to acquire scientific and technical training, which pays more because there's always a shortage of these skills. When you compare men and women coming out of college and going into the same jobs, the pay is basically the same and does not start to diverge until women leave work for childbearing.

Still, this is a hot topic. "Equal work for equal pay" is the slogan often heard. What no one has found out is just what is really equal in a market economy.

FOUR

BUILDINGS

NEVER, ever, in any previous century has there been as much construction of buildings as in the twentieth century. Yet it wasn't just the quantity of building that made the twentieth century different, but how those structures were built and what went into them. Looking at it from this angle, you find that the twentieth century was very unique indeed.

——Houses for Everyone——

Throughout human history, most people owned their own homes. Often just a hovel on a farm, but at least it was their own. But as nations like America industrialized, more people moved to towns and cities, where they lived in rented housing. This was not particularly popular, and after World War II, millions of families fled the cities for a new

---

Note: All dollar amounts are given in terms of year-2000 dollars. That is, they are adjusted for inflation and represent the dollar value at the end of the twentieth century. If you want to see what the actual money values were for a year, see the Appendix.

---

kind of private housing. The suburbs were born, and our culture has never been the same because of it.

The twentieth century saw Americans move into more and larger houses. In 1900, when the population was 75 million, there were 16 million housing units (houses or apartments). That's nearly 5 people per house, and only 47 percent were owner-occupied. At the end of the century, there are 277 million Americans and over 100 million housing units, which is about 2.8 people per house, and nearly 70 percent were owner-occupied. By the end of the century, the average house had over 2,000 square feet, with indoor plumbing, air-conditioning, and electricity. In 1900, homes were less than half that size, and most units either lacked indoor toilet facilities or shared them with another apartment. No one had air-conditioning, and most lacked electricity.

In 1900, America was undergoing a major shift in population from the rural areas to towns and cities. At that time, some 35 percent of the population was still working on farms. Most of these people had their own homes, although most lacked the indoor plumbing and electricity we now take for granted. Most of the urban population lived in rented housing. There was a burst of home building in the 1920s, a decade of growing prosperity. But the Great Depression brought a halt to that in 1929, and before the Depression was even over, World War II came along, and rationing prevented much more home building. But all the money paid out to war workers did allow more people to buy their homes. Before World War II, only 43 percent of homes were owner-occupied. The percentage had actually fallen a bit due to foreclosures during the Depression.

After World War II, a home-building explosion took place. The government provided cheap housing loans to veterans, and the tax laws allowed mortgage interest to be treated as a tax deduction. By 1960, 62 percent of homes were owner-occupied. The owner-occupied rate reached 67 percent in 1974. Then another recession, and higher mortgage rates because of severe inflation brought the owner-occupied rate down to 59 percent in the late 1970s. The rate has since gone back up to 67 percent and keeps going up. Part of this has to do with the increasing number of single adults living alone and not seeing the need for all that space of a house or the hassle and expense of keeping it up.

Condominiums have become popular, but the ideal owner-occupied residence is still a house in the suburbs.

One of the more noticeable innovations was the mass production of houses. Many techniques were used to bring this off, including the use of factory-built modules. But the most common approach was to build several dozen, or hundreds, or thousands of houses of the same design on one piece of land. Called "tract housing," "developments," or "sub-divisions" (depending on what part of the country you were in), the technique was first developed earlier in the century. After World War II, this method was used again, but for a larger number of smaller houses selling for a lower price. Developer Sam Levitt built several "Levittowns." The first one, east of New York City on Long Island, contained 17,000 homes, each selling for $30,000 to $35,000. This was about twelve to eighteen months' wages way back then, for a 750-square-foot home. This was a bit less than the average of 1,100 square feet for all houses built in 1949. The Levitt houses were meant for young veterans of World War II, eager to own their first home via the generous mortgages provided by the G.I. Bill.

When another Levitttown was built in the 1960s, the homes sold for $50,000 to $75,000, which was more like eighteen to twenty-four months' wages. These houses were larger, more like 1,200 square feet. By 1970, the average new house was 1,385 square feet, and over 2,000 square feet by the 1990s. In addition, with more and more single-person households, the amount of space per person has gone up. In 1950, the average person had 312 square feet of living space. By the early 1990s, that had gone up to 742 square feet (about the size of those Levittown houses in the late 1940s).

From the 1970s to the end of the century, the average price of a new home didn't go up as fast as the size increased. The late-1970s house cost $165,000 (average price for 1,755 square feet), while at the end of the century it cost $180,000 (2,200 square feet). The price was kept down by the building of more houses with only one story and the use of more efficient construction methods.

The children of the Levitttown home buyers, often first-time home buyers, bought houses twice as large as their parents', and the grand-children of those late-1940s pioneers had homes three times as large.

Not that the families in those Levitttown cottages (by today's standards) stayed in such small homes. They expanded their 750 square feet with additions and upgrades. Indeed, when the fiftieth anniversary of Levittown came along, it was discovered that only a few of those 17,000 houses were still their original size. By the end of the century, it became common to buy a first home as a "starter" home and then move up as income increased. Buying a used home saved about 10 percent off the price of a new home.

This was the trend for housing since World War II—more expensive and larger houses. Housing size, and cost, increased faster than income. People wanted to live in larger homes and were willing to pay for it. Those more commodious houses took longer to pay off, but confidence in the economy increased, and people were more willing to take on the debt and additional time it often took to pay it off. The family house became most families' largest asset. By the end of the century, the value of Americans' homes comprised 44 percent of the nation's net worth. Over a million new homes were being built each year, every year.

A major reason for wives' going to work, aside from having something more interesting to do than keeping house and doing volunteer work, was to pay for the larger and larger house, plus, for many families, a second vacation home. By the end of the century, over 12 million American families owned two or more homes.

The money, and work, required to maintain these larger and more lavish homes changed lifestyles. Pre–World War II families did not have as much house-centered work to do and had more time to, for example, hang out at the local saloon. Neighborhood bars disappeared as more homes with their own bars in basement rec rooms were built. There were still plenty of outside activities, but you had to spend less time at them if you were going to keep the house going. As the national housing stock grew, it also became better maintained and more frequently improved. This reached epic proportions toward the end of the century. In the last quarter of the century, Americans were spending over $40 billion a year maintaining their homes and twice as much remodeling and expanding them.

Everyone got their house, or was it the other way around?

——Cooled by Refrigeration——

The twentieth century is the century of cool air for the masses. Inexpensive air-conditioning has made many tropical areas much more livable and changed population patterns and the economy in ways no one anticipated in 1900.

It wasn't until 1902 that Willis Carrier invented what we now know as the air-conditioner. His first machines were large and expensive, but like many turn-of-the-century inventions, they would get smaller, cheaper, and more effective as the decades rolled by.

Artificial cooling is nothing new. For thousands of years, clever peoples in hot climates have developed ways to cool their homes. But the methods were expensive, requiring extensive construction, maintenance, and manpower. All that changed in the latter part of the nineteenth century as the mechanical techniques of modern air-conditioning became known. As the twentieth century opened, the race was on to engineer cheaper and cheaper air-conditioning units. By the 1920s, air-conditioning units had become cheap enough to use in movie theaters and other places where large summer crowds often became unbearably hot. Summer movie attendance went way up for theaters that could display a large sign saying COOLED BY REFRIGERATION. The term "air-conditioning" did not come into use until after World War II.

Air-conditioning remained quite expensive until the 1950s. But aided by a constantly growing U.S. economy, air-conditioning use really took off in the 1960s, as more people were making enough money to afford it. By the end of the sixties, most large office buildings had it, and the toastier parts of the United States began to cool off as offices and homes got their AC. In 1970, 34 percent of homes had central air-conditioning. Many more had room air-conditioners. At the end of the century over 80 percent of houses had central air-conditioning.

While the Southern parts of the United States were habitable before air-conditioning, it took a special kind of person to handle the heat and humidity year-round. Getting folks to move to the Southern states became a lot easier once air-conditioning was available. Indeed, once people had the option of cooling off during the hottest days, the South became quite attractive, for the weather was otherwise mild by Northern standards.

Air-conditioning changed more than just how comfortable people felt at home or at work on hot days. At home, they could sleep better in the soothing embrace of air-conditioning. They were more productive at work and enjoyed their food more when they ate out at air-conditioned restaurants. Cars were soon air-conditioned, as was mass transit. It got to the point where many people prided themselves on never having to deal with the heat of day. They went from an air-conditioned garage at home, via an air-conditioned car, to an air-conditioned garage at work, and spent the day in an air-conditioned office. And then back again. Perhaps when the sun went down, along with the temperature, they might go outside and have a cool drink in the backyard. Many of the Southern and Western states, especially in the desert areas, were quite pleasant when the sun went down and the heat quickly disappeared.

There was a price for all this. While the air-conditioners themselves became cheaper and cheaper and homeowners brought the cost down even further by installing central air-conditioning units for their homes, the cost of electricity to power the machines did not decline. While in the past, people accepted the need to pay for fuel during the cold months to heat their homes, air-conditioning now provided an opportunity to pay for cooling several months a year. Except for a few temperate months, people were now heating or cooling their homes and businesses most of the year.

Air-conditioning was worth the price, and people voted with their checkbooks. For those who could not afford AC, there were many public places with it that one could visit to hang out. And while the old-timers could remember what it was like before AC, they preferred not to dwell on it. If you lived in a tropical climate, once you got a taste of AC, there was no going back.

But that was only in America. In many other parts of the world, air-conditioning was seen as a luxury. Unlike America, where most of the population living in the Southern parts of the country had come from cooler climes, in the rest of the world people had lived the hothouse life for hundreds or thousands of years. People were used to it and, unlike Americans, were often unwilling, even if they could afford it, to pay the price of AC. This was especially true in places like Europe. With only a dozen or so really hot days a year in most parts of Europe, even offices were not always air-conditioned.

But in a $6-trillion economy, Americans can afford to spend $30 or $40 billion a year to keep cool.

——Mobile Living——

A lot of the housing built in this century had wheels on it. Nothing new here; families have been living out of wagons for centuries. But the twentieth century did it very differently.

It wasn't long after the automobile became a mass item that people found a way to drive and keep house at the same time. By the 1920s, as cars became much more reliable and comfortable, folks thought nothing of hitting the road for business or pleasure. It quickly became obvious that a slightly larger automobile could provide much better living accommodations. The first mobile homes were thus converted trucks or buses. But by the 1930s, there was a thriving business in mass-produced motor homes. The classic Airstream is a good example. All this came to a halt during World War II, as production shifted to weaponry.

Trailers also became popular, but soon these grew so large that they were house trailers in name only. At several times, up until the late 1960s, it was thought that trailer-home technology (cheaper, factory-built homes) would become a major segment of the housing market. Never happened. Shipments of mobile homes (mainly trailers) went to 60,000 right after World War II and grew steadily to nearly 600,000 units a year by 1973. But since then, sales have declined to under 200,000 units a year. Basically, house trailers got a bad reputation. The term "trailer trash" entered the vocabulary because many people at the end of their luck sought out the cheapest housing available, and that was often house trailers.

The reputation was undeserved, for the factory-built house trailers provided equivalent value to "stick-built" (built on site) housing at about half the price. This aspect of house trailers was never fully exploited, although it was tried. The housing market wanted taller ceilings, multiple stories, and many other features that were not practical for the factory-built trailer homes. There were also problems with property taxes. As long as a trailer home kept its wheels, it was still considered a motor vehicle (or trailer, of course), and thus not subject to real-estate taxes. Since these trailers were put up on foundations, they did not need moving-vehicle insurance. Basically, for all its advantages, the trailer home never could get much respect, or sales.

RVs (recreational vehicles), on the other hand, were a different story. These started out modestly before World War II; converted trucks were common, or even cars that were rebuilt up and out. But sales really got going when RV designs grew big.

In 1970, General Motors engineers were told to design the ultimate traveling machine. The new RV was to be on the cutting edge in terms of vehicle design and construction techniques. This was not to be just another recreational vehicle. The new GM RV was to be a radical change from the traditional boxy, topheavy vehicle on a truck chassis. The RV was to be introduced for the 1973 model year.

The GM designers were told to take advantage of the latest automotive technology. Thus the new RV had front-wheel drive, something still rare in car design at the time. Many key components were adapted from items successfully used in GM cars. The RV engine, transmission, and front suspension used the basic design that had been used successfully in the Oldsmobile Toronado since 1966. The rear suspension borrowed from GM's very successful designs for its line of buses. The chassis was of a robust steel-ladder design. The body frame was aluminum, and the body exterior was molded-glass fiber-reinforced plastic. This same body exterior had been used with great success in the Chevrolet Corvette.

Front-wheel drive and the independent swing-arm rear suspension meant that there were no drive shafts and axles passing under the coach. This made it possible to have a very low floor height compared to other RVs. The resulting lower overall height and low center of gravity gave the vehicle carlike driving qualities.

The new RV was built around the concept that the entertaining use of an RV is moving it around, not just living in it. Thus the exterior of the RV design was dominated by generous use of glass. Visibility from the driver's seat was exceptional, especially when compared to all existing RVs.

The new GM RV came out in 23-foot and 26-foot models, somewhat shorter than most current motor-home designs. Much space was saved by having no permanent sleeping areas; all beds were seating areas that were quickly converted to beds (much like a convertible couch). Later on, customer demand brought back permanent sleeping areas.

Many other design innovations distinguished the GM motor home. Hot water was available while moving through the use of marine water heaters. These used hot fluids from the RV engine to heat water. The refrigerator used power from the vehicle battery, although this had the disadvantage of running down the battery if the fridge was used any longer than overnight.

Unfortunately, the innovative design hit the market just as the OPEC oil embargo hit American motorists. Only 13,000 of these outstanding RVs sold before GM discontinued production in 1978. Twenty years later, over 8,000 of those RVs are still in use.

GM should have waited, as RV sales took off again in the 1980s. By 1988, over 400,000 a year were being sold. The large motor homes typified (and largely defined) by the GM design, were selling some quarter million vehicles a year by the end of the century. This was quite a jump, as this class of vehicles (costing over $100,000) sold only about 30,000 vehicles in 1970. In the end, the older-style RVs, built on truck chassis and such, lost out to the specially built motor homes. Sales of these older RVs peaked at 350,000 in 1970, and had fallen to about a third of that by the end of the century.

Unlike trailer homes and the smaller RVs, the motor home (large RVs) were seen as luxury items. No trailer trash here, not when your average motor home now costs as much as a house.

——The Automation of Housework——

For thousands of years, housework was the most abject drudgery. That all changed in the twentieth century, with unexpected results.

Early in this century, the washing machine and upright vacuum cleaner (1907) were invented. It wasn't until after World War II that these devices were cheap enough to be bought by most households, but long before their wide use, it was predicted that there would be a revolution in housework. Well, there was, but not the kind of revolution expected. Yes, women—as it was mostly women who cleaned houses and washed clothes—welcomed these appliances. But soon a pattern appeared. Rather than keeping things as clean as they were before and taking less time doing it, most women raised the standard of cleanliness they strove for. By late in the century, most homes were cleaner than few had ever been in 1900. Even then, the wealthy and their numerous servants had a hard time keeping a house as clean as the post–World War II bionic housewife could. But there was soon another unexpected result of all this household automation. Women went to work, and they used all the gadgets to maintain a satisfactory (to most of the household, anyway) level of housekeeping. But that wasn't enough for many women.

Like most great ideas, the automation of housework had unintended consequences. One was that although working wives had less time for housework, many tried to do as much housework as their mothers had. Exhaustion slowed many down, but guilt (and Mommy's acid remarks) kept many women going. The golden age of housekeeping in the fifties, when wives were homemakers and lots of tools were available to make the job easier and more thorough, haunted their career-minded daughters. A high standard was set, and it took more than a generation for a more reasonable standard to be generally accepted. As new items of household hardware came on the scene in the last half of the century, new housekeeping opportunities showed up. Increasing year-round use of air-conditioning (to heat, cool, or just ventilate, as needed) kept dust down through the use of filters. But meanwhile there was an oil shortage in the 1970s that prompted more people to seal their homes tight to conserve energy for heating. This, it turned out, also conserved all the new chemicals now available to keep things clean. The air inside the house became decidedly unhealthy unless the place was aired out regularly. That brought the dust in, and so it went.

Fastidious housekeeping extended outside the house as well. In 1958, the power lawn mower went on sale. This took the effort out of mowing the lawn, which led to more frequent mowing and more ambitious grass cultivation. The result of this was more chemicals used in the grass, which put some of those chemicals into the water supply in some areas. The power lawn mower eventually escalated to a version you could ride. After a decade or so of this, it was noted that the exercise effect of using the manual was sorely missed. Manual lawn mowers made a minor comeback in the 1990s, at least among the physical-fitness crowd.

By 2000, over two thirds of the workforce was providing services, and a growing service product was housecleaning. Not to mention groundskeeping and maintenance of all sorts.

The ultimate solution was at hand: make enough money so you could pay someone else to clean your house.

——The Robotic Kitchen——

Home automation was nowhere more popular than in the kitchen. For all of human history, most of the household tools were found in the kitchen. In the century of automation, this turned the kitchen into a little factory.

But it turned out to be a factory that had little to do.

In 1918, the first modern refrigerator (as opposed to an icebox) went on sale. It was expensive. The icebox (with a block of ice in a special compartment) remained in wide use until after World War II. The refrigerator changed home life enormously. People no longer had to go shopping as often, as with a fridge they could store food longer, requiring fewer trips to the market. Leftovers became more common, as uneaten food could be preserved and then reheated. The refrigerator also had medical benefits, as there was now less food poisoning from food gone bad. New dishes that were best served chilled now became possible. As freezers became larger, meats could be bought more cheaply in bulk. Dishes could be prepared in large quantities and then frozen, to be used gradually over the next weeks or months. This became a necessity as more women went to work and did not have time to prepare meals every night. The first consumer models appeared in the early 1930s, costing over a thousand dollars each. Thus most of these benefits did not become common until affordable refrigerators appeared after World War II.

In 1928, a more affordable item of kitchen automation appeared: the pop-up toaster. This toaster cost over a hundred dollars, but sold much better than the older manual version costing ten or twenty. The fact that people would pay a lot of money for better kitchen gadgets led eventually to a large number of electric cooking appliances. Not so much electric stoves as variations on the toaster. Things like electric frying pans, toaster ovens, and, in the 1960s, microwave ovens. But first most homes had to get electricity. This didn't happen to many rural homes until the 1930s. And these electric cooking gadgets required a lot more power than the first generation of homes was wired for. Electricians owe a debt to the inventors and manufacturers of all these electric cooking devices, for millions of homes had to be rewired so these things could operate.

In 1930, Clarence Birdseye began selling quick-frozen foods. This was a revolutionary technique that froze things like vegetables quickly enough that they were preserved yet still tasted fresh when thawed and cooked. Quick-frozen foods really didn't catch on big until after World War II, when more people had refrigerators (with freezer compartments), rather than iceboxes. Once refrigerator-freezers proliferated, Birdseye's was not the only product filling the freezer compartment. The combination of frozen food and electric cooking tools led to a revolution in American eating habits. Not a very healthy revolution, as it turned out. Although TV dinners (a 1950s innovation) were meant to be nutritious as well as convenient, food companies quickly realized that there was a bigger market out there for "fun food." Pizza, pastries, and all manner of more tantalizing frozen foods soon arrived in supermarkets. Fast food was a big hit at home, even though it meant that the only kitchen appliances being used were the fridge and the oven (often just the toaster oven).

But this did not slow kitchen automation. Although people were eating out more, and eating in with frozen foods, there was a nagging sensation that one should be preparing proper food in the increasingly lavishly equipped kitchen. So more gadgets came on the market, and they sold in huge numbers. The blender had been an early addition to the kitchen tool chest, and soon industrial-strength French models, called food processors, were added (the Cuisinart and clones). Electric can openers, dishwashers, and electric breadmakers sold well, as did electric ricemakers (long a big seller in Asian countries). Slow cookers (crock pots) and yogurt and ice-cream makers proliferated. Kitchens were increasingly equipped with everything except people cooking. Nonetheless, many kitchens were remodeled to make them more an all-purpose place to hang out. Restaurant-grade stoves, sinks, and re-frigerators were added. TVs, radios, tape players, and all manner of entertainment tools invaded the kitchen.

Toward the end of the century, catered and take-out food became increasingly popular. These items could be reheated in the microwave and consumed in the eat-in kitchen.

Who had time to cook?

——Freedom of the Road——

The automobile was the ultimate twentieth-century gadget. It was more than a better form of transportation; for many it was an addiction. But cars needed paved roads, and we got them. Nothing changed our cul-ture, and countryside, more than the automobile and its paved roads. At the end of the century, few of us have any memory of just how different America looked before the automobile came along.

It was a very different landscape back then.

It smelled different too.

In 1900, automobiles were poised to become a major form of trans-portation, ready to take advantage of America's extensive network of roads. Except there were no roads as we know them today; most were unpaved, and few got along well with automobiles. Cars could move a lot faster than horse-drawn vehicles, and to make the most of this speed they needed hard-surfaced roads. In 1900, most of the roads in America were fine for horses but obviously inadequate for automobiles. America had been settled largely by people moving along lakes, rivers, and ocean coasts. In the 1830s, railroad technology came along and provided an excellent way of moving people and goods overland. Who needed roads? Those that existed were simply local expedients for moving goods that last few miles from dockside or railroad to a store where they could be sold. Horse or oxen pulled wagons for this work, and the only ones that did long-distance work were those few Conestoga wagons that, for a few decades before the railroads caught up, were the only way across the Great Plains to the West Coast.

In 1900, America had a lot of things, but decent roads were not among them. There was no pressing need for a lot of hard-surfaced roads. Then the automobile came along, and the increasing number of drivers, many of them local notables and politicians, began to agitate.

"Get us out of the mud!" became the rallying cry.

Spending tax dollars to improve roads for automobiles was a hard sell at first. The cars were seen as a toy of the upper and middle classes. But by the 1920s, with automobile ownership becoming a mass-market thing, road improvement was all the rage. Local politicians noted that this provided them with lots of money and lucrative contracts for friends and political allies. Most important, the bus and the truck had been invented, quite by accident, and these automobile variations served everyone.

In 1912, 1916, 1921, 1944, and 1956 the federal government passed increasingly ambitious laws to improve the nation's highways. The 1956 law began the interstate-highway system, over 40,000 miles of multilane superhighway that still serves as the main road links between regions in North America. But most of the roads are in towns and cities or sparsely populated rural areas. In 1900, there were about 3 million miles of these largely unpaved roads. A major, and generally unrecognized, construction project of the first half of this century was the paving and improvement (bridges, streetlights, etc.) of these roads. During the Great Depression, the federal government put a lot of money into this roadwork as a means of providing employment. After World War II, as the population moved to the suburbs, the extent of this road network increased. But not by all that much, for by the end of the century, there were still not quite 4 million miles of roads.

What did increase dramatically was the use of these roads. In the 1920s, vehicle miles driven by motor vehicles went from 50 billion a year to nearly 200 billion a year. That's on about 3.2 million miles of roads. Most of this growth came from the increased number of vehicles on the road, but some was coming from the increasing number of miles being driven by each vehicle. This hit 8,000 miles a year in the mid-1930s and grew slowly for the rest of the century. In 2000, it was closing in on 11,000 miles a year. But because the number of vehicles was increasing so rapidly, the vehicle miles grew even more quickly. It hit 100 billion vehicles miles in the early 1920s, doubled again just as the Great Depression hit, and took nearly twenty years (till 1949) to double once more. Traffic increased a lot more quickly after that. Vehicle mileage doubled again by the early 1960s and again by the early 1980s. By the end of the century, vehicle miles hit nearly 2.5 trillion. Anyone who started driving in this century would find twice as much traffic within twenty years. So it's not just your imagination. The roads are getting more crowded.

But not as crowded as they could be. While cars killed train and bus travel, they did not stop the growth of air transport. Even though modern passenger aircraft were not built until the 1930s (the DC-3, still flying in many parts of the world), passengers took to the air in the early 1920s. By 1926, there were thirteen airline companies; by 1930, there were forty-three airlines flying 497 aircraft piling up 85 million passenger miles (one passenger flying one mile). The Great Depression and World War II slowed the growth of air travel. But by 1940, 1 billion passenger miles were flown. That year saw 2.5 million people carried, mostly by two-engine aircraft, similar to the commuter aircraft used today for local flights. But even during the war, the importance of air travel was recognized, and by 1945, 3.3 billion passenger miles were flown. When a lot of military air transports became surplus after World War II, airlines picked up many of them cheaply, and air travel grew quickly.

The major revolution, however, was the introduction of jet transports in the late 1950s. By the late sixties, 100 billion passenger miles were flown by over 150 million people. By the late 1970s, passenger miles doubled, and they doubled again ten years later. At the end of the century, nearly half a trillion passenger miles were flown, with nearly half a billion passengers carried.

This was a tremendous number of people being kept off the roads, although there was a lot of car traffic going back and forth to the airports. Though it wasn't just car traffic that was being thinned out by air travel, but truck traffic as well. As early as the 1920s, freight was being carried by air. At first, it was high-value, lightweight stuff, like mail. But ton miles (one ton flown one mile) went from 1,000 in 1926 to 3.4 million in 1940. By the mid-sixties, 1 billion ton miles a year were moving through the air. Then things really got going. Air freight was more expensive than truck, rail, or sea, but speed had a higher and higher value as economic activity got more efficient and shippers grew more conscious of the need for speed. Ton mileage flown doubled by 1970, doubled again in five years, and doubled again by the late 1980s. At the end of the century, nearly 20 billion ton miles were being flown. Trucks and rail were feeling the pressure.

In 1900, rail was king when it came to moving people and goods. There were 258,000 miles of track in operation, the largest railroad network in the world. The net grew for the first three decades of the century, peaking at 430,000 miles in 1930. Then the decline began. Freight carried hit 1.3 billion tons in 1929. The economic slowdown of the Great Depression saw freight levels drop to 630 million tons by 1932, after which they slowly grew again, and grew even faster during World War II, reaching 1.4 billion tons in 1945. The all-time peak was 1.5 billion tons in 1947. Then the trucks, and later cargo aircraft, began to take freight away from the railroads. Tonnage dropped to 1.2 billion tons by 1958, and then things began to turn around, heading for 1.5 billion tons again by the end of the century. At that point, there were about as many miles of track as existed in 1900.

In this century, the railroads were the cause of many of their own problems. The government had granted railroads thousands of square miles of free land on which to build their transcontinental lines in the late nineteenth century. When the railroads were the only transport game in town, they got lazy, lowering service and hiking rates. With all that free government land, and years of no competition, managing a railroad was a no-brainer, and eventually the industry attracted managers with few smarts. The automobile and aircraft industries attracted all the best talent after World War I. Meanwhile, railroad customers responded by moving as much business as possible to trucks, river barges, or aircraft. It was only in the 1950s and '60s that the railroads hit rock bottom and had nowhere to go but up. At the end of the century, there was a much chastised and more efficient set of railroad companies operating.

Railroads had not only trucks to worry about but also the increasing use of pipelines for moving petroleum and barge traffic along rivers and coasts. In 1941, just as the economy was getting over the Depression and just before America entered World War II, railroads moved 63 percent of the freight traffic. By 1950, that had declined to 57 percent, with the biggest gains by waterways and pipelines. Remember, the interstate-highway system did not get going until the late 1950s. By 1965, truck traffic was making itself felt. In that year, railroads moved only 44 percent of freight, while trucks moved 22 percent. Trucks were now moving more tonnage than barges or pipelines. By 1990, rail still moved 38 percent of freight, but trucks were moving 26 percent, barges 16 percent, pipelines 20 percent, and air a (very valuable) fraction of a percent. By the end of the century, rail had gotten back some of the lost ground but was nowhere near the dominance it held in 1900. Still, the railroads made remarkable progress in a century. Automation, more modern equipment, and better management enabled the railroads to move over four times as much freight over the same amount of track.

In a century, Americans went from being not much more mobile than humans had been for thousands of years to traveling hundreds of miles a week. This had never happened before, and no one ever expected people to be moving around on this wide a scale. In the past, only sailors traveled that much, and these mariners were only a minuscule portion of the population. But traveling appealed to something within people; otherwise, millions would not so willingly drive or ride so many miles year after year. All this movement has changed us in ways that are hard to understand, for never before has there been such a large and mobile population. The landscape changed to accommodate this increased mobility. Millions of miles of roads were paved, acres of parking lots appeared, and thousands of airports were built.

Retailing moved from the downtown areas of towns and cities to the outskirts, where there was more parking and fewer traffic jams. People spread out as they never had before, with the "commute" becoming a major part of many people's lives.

The automobile was more than just a new form of transportation. It was the machine that changed the face, and lifestyle, of America.

——You'll Never Walk Alone——

Solitude has long been recognized as an excellent way to regain one's peace of mind. To catch one's psychological breath. To take a break from the hurly-burly of life.

Then came the telephone.

And then it got worse.

We take telephones for granted at the end of the century, but in 1900 they were still few in number and labor-intensive to use. For the first half of the century, the telephone system was the major high-tech industry, and progress was swift.

In 1905, the dial telephone was perfected, and the telephone network as we know it was still taking shape. While the basic telephone technology had been made workable in the 1880s, in 1900 the telephone "system" was still nothing but many different companies, often competing with each other in the same area. Subscribers to local telephone companies called human operators in order to be connected to other subscribers. At the time, this was considered as amazing as computer networks are today.

In 1878, two years after the first practical telephone device was demonstrated, the first local telephone exchange (in New Haven, Connecticut) was opened. By 1900, you could, with the aid of one or more human operators, call between most major cities. In 1915, the first transcontinental telephone "net" between New York City and San Francisco opened for business. The first transoceanic telephone call was placed in 1926, between New York City and London. The dial telephone was not invented until the late 1890s and did not replace the "ring up the operator and make your call" system for several decades. In fact, the last hand-cranked telephone exchange did not go out of service in the United States until 1983. The telephone companies did not become sufficiently automated to allow long-distance calls without operator assistance until 1951. But the automation continued, and that's what made those less resourceful telephone-company robots more vulnerable to deceit than the traditional human operators.

But it's been only in the past few decades that all the telephone systems have been computerized. Before that, there were a lot of people you had to go through in order to connect with someone far away. Once computers were put in charge, it was soon discovered that the computer programs could be fooled with tricks that would have never worked on human operators. These hackers didn't use personal computers to attack the phone network, because personal computers hadn't been invented. Rather, the "phone phreaks" of the 1960s used hand-held, battery-powered devices that emitted the various electronic tones that the telephone company used to control the long-distance phone net. Some of the phreakers could whistle the tones, but anyone could use the various electronic boxes. All one could really do with this phreaking was to make long-distance calls for free. But that was enough to attract a lot of people to phreaking. This battle between telephone companies and phreakers goes on to this day, even though the phone-system attackers equipped with personal computers get most of the attention.

Computers and telephones were too potent a combination to ignore. In addition to making telephone companies cheaper to run, and thus more profitable, there was also the potential of many new services. Starting in the 1960s, computers could do things like forward calls, provide the number of the last person to call you, redial automatically, and so on. Customers could be charged small amounts for each of these services. Because the computers were doing all the work, the cost of providing these items was very low and the profits quite high.

The Japanese had been the great innovators of consumer electronics for the last third of the twentieth century. They were driven not just by a desire to export huge quantities of this gear to America but also by their own gadget-crazed population. One result, in 1979, was the cellular phone. It was a daring idea at the time. After all, who would pay several dollars a minute for a phone call? Nearly everyone, it turned out. The first U.S. cellular system went on-line in 1983. By 1984, there were 91,000 U.S. users; in 1990, there were over 7 million users; and by the end of the century, there were over 70 million users in the United States alone. By the end of the century, there were planetary cellular networks, using dozens of satellites to handle the messages. For the less ambitious systems, the price had come down to the point where it was not much more expensive than noncellular systems. People were beginning to drop their regular phones and depend just on their cell phones. In some still-developing countries, it was found more efficient to install a cell-phone system than the more conventional ones based on stringing wire.

Cell phones were the ultimate communications convenience. You could reach out and contact anyone with a phone, and do it no matter where you were or what you were doing. And then there was the increasing incidence of telephone tag. As more busy people got telephones, they found themselves calling each other and getting a busy signal. By the 1960s, the majority of business calls did not reach the person for whom they were intended on the first try. People knew the intended callers were spending a lot of time away from the phone doing not particularly interesting things. Like commuting, having lunch, or walking down the hall. Prime phone time was going to waste, until the cell phone came along. Far fewer wasted moments.

But were these moments really being wasted? Was the commute to work or walk down the hallways lost time? You could think, read, nap, daydream, or, as many rail commuters fondly recall, have a game of cards or a drink in the bar car. You can still do all that, but subject to an abrupt interruption as your cell phone krills for attention. Those people who crave that kind of attention were the first to rush out and get cell phones, the first to take calls while dining out or attending the theater, and the most likely to make and take calls while walking down the street. We've all seen them, and most of us cannot imagine carrying on like that.

Most users are more selective in their use of their cell phones.

Women like the idea of having one in the car or in their purse, in case there's an emergency. Parents like the idea of being able to keep after their adolescent children, and the kids are willing to suffer more parental supervision so they can carry around a cell phone (even if it does not have many minutes available for their recreational use). Cell phones provide a sense of connection to the more familiar. Users can, and do, turn them off a lot. And even if you don't turn them off, the batteries might run down and leave you in peace anyway.

For over a decade before cell phones arrived, there were beepers. When beepers got cheap, parents had their kids carrying them. Beepers were one-way; beepees had to go find a phone to return the beep. Cell phones were basically beepers with the phone built in. The beepers are still very popular at the end of the century, not just because they are cheaper to operate but because they are less intrusive. There are more options when you want to ignore the beep, or at the very least just answer it on your terms, in your time.

While you can turn off your cell phone, once it is known you have one, it's assumed that you are committed to being available all the time. The cell phone has become a badge indicating that you're operating in the fast lane of 24/7 access. It's no coincidence that the term 24/7 (24 hours a day, 7 days a week) became common at about the same time cell phones did.

Naturally, as cell phones get cheaper and cheaper, many less driven people will carry them. Just for the convenience, not because they want to be reachable 24/7.

It won't work out that way. Cell phones are just one more element in the pattern of twenty-first-century communications. It was always considered science fiction that there would come a time when everyone would be reachable all the time. The present is catching up with the science fiction, as it has done so often in this century. It's more than cell phones and beepers. It's also e-mail, ATMs, surveillance cameras, E-Z Pass, and tracking devices. And software. Software that collects data from stores, both on-line stores and off-line ones. Software that searches data to find patterns. Patterns of what you do, when you do it, and how likely you are to do it again.

Which brings us back to telephones, and telemarketing. The latter has become one of the more potent selling tools of the twentieth century. Selling by phone is nothing new; it was one of the first uses of the telephone. What takes telemarketing beyond simply using the telephone to make a sales call is the use of computers and data. Lots of data, and very powerful computers. Figuring out what you're likely to buy from records of what you've bought in the past, computers construct a script for the sales rep to read, complete with likely questions you will ask and the best answers to them.

But it doesn't stop there. At the end of the twentieth century, the computer can do the talking, listening, and answering in a human-sounding voice. Too new to be true? It's already been used by telephone companies and aircraft-electronics firms for some years now. It's only a matter of time before a telemarketer judges it ready for a trial run. While this won't work for many people, it will work for some. What keeps telemarketing going is the small but profitable number of people who do respond to the phone pitches. If having voice-recognition and voice-synthesis software, backed by a lot of market research and artificial intelligence, do the pitches brings in more money, it will be done.

But getting hustled by talking software is the least of your worries. All of these twentieth-century communications gadgets have another worrisome side effect. Taken together, they can tell the wrong people where you are and where you've been. Communication is a two-way street, and with enough communications devices operating, you'll never walk undetected. Consider the pattern of location information you leave behind you when you use this stuff. It's always been the case that a telephone call left a record of where the phone was. Cell phones do the same, for they send their signals to a specific receiver, whether it be a small antenna on a telephone pole or a low-flying satellite. ATM transactions are linked to a location. E-mail can be traced to a specific location. And there's a lot of e-mail to trace. At the end of the century, over 5 trillion e-mail messages a year (compared to about 100 billion pieces of first-class mail) were being sent in the United States alone. Two-way beepers now give the same information as cell phones. E-Z Pass—that transponder device you put on your windshield so you can zip past the toll both—also keeps when-and-where-type records. Credit-card transactions, which use telephones, also track your movements, not to mention your spending habits.

Someone knows where you were and when. And with the right connections, that person can know very quickly. A hundred years ago, it was easy to get lost. Today, you have to give up quite a lot to maintain some degree of stealth and privacy.

——Miles of Aisles——

Ever think about how much time you spend in stores? It's a lot of time, and it's no accident. A century of clever store design has sapped your willpower. Come in, shop, resistance is futile.

People love to shop, and in the latter half of the twentieth century, shopping became a really big business, as well as a major form of entertainment. But we did it in fewer, and more attractive, stores, and at lower prices for a much larger array of goods.

To put this in perspective, consider the population per retail store and how it changed. In the first half of the century, there were about 70 to 80 people per retail establishment. The average number of employees per store was two or three. There were a lot more stores back then, and they were smaller than the ones we shop in today.

After World War II, the situation changed dramatically. Up through the late 1970s, the population per retail outlet grew to nearly 150. The average number of employees per store went to about ten per store. After stalling in the wake of the Vietnam War, the economy began another boom that went from the late 1980s to the end of the century. One interesting development during this period was a rapid increase in the number of retail outlets. At the end of the century, the population per store was moving toward 120, with about eight employees per outlet.

Two developments made the shopping boom possible. First was the development of the department-store concept. This is actually an ancient idea, examples having been found in antiquity. But the modern version appeared mainly in large American cities (particularly New

York) in the nineteenth century. The department stores were, in effect, urban malls. Most customers came on foot or by public transportation, and the stores provided a delivery service for purchases.

By 1900, the layout of department stores was well established. In the basement there were small odds and ends (notions). On the first floor were women's accessories and cosmetics. The second floor featured women's clothes, while on the third floor were children's clothes. On the fourth floor were men's clothes. The fifth floor held furniture, and the sixth floor contained appliances. This layout was developed based on what it took to draw customers in and keep them there. The goods on the first floor were those that most appealed to women and were largely impulse items. This drew shoppers off the street. Any woman coming into the store had to run the gauntlet of all those accessories and cosmetics to get to anything else.

The first department stores appealed to upper- and middle-class women who did not work. But as the twentieth century got older, more married women worked, and working women in general had more money to spend. The department stores' first response to these changes was to convert the lowest floor to the bargain basement. The notions goods were sold more conveniently and at lower prices in the Woolworth type stores, so the department store conceded that category.

By the middle of the century, there were noticeably fewer married women with time to shop, and these women were more price-conscious. The original department store had depended more on presentation, convenience, and atmosphere than on low prices. Department stores had, and still have, a rough time dealing with the price issue.

The department-store idea was gradually adopted by retailers in most American cities, where by the end of World War II you could find department stores in cities everywhere, but rarely in the suburbs or rural areas.

Another innovation was the chain store, that is, one company that had many stores of the same type all over the country. Chain stores also go back a long way, and the earliest one in America is the Great Atlantic & Pacific Tea Company, founded in the mid-nineteenth century. A&P had hundreds of relatively small grocery stores all over the country. This had the same effect on small-town shopkeepers as the twentieth-century Wal-Marts did. The A&P stores were bigger and had lower prices. In the latter half of the twentieth century, A&P would close many of these smaller stores and convert the rest to supermarkets.

In the 1950s, retailers noted that the money was moving to the suburbs, but there were no department stores there to make use of all that wealth. Moreover, the automobile had changed the way people lived in the suburbs. From the late 1800s, there had been suburbs connected to cities by railroad and trolley lines. But once most people in the 'burbs began to commute by car, they realized they could go anywhere to shop, and did.

In response, a lot of new stores were opened up all over the suburbs. Many were freestanding, all alone off the side of a local road with adjacent parking. Others were built together in the first "strip malls." These were not true malls, simply a convenient way to build several stores in one place. These strip malls did have more parking, but they had to or many potential customers would not come.

But this got some developers to thinking, thinking about the differences between shopping in the city and in the suburbs. The difference was cars, and parking. A lot of city shoppers came via foot, bus, or train and left the same way, often having purchases delivered later. In the suburbs, everyone had a car, and people took that car with them when they went shopping. The downtown shopping areas of the new suburbs did not have parking for all the cars the new suburban residents were using. By the 1950s, several developers in different parts of the country came to the same conclusion. The basic idea was to expand the strip-mall concept, put a roof over it, and add lots of parking. Other features quickly appeared. One or two major national retailers had to be enticed to move to the mall in order to "anchor" it and provide a major reason for people to come to the mall. The most popular anchors were the big-city department stores (like Macy's) or clothing stores that were branching out all over the country. The rest of the stores were selected so that all a customer's shopping needs were covered. Retailers quickly realized that the mall was a great place to be, but the mall operators demanded, and got, a share of the mall stores' sales and adherence to a long list of rules and restrictions.

By the early 1960s, those first few malls proved to be extremely popular, and profitable. The malling of America began. By the end of the twentieth century, the second-generation malls began to appear. These included not just shopping opportunities but entertainment as well. First it was movie theaters, then multiplexes, skating rinks, gyms, and amusement-park-type rides. The mall has gone from shopping center to entertainment complex. Mall developers realized, perhaps before market researchers picked up on it in the 1980s, that shopping was a hugely popular form of entertainment. So by combining traditional mall shopping with pure entertainment, the malls became irresistible attractions for the surrounding population.

Malls became so popular that, by the 1980s, they were being built inside towns and cities, along with massive, multistory, above- and below-ground parking facilities.

The malls changed American retailing in ways that are not so obvious. Malls gave new life to specialty stores. These are retail outlets that carry a large number of items of one type of merchandise (such as flowers, sporting goods, shoes, fabrics, or books). Stores that specialize even more, like selling athletic shoes or books on a particular subject, thrived and were called superspecialty stores. America, of course, is the nation that pioneered the building of "general stores" that had a little of everything. This was the typical type of store in small towns that could not support more than one or two stores of any type. Department stores are basically much larger versions of the general store, designed to take advantage of the larger number of customers available in big cities. But despite the success of department stores, there were still a large number of specialty stores in cities and large towns. What malls did was to make it possible for more specialty stores to exist. Malls catered to people with cars who were willing to drive a bit farther for the "mall experience." With more shoppers in one place, it was possible for more specialty stores to prosper. This was made easier when many famous big-city specialty stores opened branches in malls. Clothing (Brooks Brothers and many women's clothing stores) was particularly popular. Heavy mall customer traffic made a lot of super specialty store concepts viable.

Department stores are, in effect, malls. Their many different departments function much like the separate stores in a mall. It's no doubt only a quirk of history that some department-store executive didn't think up the mall concept first, but with the twist that the entire structure (usually three or four levels and over a hundred thousand square feet) was actually one big department store. It probably would have worked, as many department stores did later adopt mall design ideas with some success.

Department stores are also an ancient idea. For thousands of years, very successful merchants eventually built themselves huge structures where they sold a wide variety of goods, all segregated by type. The European department stores came from this ancient tradition and as a result featured an extensive food department. In effect, these department stores were the first supermarkets. American department stores were slow to pick up on this angle and only began doing so at the end of the twentieth century.

One thing department stores did pick up on from the European stores was the inclusion of a restaurant. The malls took the food angle one step further, by inventing the "food court," a portion of the mall containing several restaurants (mainly fast food).

One of the hallmarks of twentieth-century American life was the increasing variety and declining price of food. This is what attracted A&P to open all those food stores in the nineteenth and into the twentieth century. But the A&P outlets, like many independently owned stores, were never more than a few thousand square feet. While these stores carried a little of everything, they did not have a lot of selection in any one category.

Michael Cullen changed all this in 1930 when he opened his first King Kullen supermarket. It was a roaring success, even in the midst of the Great Depression. Part of the reason was that, in addition to carrying many more items than conventional food stores, Cullen depended on volume to make him a profit on his lower prices. Cullen also offered convenience. You could get any kind of food in his stores, as he had created a food department store. He divided the store into departments that for thousands of years had been independent stores (meat, produce, baked goods, groceries, and, after World War II, delicatessen, and nonfood items). By the 1960s, supermarkets ranged in size from 15,000 to 35,000 square feet, and they typically stocked over

10,000 different items. By the end of the century, there were over 25,000 different items available to be sold, including over 200 kinds of cereal alone.

The King Kullen chain, by its very success, forced the other food chains (like A&P) to convert their stores to the supermarket model. While the consumer loved the supermarkets, this development was devastating to smaller food stores. On average, each new supermarket would put over a dozen smaller stores out of business. After World War II, the supermarket concept spread to Europe and then around the world.

In the 1970s, Europe returned the favor. In France the Hypermarché (hyperstore) was developed. These were larger than supermarkets and included additional features like dry cleaning, laundry, drugstore, and fast-food restaurant under one roof. There was even larger selection and lower prices (because of bulk sales to customers). The concept was nothing new, but the scale was. There were similar trends developing in the United States, but with a different array of merchandise.

In 1900, there were hundreds of "variety stores," the most famous of these the Woolworth "five- and ten-cent stores." The last of these were closed in the late 1990s. The cause of their demise was a 1960s development of the variety store, the "big box" store (because of the bulk quantities and larger items available, and the huge, boxlike shape of the stores themselves). The best examples of this were Wal-Mart and Kmart. Both opened the first of their super variety stores in 1962. Woolworth was too late getting into this business, and this is the main reason the Woolworth stores eventually disappeared.

Wal-Mart stores became the most successful of this type because, like the chain of variety stores they grew out of, they stayed away from the major metropolitan areas. This was a wise move. There was not much competition out in the countryside. Many people were moving to the cities and suburbs, making the retail outlets in all those shrinking small towns very vulnerable to a Wal-Mart's opening nearby. Wal-Mart brought lower prices and wider variety, something the folks out there, with smaller budgets than people in the urban areas, could appreciate. Some activists opposed the entry of a Wal-Mart into their area, knowing that many of the existing retail outlets were likely to go out of business. In a few cases the opposition succeeded, but in most cases the people got what they wanted: a Wal-Mart.

Kmart developed from a variety-store chain founded in 1899 by S. S. Kresge. Previously overshadowed by Woolworth, the new, better managed Kmart chain was expected to beat Woolworth, and it did just that. But there was a lot more competition in the urban areas Kmart favored, and it did not do as well as Wal-Mart. Kmart got hammered by the new specialty superstores for high-ticket items like electronics, as well as by the factory-outlet stores. Kmart was able to take advantage of the denser retailing environment also, but in the end, this was not enough. In the 1950s, they began putting their stores in malls. But this meant they had to spend more on advertising to deal with the competition, something Wal-Mart could neglect.

Wal-Mart had much less of this competition in the thinly populated countryside. Thus they were able to depend more on word of mouth and less on advertising. Moreover, Wal-Mart was one of the best-managed retail chains in the country, applying in their operations the habits of hard work and hospitality found in the rural areas. Watching what new ideas were working, and not working, in the more competitive urban markets, Wal-Mart emulated the ideas that worked and executed its entry into new types of retail stores, like wholesale clubs, superbly.

Wal-Mart also led the industry in using computers and linking store registers, via the store computers, directly with suppliers. Wal-Mart had less inventory, fewer items out of stock, and higher customer satisfaction and profits. Wal-Mart, like any other large chain, was able to buy goods in vast quantities, and thus more cheaply. With lower wages in the rural areas, where the cost of living was lower, the selling prices of their goods were about as low as they could go.

The success of Wal-Mart's low-price stratgy led to stores explicitly called "wholesale" stores, for the rock-bottom prices and no-frills atmosphere in which the goods were sold. These stores had to be a certain size to be cost-effective, so there were not many of them and most were located in high-density urban and suburban areas. While fewer in number, very large stores became popular in major markets, some over 200,000 square feet in size and containing grocery- and department-store merchandise, all available in bulk quantities at low prices.

A related type of store, also fewer in number for different reasons, were "off-price" stores. These specialized in merchandise that was not moving quickly in the regular stores. There were also discontinued items that manufacturers wanted to get rid of, as well as items that did not meet the quality standards of the producer. These "irregulars" were often just items that were overproduced. But the customer didn't care; they were good enough (the defects were usually not detectable at a glance), and the price was right. The price, in fact, was usually below the normal wholesale cost, as the manufacturers dumped these goods for less than it cost to produce them in order to raise cash for new product lines.

After World War II, millions of newly affluent people moved from the cities to the suburbs. One thing they missed, aside from the department stores, was the convenience store. In cities there was always a store that sold, at all hours, things people needed at all hours: newspapers, over-the-counter drugs, beer and soft drinks, some food items, and the like. Cities were, and are, full of stores like this. But out in the suburbs there were none, at first. Then local entrepreneurs began setting up convenience stores, or service stations added convenience-store items. There were already some convenience stores out there. In the 1930s, 7-Eleven stores began to show up in the Southern and Western states, after the first one got started in Dallas in 1927. Others followed, but it wasn't until the great migration to the suburbs after World War II that convenience stores became a big business in residential areas and not just something for lonely stretches of the highway.

Shopping, and prowling around stores, occupies much more of people's time in 2000 than it did in 1900. Not just because there's a lot more money to spend, but because the layout and management of stores has become more methodical and effective.

We have become a nation addicted to shopping, and it's one addiction that is unlikely to be outlawed.

——Malling the Landscape——

The pyramids defined ancient Egypt, the cathedrals defined medieval Europe. The twentieth century leaves behind malls for future archaeologists to puzzle over. Huge, multilevel structures surrounded by parking lots, they have replaced downtown in many towns and villages. All because downtown and the automobile could not coexist.

Shopping malls, to a historian, are nothing new. For thousands of years there have been markets where many merchants offered their goods under covered "malls," along with food courts and their own security force. But these ancient malls were in cities; the twentieth-century mall is outside urban areas. And therein lies the big difference.

The mall evolved gradually over several decades. In the 1920s, as more people had cars and more families were living outside the city in suburbs, the strip shopping centers appeared. These were what they still are, a row of stores along the side of a street, with parking in front and often in the back. In 1928, a very large strip shopping center opened in Columbus, Ohio. It had thirty stores and parking for four hundred cars. The customers were still out in the open as they went from shop to shop, but it did show that you could build an "instant downtown shopping district" outside a city. If you provided enough parking places, the shoppers would drive over and shop. In 1931, a Dallas-area strip mall appeared with the stores facing one another across a courtyard. Shoppers were still out in the open, but it was almost a mall.

The Great Depression and World War II stalled the development of new shopping concepts. But by the 1950s, there were many retailers picking up where they had left off twenty years earlier. In 1956, in Edina, Minnesota, the first enclosed mall was built. The concept caught on immediately and in a big way. In the next twenty years, over 13,000 malls were built in the United States.

In 1976, the Faneuil Hall Market was built in Boston. This project proved that a mall can thrive inside a major city. Many more followed. Then, in the 1980s, the Mall of America was built in Wisconsin, with 4.2 million square feet of space. It was the largest mall ever built, and it was a success.

The mall was a development of the department store. Before the automobile came along, a department store could survive only in a city, where there were enough customers walking in to make it profitable. Out in the countryside, where people walked or went by horse or train, general stores were scattered all over the landscape. The automobile changed all that. Cars quickly became extraordinarily popular, and people quickly bought millions of them. People loved to travel, and they didn't mind driving an hour or more just to shop. This was a double plus for most folks; they got to go for a ride and shop in one trip. As more people got automobiles, more could travel farther to shop. This allowed retailers to draw on a larger audience, and even in the 1920s it was noted that if you provided parking, drivers would pull off the road and check out your store.

After World War II, as the veterans came home and found that the Great Depression really was over and the government was offering them college scholarships (through the G.I. Bill) and cheap VA mortgages, they used their college educations to get better jobs and move to new housing developments in the suburbs. By the early 1950s, new towns and villages were literally springing up by the thousands all over the countryside. These were the suburbs. Technically, many were additions to existing towns and villages, but in reality these suburban tract-house developments were new settlements, and they created a demand for many new stores. While the existing Main Street stores did a booming business initially, the new suburbanites quickly grew tired of the lack of parking space. Thus the strip malls became ever more popular, even if they lacked the charm of Main Street shopping. At least there was parking, and shopping was shopping.

People went where the goods were, as long as they could find a parking space.

The first enclosed malls changed all that. Here was a shopping environment that outdid Main Street in terms of charm and convenience. No bad weather to worry about, which had something to do with the first enclosed malls' showing up in places with nasty winters, like Minnesota. But more than the weather was controlled. "Undesirable activity" was kept out of the malls because they were private property. The mall owners considered the entire mall to be the inside of a building, which it was. But the mall was designed like an idealized version of

Main Street, with only foot traffic allowed and nothing but shopping on display. No rain, no beggars, no drunks, no rowdy behavior. Air-conditioning made malls the perfect place to spend some spare time. Malls were comfortable, they were safe, they were all over the place. It was a concept that made spectacular sense to most suburbanites.

Malls continued to develop. At first, they just got bigger and built more stores with more lavish materials. But they also added different attractions like movie theaters, supermarkets, and even housing. Malls were much quicker to innovate than the old downtown area had been. Mall management is unified; all the stores are tenants. Zoning restrictions are few, and no voters need be consulted. The shoppers vote with their money and the stores with their willingness to renew their leases. This ability to respond quickly to changes in society is one of many reasons that malls are so successful.

While many types of structures can be said to define the twentieth century, malls are the ones that are everywhere.

Sure, skyscrapers are impressive and tract housing is where many of us live, but the mall is one place most of us want to be.

FIVE

TECHNOLOGY

MANKIND has always used technology to adapt to, and change, his surroundings. The rapid and widespread rate of change in the twentieth century was a result of the unprecedented development of new technology. Moreover, only a small portion, less than 20 percent, of the world's population was responsible for creating most of this technology. The twentieth century played host to two vastly different populations, one living amid a growing flood of technology, the other living much as they had for thousands of years. But the other 80 percent have been catching on and catching up. What happens when we have to live with *their* new technology in the twenty-first century?

Note: All dollar amounts are given in terms of year-2000 dollars. That is, they are adjusted for inflation and represent the dollar value at the end of the twentieth century. If you want to see what the actual money values were for a year, see the Appendix.

——The Real Scientific Revolution——

The major scientific breakthroughs of the twentieth century had nothing to do with scientists.

While the twentieth century has been a time of enormous scientific progress, the more important revolution has been in the unprecedented ability to turn scientific discoveries into practical applications. Every past century has had a few scientific geniuses, and we have thousands of years of written records of their brilliant ideas. But because of a lack of engineering, few of these ideas were put to practical use. What was also missing was the management skills to make it all work and mass-produce it so many could benefit. One scientist can think up some marvelous new gadgets without any help. But bringing an idea to life takes a lot more people with the ability to manufacture the components, put them together, and manage the whole process. In the past, many of the breakthrough ideas required materials (like harder metals) that didn't exist yet or techniques (like welding) that had not been dreamed up yet. Moreover, most of the modern engineering marvels require first dozens, then hundreds, then thousands of different parts. Getting all those parts together efficiently required management skills that never existed in the past. All that began to change in the last two centuries, and especially in the twentieth. This century was a golden age for engineering, manufacturing, and management. Not only do we have a lot more scientists, but we have even larger numbers of engineers, technicians, and managers who can figure out how to make something useful out of scientific breakthroughs. This was a sharp change from past practices, where "thinkers" were reluctant to get involved with the lesser "engineering" and "craft" skills.

Management as we know it did not even exist until recently. But this changed in Europe over the past few centuries. Engineering became a respectable profession, not just something a few skilled craftsmen did. Moreover, in Europe there developed what we now call "management skills." Supervisors, proprietors, and foremen turned into managers.

Modern engineering is more than a lot of clever engineers let loose on a project. The really key ingredient is the ability to manage these projects. Modern management has become a pervasive element throughout our culture, but it was particularly critical in making modern engineering projects possible.

In this century, we have seen many examples of how crucial engineering and management skills are. When the Soviet Union got going in the 1920s, they paid a great deal of lip service to scientific progress. The Soviets put a lot of people into engineering schools and provided the means for many scientists to do important research. But the Soviets were never able to pull off the vast array of engineering projects found in the West. What was the difference? The Soviets never developed a modern management class. They had plenty of bureaucrats, but few managers who could do whatever needed to be done to bring off complex projects.

Another example is Japan after World War II. Realizing that whatever they were doing before World War II did not provide them with the most effective industry and economy, the Japanese studied how it was done in America. Before World War II, Japanese engineering tended to be a bit haphazard. This was seen in the manufacture of their weapons during World War II. While the Japanese (like the Soviets) could do some engineering very well, they were not able to maintain a consistent level of excellence in engineering, as did American and other Western engineers. By the 1960s, the Japanese had adopted American-style engineering management and proceeded to outdo their mentors. Ironically, in the 1980s, American managers finally woke up to this and cleaned up their act. Thus we had an economic boom in America throughout the 1990s.

We still have examples of the ancient bad habits that prevented great ideas from being engineered into useful items. A constant problem with managing software development is the tendency of many of the best programmers to get sidetracked with clever ideas that get in the way of finishing the program. The thing software development managers hate to hear is "Hey, look at this neat stuff!" This means the programmer has come up with some jazzy new piece of code and, now in scientist mode, has little interest in doing any software engineering. This is an ancient problem, and the popularity of comic strips like "Dilbert" that skewer managers only emphasizes how rare good engineering managers are. But there are a lot of such managers out there; otherwise, we would not have so many neat gadgets that do work and make our lives longer, easier, and more pleasant.

While taking nothing away from the scientists, it was breakthroughs in engineering and project management that provided twentieth-century scientists with the tools they needed to achieve *their* next breakthroughs. This was the catalyst that turned loose the scientific genius that has always been present in the human race and produced a flood of scientific advances never before seen.

——The Really Important Inventions——

By the end of the century, it was widely noted that most of the scientists who ever lived were currently alive and practicing their craft. The result was millions of inventions. But some were more useful than others. Some inventions were much more than useful; some were essential for entire categories of later inventions, and others radically changed the lives of so many people. Here is my list of the century's most defining inventions.

- Air-conditioning came along in the first decade of the century, and within a few decades a large part of the planet, the tropics, became more habitable. Subsequently, millions of people moved, got good jobs, and completely changed the look of many of these tropical areas. We may take air-conditioning for granted, but just try to live in a hot climate without it.

- DNA, the blueprint of living creatures, was discovered in the early 1950s. Over the next four decades, this discovery emerged as the beginning of a string of breakthroughs on how the body worked and how better cures for diseases could be developed.

- Intelligence testing had been around for some time, but not in a really systematic fashion. That all changed in the first decade of the twentieth century, when the IQ test was developed. This led to the creation of many other tests to classify people according to their actual or potential abilities. While much detested by many, the tests have changed schools and the workplace for the better. The testing puts more emphasis on fairness in selecting students and employees.

• The laser was developed during the 1950s and patented in 1958. This device—actually it was a technique—put light to work as never before. You now find lasers everywhere. Fiberoptic cables carry messages and movies; CD players use lasers to read data; lasers are used for range finding and for cutting material. No light saber yet, but the twenty-first century is still young.

• Penicillin was discovered in 1929. This was the most momentous medical discovery in human history. Penicillin was a universal antibiotic; it killed bacteria that had killed hundreds of millions of people over the centuries. Pneumonia, gangrene, leprosy, blood poisoning, and the Black Death were all caused by bacteria, and all were now brought down by penicillin. It took more than a decade to figure out how to mass-produce penicillin, just in time for World War II. After the war, medicine was fundamentally changed by penicillin. People now had faith in drugs, where before, many such cures were basically scams. Work proceeded on more drugs, especially vaccines that would prevent dangerous illnesses. A vaccine for typhus had been developed in 1909, but it wasn't until after World War II that vaccines appeared in large numbers. One for measles showed up in 1954, for polio in 1955, and for meningitis in 1987. Perhaps more ominously, the availability of antibiotics led to a lot more surgery, for before that, the threat of infection made surgery too dangerous except for the most desperate of situations. The bacteria eventually adapted and fought back, but work also continued on drugs similar to penicillin, saving the lives of a goodly portion of the people currently alive.

Smallpox, one of the major scourges of the human race for thousands of years, was eradicated in 1979. A major disease had never been wiped out before, and the elimination of smallpox was the result of decades of work by international medical organizations. This example provided the incentive needed to go after other major diseases, and we can expect to see more of them disappear in the twenty-first century.

• Magnetic-tape-recorder technology was invented at the turn of the twentieth century. It wasn't perfected until the 1930s in Germany and didn't reach America until after World War II. In the second half of the century, this form of recording, which was far superior to the wax-cylinder type available early in the century, changed the way people dealt with information and entertainment. First sound, then video, then computer data were recordable. Never before had people been able to record, distribute, and use so much data. We take it for granted now, but without this recording technology we would be living quite different lives.

• The radio telephone, or "wireless," arrived in 1900. Communications have never been the same since the appearance of this seemingly magical technology. Out of it came radio, television, cell phones, satellite communications, and more in the future.

• Television—one version of it anyway—was invented in 1923 and publicly demonstrated in 1926. Crude at first, but full of obvious potential. Especially since radio was undergoing explosive growth at the same time. Television was seen as the "next radio," and it was, and even more than that, spawning many technologies and lifestyle changes.

• The transistor (solid-state electronics, like the microprocessor) was invented in 1947 and moved the electronics business to heights never imagined. The vacuum tube is largely forgotten at the end of the century; it was replaced by the transistor. Even the CRT (cathode-ray tube) used for televisions is being replaced by transistor-based flat screens. But before the transistor, electronics depended on tubes. Although tubes had shrunk from fist size at the turn of the century to finger size (and a bit smaller) after World War II, they were still too big and produced too much heat. The first transistors replaced vacuum tubes on a one-for-one basis, with the individual transistors the size of a grain of rice or corn. But within twenty years, a way had been found to put first dozens, then thousands, and, at the end of the century, millions of transistors on a piece of silicon the size of a fingernail. Smaller electronics meant cheaper and more powerful devices.

- Uranium fission, the key breakthrough needed to build an atomic bomb, took place in 1942. This led to nuclear weapons and nuclear power. The former played a large role in preventing war between the major powers in the second half of the twentieth century. The latter brought a new, safer, and cleaner, although controversial, source of energy. But the most important result of nuclear weapons was an unprecedented period of peace. Never before had there been such a long span of peace between the major nations. It was a balance of terror between the nuclear armed powers. It wasn't pretty; in fact, nuclear weapons were terrifying. But that was a decent trade-off for avoiding another world war. There may still be a nuclear war, but for the moment, we are getting the peace dividend. In advance.

There were many other notable inventions that brought somewhat lesser benefits. There was xerography in 1938, which was a mixed blessing. The first human heart transplant took place in 1967, which led to new techniques for a wide range of other transplants. Radiocarbon dating was developed in 1947, which allowed us to more accurately date ancient artifacts. Vitamins were discovered throughout the century, vitamin A in 1913, vitamin B in 1916, vitamin C in 1928, vitamin D in 1922, and so on. Other inventions that had a profound effect on twentieth-century life, like the automobile, were invented in the late nineteenth century. There's a lesson in that, for one of the many curious scientific breakthroughs of the late twentieth century may turn out to have as enormous effect in the twenty-first century as the automobile did in the twentieth.

It was a century of invention, unlike any century before. Invention has become a part of our culture for the first time. We take it for granted, forgetting that such acceptance of the new and novel is a uniquely twentieth-century custom. It has changed our lives and will continue to do so for the foreseeable future.

——The Age of the Automobile——

The automobile is the most visible technology of the twentieth century, and the one that has changed culture and lifestyle the most. We are still trying to work out the implications of all that as the century comes to an end.

In 1900, there were 8,000 automobiles registered in the United States. About half of those had been registered in that year. It was the dawn of the automobile age, and cars were still seen as something of a novelty. But something powerful stirred in the hearts of men once they saw an automobile.

The reasons for automobile mania were more obvious in 1900 than they are today. A century ago, the other forms of personal transportation were obviously inferior to the automobile. There was the horse, either ridden or pulling a carriage. But horses were tricky to work with and required a bit of experience to handle safely. Horses had to be fed and exercised regularly. Getting a horse ready for travel took time. You either had to put a saddle on or hook up the beast to a carriage. Traveling by horse was far more dangerous than going by automobile. Horses were also slower than cars.

Trains and trolleys were popular, but people could only go where the tracks went, and they couldn't do it on demand. Boats were convenient, but slow. Of course, there was also walking, and back then many people did so a lot more often and over longer distances than is the case today. But walking was slow, and it took a bit of effort.

Seen in this light, it's no wonder the automobile became so popular so quickly.

By 1910, there were 468,000 cars registered. Thus in a short ten years, the car had gone from rare curiosity to something just about everyone had seen and many used. This despite the fact that a car cost over a year's household income.

In 1910, 181,000 new cars were registered. This was a tremendous jump, and due largely to one man, Henry Ford, and his inexpensive, mass-produced cars. In 1908, a Ford cost about $17,000. Fairly typical for cars back then and not all that pricey for 1908, for although income was about half what it is today, there were a lot fewer things to buy. People lived simpler, less expensive lives. But the automobile appeared to be the sort of thing to splurge on. And the automobile was also the first major consumer item to be bought extensively on credit. Yes, we have been making monthly car payments for the entire century.

This trend did not go unnoticed. Between 1904 and 1908, 241 companies started to manufacture automobiles. At the same time, Henry Ford developed mass-production techniques for manufacturing, and this brought the cost of cars down to the point where a large segment of the population could afford them. By 1913, Ford had refined his mass-production techniques to the point that he could make a good profit selling his cars for about $10,000, although in the 1920s he had a bare-bones model going for about $5,000. A $5,000-to-$10,000 price made the car affordable for most families in America, and year by year more and more of those families decided that they just had to have an automobile. The $10,000 price tag for a mass-market car has not changed much throughout the century. The average price has gone up; indeed it just about doubled by the end of the century. But you can still get a basic, few-frills new car for that price, although usually in a developing country where the male population is just getting started in expressing their innate passion for automobiles.

The popularity of cars was more than just keeping up with the neighbors; the freedom to travel provided by the automobile struck a fundamental need in people. Well, at least in men. Women did not have much to do with cars, except as passengers, during the first half of the century. While women were still largely housewives, men saw the opportunity to vastly increase their mobility with the automobile. And so they did. And in the latter half of the century, women did the same.

With so many cars careening about, it wasn't long before traffic-control measures came into use. Laws were passed, and, in 1914, the traffic light was introduced. Traffic jams arrived early, for the simple reason that the more mobile cars could get into towns and cities far easier than horse-drawn transport. While there were trains and trolleys one could take into town, people preferred to drive in and put up with the traffic jams and difficulty finding a place to park. Traffic jams are not unique to the twentieth century; they were reported in large cities thousands of years ago. But never have there been so many traffic jams in so many cities. And so few—in fact, no—solutions to the problem.

Because of Mr. Ford's innovations and all those new car manufacturers, by 1920, there were 9.2 million cars in use. Even the slow learners could see that the horse was history. By 1930, there were 26.7 million vehicles in use in America alone. The 1920s had been a time of prosperity, innovation, and optimism. Sort of like the 1960s, but in the 1920s there was even more technical innovation. Radio broadcasting was introduced, and this spread the excitement about the new automobiles faster and more convincingly.

Despite the sour economic conditions of the Great Depression, by 1940 there were 32 million vehicles (mostly cars) in use. Even during the Depression, new-car registrations never fell below 1 million a year, and they hit nearly 4 million in 1937. Vehicles in use declined during World War II because production was halted due to wartime rationing (of fuel, tires, and other parts). In 1945, there were only 31 million vehicles in use (from a 1941 peak of 34 million). There was a huge pent-up demand for cars, so by 1950 there were 49 million in use. It kept going; 74 million in 1960 and 108 million in 1970. Then things began to level off. By 1980, vehicles in use grew to only 122 million, then 144 million by 1990, and over 160 million at the end of the century.

Until World War II, the United States was the only nation with widespread car ownership. But from the 1950s on, most nations got a taste of automobile fever. Same pattern as in the United States. First the men decide they have to have a car, and before you know it, you have traffic jams. In poorer nations, motorcycles caught on first, but nearly everyone wanted to have a car.

The automobile has since established a love/hate relationship with its owners. While people are really, really in love with the personal mobility and convenience cars provide, they hate the fact that everyone else is clogging the roads as well. Reformers preach the virtues of mass transport and claim that the failure of those more efficient forms of moving people is the result of a clever conspiracy by the automobile and oil companies.

But people want their cars, and they will continue to have them. Logic has nothing to do with it.

──Operations Research──

There were a few key concepts that made the flood of twentieth-century technology possible. One of the most important of these items was "operations research" (OR). Despite OR's success, it's still unknown to many and controversial to some.

Operations research emerged as a profession in the late 1930s, when British scientists developed mathematical methods to deal efficiently with making complex technology work within equally complex military organizations. The British called it operational research, but the American term became more common, if only because there were more Americans doing OR. Much of what major American corporations were doing in the 1920s and '30s was OR without its being called that. Many of these corporate OR specialists were drafted or otherwise brought into government service during World War II.

The impact of OR was often immediate and nearly always very impressive. OR can best be described as a combination of the centuries-old scientific method (systematic research to prove, or disprove, an educated guess), modern engineering methods (a lot of math and statistics), and plain old common sense (which, as you know, is not all that common). A good example is an OR project carried out early in World War II. The British noted that their fighters and bombers were often limping back to base shot up with enemy bullets and shell fragments. It was suggested that some armor be added to the aircraft to minimize the damage. The OR boffins (the British term for a technical expert) were turned loose on the task. Since aircraft cannot carry a lot of armor without sacrificing performance, the idea was to work out where the minimal amount of armor should go to do the most good. Hundreds of damaged aircraft were examined. The location of the damage was noted and statistics were developed (how much damage in the wings, fuselage, engine, etc.). But one of the OR folks also applied a little common sense. He noted that they were unable to examine many of the aircraft that had not come back. These had been shot down over the English Channel or German-occupied Europe. But all the damaged aircraft that had come back had been damaged in places that had not done so much damage that the aircraft were brought down. Thus the areas that were *not* hit were noted. Given that hundreds of aircraft were examined, by combining all this information, the OR folks noted certain key areas that received little or no damage in the aircraft that had returned. These must be the crucial areas that should be better protected. And so they proved to be. Certain control (cables and electrical wiring) and engine (hydraulic and fuel lines) components were rarely harmed in returning (but damaged) aircraft. Doing a little more math and organizing information from aircrew on what types of damage caused them the most problems, OR work made it possible to provide substantially increased protection to aircraft with a minimum amount of armor. When the newly equipped aircraft went into action, a higher percentage returned. And many of these had dents in the armor protecting the key areas.

Another example of OR involved coming up with the best way to hunt for enemy submarines after they had attacked a convoy. There were never enough armed escorts for these convoys, and one of the few times these warships got close to an enemy submarine was when a convoy was attacked. The subs, naturally, wanted to get away as quickly as possible. The subs could go in any number of directions. How could one improve the odds of warships' detecting the fleeing subs? It was a mathematical problem. Since the warships could move in any number of directions while searching, math could be used to work out what the most efficient patterns would be (after taking a few other factors into account, such as the location of other warships and surviving ships in the convoy). These search patterns were expressed in simple, straightforward instructions for the warship skippers. The number of German subs detected and sunk went up dramatically as soon as these new patterns were used. The Germans thought the Allies had some dramatically new and improved detection equipment (sonar), and were chagrined to discover that they'd been done in by some simple math. The Germans could have developed optimal escape patterns, but they didn't. This would have reduced the effectiveness of the new Allied search patterns, but not given the subs a whole lot of additional protection.

OR was used in many less exciting areas, such as setting up factories, moving supplies, and organizing the building of the atomic bomb. One of the less well known scientific techniques applied to winning the war, OR went on to be a key spark plug in the economic boom that took place after World War II and continued until the end of the century. OR made its reputation, and acquired a bit of glamour, from its use in World War II. But more than anything else it was an apt expression of the merger of science, engineering, and management during the twentieth century.

After World War II, the OR folks came back to civilian life determined to make OR shine as a peaceful tool. Engineering and business schools were the most common places to find OR taught. The M.B.A. (master of business administration) degree soon became the most visible badge for someone who had become an OR practitioner. The engineering-school graduates actually turned out more OR experts, but the M.B.A. grads were more likely to have a press agent. The M.B.A. crowd also acquired a sinister reputation. Few understood exactly how all this OR stuff worked, and the media did a miserable job of explaining it. Indeed, the press decided that M.B.A.'s and OR made excellent villains, and that, unfortunately, is how things have remained for over half a century.

Science created all the good things in life and got no respect.

But that's another story.

Where the Personal Computer Came From

Personal computers came out of nowhere. No one expected them, and the experts dismissed the concept of "personal computers" as totally off the wall. The experts were wrong. Again. Keep that in mind.

Personal computers first appeared in the mid-1970s. These were new toys for the electronic hobbyists, and no one really thought much would come of them. This was not the first time the conventional wisdom was so far off the mark.

The first computer was designed in the nineteenth century. But, as with many great ideas, the tools were not yet available to build it. Even when the engineering capabilities (electronic components like vacuum tubes) for building a computer became available early in the twentieth century, there was still no obvious need. At least no need so compelling to justify the enormous cost.

Then World War II came along, and there *was* a need. The Allies had found a way to decipher the secret codes in which the Germans sent their radio messages. But it was a slow process, often too slow to be of any use. Then some of the scientists involved remembered the nineteenth-century computer-design efforts, and they took another look at the state of current electronic technology. By the end of World War II, there were several large computers, taking up thousands of square feet and costing millions of dollars. Mostly for code breaking, but now that the computers existed, people began to see still more uses. These huge machines had less power than the first personal computers, but at the time they were very useful. Work continued on computers after World War II, mostly for scientific and business use. Even by the 1950s, when IBM was busily building commercial computers, the thinking was that the market was very small, from a few hundred to a few thousand machines.

It's important to remember this narrow-minded thinking about the first computers, because you never know when some similar innovation will come along and take everyone by surprise. Then again, it was a lot of fun and pretty exciting to see the way PCs lurched into the market-place.

The hardware designers and programmers of the 1950s and '60s developed the hardware theory and software tools that made it possible for PCs to get right to work when it became possible to build them. And that became possible in the early 1960s, when transistor technology was taken one step further. Using a combination of high-resolution photography and thin layers of different substances (mainly silicon, otherwise known as sand), engineers managed to put the hundreds of different transistors normally needed for computing functions onto one fingernail-size "chip." These were called integrated circuits (more than one transistor function etched onto a sliver of silicon). By the early 1970s, integrated circuits were complex enough to contain all the functions necessary to have a "computer on a chip." This was called a microprocessor, and one of its first uses was to run handheld calculators. By the early 1970s, there were minicomputers, still the size of a refrigerator, but many times smaller than the current "mainframe" computers, using microprocessors. The minis first appeared in the late 1950s, using transistors but designed to be mass-produced and sold at much lower prices than mainframes. This was not saying much, as a 1970s mini would cost $50,000 to $100,000. The mainframes were selling for $1 million and up (way up).

By the late 1970s, personal computers, using microprocessors, were selling for about $4,000. These were really minimal devices by today's standards. The first Apple II cost $3,800, and for that you got an 8-bit CPU with 64,000 bytes of memory and data stored on a cassette player. With some of these PCs you could use a TV set as a display; with others you bought a low-end black-and-white display. You could also buy diskette drives, holding 40,000 characters of data, for $1,200. In the early 1980s, hard-disk drives became available. A 20-million-byte unit would cost about $5,000. The first IBM PC, in 1981, cost $2,600 for the bare-bones model. A more useful system cost twice as much.

In the mid-1990s, PC prices finally began to plunge. Until then, PC power had steadily increased, but the price was stuck at about $3,000 to $4,000. Twenty years after the first PC appeared in the late 1970s, the price of PCs (adjusted for inflation) had fallen by more than 50 percent. By the end of the century, there were over 100 million PCs in use worldwide.

By the late 1990s, you got a lot more for your money. Typically, for less than $1,000, you got a 32-bit CPU that is about 3,000 times faster than early models and has 32 or 64 million bytes of memory. Storage is via a 6- to 10-gigabyte hard-disk drive. For under $500 you could get about 80 percent of that computing power. At the end of the century, there were handheld computers far more powerful than the first bulky PCs of the late 1970s.

But in the early 1980s, there were only a few million PCs out there.

IBM entered the PC business in 1982, and only then did PC sales really take off. Most current PCs are developments of those first IBM PC designs. You can run much of the software for those early IBM PCs on current PCs. But it wasn't just IBM's putting its seal of approval on PCs that goosed sales. There was also some unique software that made PCs a must-have item for many businesses.

The first of these breakthrough software products was VisiCalc. This was the first spreadsheet program that allowed business folks to play with numbers painlessly. For centuries, one of the most useful, and tedious, management tasks has been adding up columns of numbers. Then looking at the results and wanting to know what the totals would be like if one or more numbers were changed, and then having to do the math all over again. VisiCalc changed all that. If you changed a number in VisiCalc, the program automatically recalculated the totals. You could also put in formulas instead of numbers, and these would be recalculated too when another number was changed. Millions of PCs were bought through the 1980s, just to run VisiCalc (and succeeding programs like Lotus 1-2-3 and Excel).

Just as the minicomputers had taken a lot of business from the original mainframes, the PCs took away business from both mainframes and minis. But PCs did more than that. By the 1980s, thousands of new firms had sprung up to write software for the millions of new PC users. The success of VisiCalc was noted, but there was also a steady demand for more mundane programs (databases and word processors) as well as more exotic stuff for the many different companies that had never used computers before. But now just about every firm could afford PCs, and many of these new users plunged right in.

At the end of the century, PCs were still difficult to use and keep operational. While PC manufacturers liked to describe their machines as "appliances," PCs are not as easy to operate as your average appliance. What this is leading to is more specialized computers that do fewer things, cost less, and are more reliable. A good, and early, example of this is the game console. First sold a few years before the PC arrived on the market, these consoles have become more and more powerful. Surprisingly, most people don't realize that these consoles are simply specialized PCs. Palm-size computers arrived in the 1990s as another example of specialized PCs that place a strong emphasis on ease of use and reliability. Voice recognition, even smaller PCs, and eyeglass displays show where the PC is going. Integrating TVs and PCs is another trend.

Basically, the PC won't become an appliance as much as most appliances will take on the characteristics of PCs.

BASIC, Macros, and Roll-Your-Own Software

The twentieth century had its own unique language, although it didn't appear until the second half of the century. It's the many languages of computer programming. Mostly bits of recognizable English, it was first thought that only specialists would learn this stuff. But programming quickly spread to the masses.

It's still uncertain where this will lead.

The very first PCs were kits for hobbyists. You programmed them the same way you did the very first computers, one instruction at a time via switches. But in 1964, several college professors at Dartmouth developed the BASIC programming language. This was meant to be an easy-to-learn programming language for getting people started. It worked, and by the time PCs began to appear ten years later, many computer enthusiasts were already familiar with BASIC.

In 1975, a small version of BASIC (Tiny BASIC) was developed for one of the first PCs (Altair). Bill Gates and Paul Allen, who went on to found Microsoft, created a more full-featured and bug-free version of BASIC for PCs and successfully sold it to most of the PC manufacturers for inclusion on their machines. BASIC was one of the main reasons PCs took off. Rather than wait for commercial software to be available for the PCs, users could and did roll their own using BASIC. This was not a powerful programming language, especially when compared to the then industry standards like COBOL and FORTRAN, but BASIC could get results, and users proceeded to create thousands of programs each year. Most were for personal use. I taught myself BASIC in 1978 and proceeded to write several dozen useful programs. But before that I, and many other future PC users, had used programmable calculators (first out from Hewlett-Packard in the mid-1970s) to create our own (however limited) software. I was not alone, as these calculators sold quite well, even though they cost as much as a PC does today. So the user enthusiasm should not have been a surprise. And to a certain extent it wasn't.

It wasn't BASIC that got a lot of people into programming, though, but rather spreadsheet programs. The first one, in 1979, was VisiCalc, and it allowed users to write short series of commands called macros. As other companies rushed to create their own spreadsheet programs to compete with VisiCalc, one of the common features added was the ability to write BASIC-like macros within a spreadsheet. Spreadsheets like Microsoft's MultiPlan offered this and shortly thereafter so did the groundbreaking 1-2-3 spreadsheet. Before long, people who barely knew what programming was were writing their own software. While the pros did not consider the increasingly user-created macros to be programming, it was. And it was, from the users' point of view, the best kind of programming, for it was what they wanted, and as soon as they could figure out how to do it, they did.

The impact of these self-taught programmers was immense. Between the late 1970s and the mid-1980s, the number of people creating useful (at least to themselves) programs increased over ten times. We'll never know exactly how many people became programmers, but it was easily in the millions. A sense of how big the programmer explosion was can be gained by looking at the sales of Turbo Pascal. This is the program that got Borland International going, and Turbo Pascal was basically the Pascal programming language with a easier-to-use front end. Millions of copies were sold, and so popular did Pascal become that it replaced BASIC as the standard "instructional language" for teaching high-school students how to program. Meanwhile, millions of small businesses and departments in larger firms began to use homemade software and spreadsheets full of macros to run their operations.

Maintaining this locally produced software became a major problem as time went on. One thing that makes a professional programmer a professional is the ability to build programs that will not only work but will keep working and will be maintainable. To make software that is easy to fix and upgrade, programmers have to put plenty of comments in their code and avoid sloppy practices. A lot of the amateur stuff was thrown together during intense sessions of creativity and urgency. Either these programmers did not know about how important it was to insert comments while writing the program instructions, or they didn't want to be bothered. Such new programmers learned the value of these comments the first time they had to fix one of their own programs several months later and were faced with a lot of stuff they no longer remembered the details of. Many anguished hours were then spent trying to reconstruct the original logic of their program.

This spotlighted the second big problem, which was that the part-time programmers were eager to get their software working any way they could. Most did not know about how to lay out their programs for ease of maintenance. Few knew that most of the cost of software development went into planning and testing. Amateur programmers did a minimum of either. Few of these people knew that over the life of a program, most of the expense would go to fixing and upgrading the program, not creating it in the first place. So the amateur programmers tended to do what was expedient, not what would make it easier to change or fix their software in the future.

The BASIC programming language, designed as it was to be easy for students to learn, accomplished much of this ease of use by allowing the programmer to write the code instructions in a haphazard fashion. Most other programming languages were quite specific about what instructions had to be put where. This gave every program done in these "professional" languages a sense of order no matter who wrote the program.

The publishers of programming tools noted the problems their part-time programmer customers were having maintaining their home-brewed software. These publishers, especially Microsoft, observed how many millions of amateur programmers there were and thought, with some justification, that there might be more of them out there. Thus more powerful yet easy-to-use programming languages were constantly brought out, and then updated. The original BASIC had turned into Visual Basic by the end of the century.

There were also a slew of products to clean up after the amateur programmers, but there were too many amateur programmers using whatever was at hand to turn out ever more software for business use. While some of these hackers turned into data-processing (DP) professionals, with a professional attitude toward their code, most continued to program as they always had, and a lot of their creations were crucial parts of many companies' operations. When the authors moved on, the users soon found they needed the software updated or fixed, and no one knew what was going on inside it. Worse still, users did know what data was entered and what came out, but they had only a vague idea of what was happening in between. Publishers, sensing a hot new market, produced programs that automatically dissected BASIC programs or spreadsheet macros, while consultants abounded to fix the problems (or at least convince publishers that the best solution was to hire them). But there was too much amateur code that was not attended to, resulting in thousands of critical software programs waiting to fail in catastrophic and unpredictable ways.

The spreadsheet macros caused a lot of problems, and even a few lawsuits. The macro capability was never meant to support heavy-duty programming. But the spreadsheets were so easy to use, and so unintimidating, that many a desperate businessman (and they were overwhelmingly men) began crunching numbers on his spreadsheet and just kept adding things. Naturally, these situations eventually got out of hand and didn't stop until the spreadsheet file got too big for the user's PC or until unfixable (by the creator) errors crept into the massive spreadsheet model of a small business or part of a larger one. Newer versions of the spreadsheet programs, PCs that could handle larger spreadsheet work files, and a lot of "we'll fix it" consultants kept things from getting completely out of hand.

But there was a better solution in the offing.

Along came the RAD (Rapid-Application Development) tools. Visual Basic is one of these. A RAD is a programming-language package that has a front end an idiot could love, or at least understand. The whole idea behind RAD is to provide a point-and-click approach to creating new programs. Speed was never an issue with BASIC (which always had the slowest programs of any language), as users were brought up short very quickly when the lack of speed told them they had to use a faster language. The newer versions of BASIC create much faster programs, and the new generations of hardware gave most users speed to spare. But most important, the RAD programs brought order to the code and made it easier to maintain after the author moved on. RAD programmers are continuing to create needed software for businesses and organizations. PCs gave a lot of people who didn't know they were programmers an opportunity to find out that they were. Thus from the original BASIC to the current RADs, these largely unknown programmers continue to change the world we live in.

Bringing programming to the masses became a viable concept as the century closed. In a way, it was inevitable, for computers have proliferated to the point where they are everywhere. Appliances (with at least one microprocessor) and automobiles (with over a dozen) were typical of machines that people had to use and, for all practical purposes, program. One of the best examples of how this has worked out is to be found in the VCR and microwave oven. Both can be used just by turning them on, but both are far more useful if you know how to program them. Both of these items became more common during the last two decades of the century, and both acquired reputations for being difficult to use to their full extent. It was not easy for the average person to create programs. But as the century ends, solutions have been found. One solution was to do a lot of research on how people approached these devices, and their programmable aspects, and then to create "intuitive" controls. Alas, what was intuitive for some people was perplexing for others.

The solution to that problem, not quite ready for prime time as the century ends, is appliances people can talk to. This voice-recognition technology was available as early as the mid-1980s, but it was crude. Not quite ready for mass-market appliances. But like all the new twentieth-century technologies, it has matured year by year. Early in the twenty-first century, it will be common for people to tell their appliances what to do, with the machines talking back if they don't understand and leading the user through the correct string of choices so that the appliance does exactly what the user wants. Similar systems are planned for programmers, especially the amateurs whose numbers continue to grow year by year.

Salvation will appear when the computers can talk back.

——Workstations——

What drives technical progress and innovation is what we call "intellectual capital." That is, people thinking and then putting their thoughts into action. But thinking is like any other kind of work; you can get a lot more done with powerful tools. The tool of choice for the late-twentieth-century innovators was the computer workstation. This one item was largely responsible for the blinding rate of technological change in the last few decades of the century.

In the early 1980s, several entrepreneurs noted that the same technology going into PCs could be used to build some highly muscular desktop computers for really, really serious computing work. Soon companies like Apollo and Sun were in business, and the machines they turned out were called "workstations." Basically these were PCs built to a higher standard and equipped with the most powerful (and much more expensive) components available. In terms of computing power, the workstations were usually a year or two ahead of the current top-of-the-line PCs. Going into the 1990s, that spread began to narrow, but the workstations had other things going for them. They were built for a very discriminating market that was willing to pay a premium for extra performance and the kind of special attention to their needs that the workstation companies were eager to provide.

Workstations were equipped to handle jobs that few PC users would be interested in. Things like computer-aided design (CAD, for designing all sorts of things, including buildings) and computer-generated imaging (CGI, for creating special effects for movies, ads, and presentations). Both of these graphic applications required a computer with powerful graphics capabilities and a large CRT. These two items often represented half the cost of a workstation. The faster microprocessor, more memory specially built to support the faster microprocessor, and a larger hard disk all pushed the cost up to three to five times the cost of the most expensive PC.

But there was a demand among architects, equipment designers, and scientists for this kind of computing power. Many users also wanted the most powerful machine for network servers. All these people were willing to pay the premium for it. Moreover, many software publishers promptly began creating programs to utilize it. Once the workstations began to appear, new, more powerful models followed each year. The workstation manufacturers knew that the PC companies were right on their tail and that workstation users knew this. The race went on until the mid-1990s, when the two things happened that doomed the workstation market. First, PC developers had, since the late 1980s, been offering their high-end machines with the special graphics abilities and the large monitors to firms who were willing to get a little less performance at a much lower price. Then, going into the 1990s, the top-end PCs began to close the performance gap with workstations. One by one, the workstation companies began to weaken from the price competition and fall by the wayside. Most stayed in the game by taking the latest PC components and configuring them as super-PCs, otherwise known as workstations.

Thus, even when all the workstation manufacturers are gone, there will still be a class of high-end PC, decked out with maximum memory, a huge hard disk, the best possible video capabilities, and a large CRT, that will be referred to as workstations.

And that's what they will be.

——The DP Empire Strikes Back——

Personal computers have not been popular everywhere. And among many data-processing professionals, they are seen as a danger and a threat. Unknown to most people, there has been a war going on for the last two decades of the twentieth century, a war between PC users and those who preside over corporate data networks. As the century comes to an end, the DP empire is striking back.

Big time.

The DP professionals who grew up with the earliest computers had good reason to fear the PC. For the first time, the user of computing services was operating the machine. This had not been the case with earlier computers, which used professionals to operate the hardware and run the programs. PCs really were *personal* computers, and this changed everything in ways that few could imagine when the PCs first appeared in the late 1970s.

Until PCs came along, the closest anyone got to a computer was via a TV-like device with a keyboard attached. Arcane commands were needed to get anything out of these terminals, and specially trained operators were needed to enter data. Even this was not universal when the PC arrived. Most data was put into the early mainframe computers via punch cards. These cards, with their data punched into them by means of small rectangular holes in the card, were handed over to the DP department for loading into the computers.

The DP people had become quite protective of their machines. Few users really understood exactly what the DP crew was doing most of the time. Early on, computers had been used for complex, and previously labor-intensive, tasks like billing, accounting, inventory control, or making scientific and engineering calculations. Because using the early computers was so cumbersome, the DP staff was very strict about what went into its databases. Getting new programs written was particularly difficult, and expensive. The DP professionals were, after all, professionals, and they were very careful about how new programs would work on their machines. These mainframe computers cost millions of dollars, and running them was equally expensive. To make the expensive hardware cost-effective, it was usually run around the clock. The machines were built for this kind of duty, and the DP staff was there to make sure no sloppy software or amateur interference via the data terminals created a dreaded "crash" of the system.

PCs suddenly showed many mainframe "customers" what a computer could really do if only the user could gain full control of the machine. While the early PCs were cranky and prone to crashes, the PC users didn't mind all that much. For they had control of the machine. It was indeed a personal computer. PC users were also able to run the software of their choice, and the truly ambitious users could create their own software. The general attitudes toward computers in business began to change. And the DP people did not like it one bit.

The DP empire struck back early and forcefully. Management was told that since PCs were computers, their purchase and use should be controlled by the DP department. Where this argument was accepted, few PCs got into the company. Even then, employees got around the restrictions by buying PCs disguised as calculators or word processors in their purchase orders. There were some heavy-duty calculators available twenty years ago. Also, the availability of microprocessors had also created a large industry supplying PCs that were dedicated word processors. That's all these PCs did, and the DP department did not consider them computers. DP departments soon became aware of these guerrilla tactics and fought back as best they could. But the users were beginning to show results, and soon embarrassing questions were being raised. For example, while there were mainframe-based spreadsheet-type programs available a few years after VisiCalc appeared, the mainframe programs were slower, harder to use, and lacking in many features of their PC competition. Users also pointed out how they got projects done using PCs that would have taken much longer and cost much more for special software using the mainframes.

By the mid-1980s, the DP departments were in retreat on the PC front. By the late 1980s, many companies were replacing their mainframes with networks of PCs. What turned the tables was the relative cheapness of the PCs, the larger and ever-growing array of software, and the much lower costs of creating custom software for the PCs.

At this point, it looked as if the DP pros would go the way of the dinosaur. Not so. Networking was the DP department's salvation. PC networks (LANs, or local-area networks) came along in the early 1980s. Put simply, networks were nothing more than a system of wires going from PC to PC. Each networked PC had a special card in one of its slots and software that enabled each PC on the network to communicate with the others. Often, one well-equipped PC acted as a "server" for the other PCs in the network. The server PC would have a larger hard disk. The other PCs usually had none at all in the early 1980s, which was a major reason for using a network, since hard disks were so expensive. The network was also used so that many PCs could share the same printer.

Networks were not completely new. Minicomputer-based networks had been around since the 1970s, for the same reason PC networks came along, to keep the "per screen" cost of the computer systems down. But the mini-based networks had started off using DP staff to run them. The 1970s minicomputers had about the same computing power as the 1980s PCs, and the operating systems used by minis were not as user friendly as those found in PCs. So it took a DP professional to get the thing turned on and functioning. But mainly the DP pro was there to fix things and to keep the network up and running.

The PC networks came from a different direction. From the beginning, both hardware and software manufacturers stressed "ease of use" in their products. After all, you could hardly try to sell *personal* computers by urging owners to hire a trained operator to run the thing. PC users found out the hard way that some special skills were needed to operate a PC, but many of the early PC owners considered this a form of entertainment and education. Unfortunately, publishers of network software took the same approach. While they stressed some training for key users (the systems administrator or "sysadmin"), in practice they let it be known to potential buyers that the sysadmin could be anyone in the office with a little free time and some practical experience with PCs. That worked, sort of. But as the PC networks became larger and more powerful, there developed a growing demand for better-qualified sysadmins. By the early 1990s, the DP departments were getting involved with training and supervising the sysadmins for LANs, as well as tying them into WANs (wide-area networks, essentially linking LANs to LANs and the Internet). The mainframes did not disappear, but they became cheaper and more like PCs. Many mainframes became very reliable servers for PCs.

However, the PCs are still PCs. Users can still put their own software on their LANed, WANed, and sysadmin-supervised PCs. But not for long. Through the 1990s, more and more companies provide "security" programs for sysadmins. One form of this software operates like antivirus software, except it looks for games instead of more malicious programs. Like antivirus software, the "game sniffers" are updated every few months as new games come out. There are also sniffers to look for naughty stuff that can be downloaded from the World Wide Web.

Corporate users cannot do their own thing anymore.

The DP pros had a rough time through the 1980s, but they fought back. The DP departments do not dominate computer operations the way they used to, but they are still in charge. They provide things PC users need, like technicians to answer questions and fix PCs. They will stock spare parts and spare PCs, so that if someone's machine dies while working on an important project, the DP department will be right there to get things going. DP departments also take charge of backing up everyone's data. PC users are quite prone to trashing a file by accident. But the DP department is always there to get you a backup copy. Yes, DP departments survive by making themselves useful.

And it's still not a good idea to get into an argument with them.

Many PCs that entered businesses early on were used in firms that had never operated computers before. Small businesses were particularly quick to try out computers, especially small businesses run by entrepreneurs. Farmers were among the earliest and most avid users of PCs. Many of these firms never got into LANs, needing only a few PCs. Others grew with PCs, and some formed a department to deal with supporting their computers, appointing a PC-savvy employee to run it. These DP pros were somewhat different than those found in companies that had had computers for decades. The more recently formed DP shops knew little or nothing about minis and mainframes, and they could care less. Very aware of the shortcomings of PCs and LANs, these generally younger DP pros developed new solutions to managing PCs. They were not afraid to outsource things that traditional DP shops always kept in-house, like technical support and programming. The new DP (or "IT," for information technology) departments were still out there trying to make PCs a little less personal.

PCs are a lot more personal at home than at business. In the workplace, personal computers are company property, and the company usually has a DP department to make sure the PCs get the job done. And that's how the DP pros survived.

The Greatest Thing
Since Sliced Bread

During the latter half of this century, the phrase "the greatest thing since sliced bread" has been used to describe a very useful innovation. Until 1930, if you wanted sliced bread, you had to do it yourself, with a knife. But then the bakers finally woke up to the fact that mothers with many mouths to feed saw slicing bread for the kids as a chore, especially with the average family size larger then than now. So simple machines that sliced bread at the bakery saved everyone a lot of time. The Wonder Bread company took the lead in the sliced-bread revolution. At the time, most bread was still baked locally in small shops or plants. The bakery-shop owners thought it was a travesty to preslice bread. By doing so, much freshness was lost, and the bread went stale more quickly. But the customer was right in this case, so right that this simple innovation became a watchword for innovation of any kind.

The Hundred-Year-Old
Answering Machines

Some inventions seem so obvious, so widely needed, that it is often astounding that the gadget didn't get on the market right away. The answering machine, a most common household device at the end of the century, was invented in 1900. Nothing radical about the idea at the time, but recording technology was expensive until the appearance of cheap cassette-tape drives in the 1980s, and AT&T (the nationwide telephone company) banned the use of answering machines until the courts declared otherwise in the late 1940s. You could still use the machines on non-AT&T (often private) phone networks, and that kept the industry going for the first half of the century. There was a large demand for the machines. Many small businesses needed to take phone messages around the clock but could not afford to hire that many people just to answer the phone. Patients and clients often preferred leaving messages with a machine, rather than talking to some employee, if they could not get through to their doctor or lawyer.

AT&T wanted people, not strange machines, using its phone system.

The early answering machines were crude, using one cylinder or disk to play the outgoing message and another to record the incoming message. Recordable, but quite low-fidelity, records and cylinders were common before tape was introduced. Even the cheapest answering machines were fairly expensive, at $500 and up. More reliable and heavy-duty models went for twice that. It was common for the machines to be rented. A typical rental in the 1950s (when fewer than 50,000 were in use) was about $90 a month (including $10 to $20 going to the phone company for special equipment to prevent damage to its telephone lines). There was an installation fee of $100 to $200.

Taking advantage of cheaper and more reliable tape technology, more manufacturers began to introduce answering machines in the 1960s. Reliability went way up, although the price did not come down as much. By 1975, the average price of an answering machine was still about $600.

Things changed in the early 1980s. AT&T was broken up, and with it went a lot of those annoying fees and regulations the phone companies had always charged for any non-telephone-company equipment attached to the system. Cassette tapes and integrated circuits made it possible to create cheaper and more reliable answering machines. Many more companies entered the business, and prices plunged. But other factors were at work to increase sales. More wives were working and more people living alone. Simply put, there were fewer people to answer the phone, and the inexpensive (under $200 by the 1990s) machines were, so to speak, the answer.

SIX

THE MILITARY

AMONG its other distinctions, the twentieth century was noted for being the most heavily armed in history. Several hundred million men, and a much smaller number of women, served in the armed forces. Naturally, with all those people under arms, there were a lot of wars. Over a hundred, to be inexact; an exact count is difficult, because what exactly passed for a war in the twentieth century became difficult to determine. With so many weapons, so many people and so many things to fight over, the line between civil disorder and war became very blurred. Naturally, all that fighting spurred much progress, for want of a better term, in military technology. In this century we saw the two largest wars in history, and more changes in how we fought than in any previous century. But the changes weren't all we think they were, which leads us to some very interesting items.

Note: All dollar amounts are given in terms of year-2000 dollars. That is, they are adjusted for inflation and represent the dollar value at the end of the twentieth century. If you want to see what the actual money values were for a year, see the Appendix.

The Twentieth-Century
Military Breakthroughs

You'd think the major reasons for all the military activity in the twentieth century had to do with weapons. Not so. The key items that drove military technology in this century, for the most part, were not themselves all that dangerous.

Every century has breakthrough developments in military operations. The nineteenth century saw the modern rifle and machine gun; the century before that saw a practical musket design and modern military organization. And so on. The twentieth century had more than its share of developments, which is understandable considering that over 95 percent of all the scientists who ever lived were alive and working in the twentieth century. But take a look at what the most important items were:

- Trucks. Yes, trucks, which first appeared at the turn of the century. Faster than horses and easier to "feed" (refuel), trucks made it possible to move troops and supplies faster and farther than ever before. Moving stuff has always been a problem in warfare. Until the railroad came along in the early 1800s, large quantities of supplies could not be moved except by ship. And in that case a navigable river or ocean coast was needed to do it, not to mention ships and the absence of a hostile navy. Once troops marched away from the water, they left their supplies behind as well. Railroads were an improvement, but track had to be laid first. This takes time. Trucks could run cross-country if need be. The difference trucks made can be seen in the kinds and quantities of supplies used during World War I and World War II. During the first war, most of the supplies moved consisted of food for the horses (twenty to thirty pounds a day per animal). Trucks became more prominent as World War I went on, but it was basically a horse-powered war. In World War II, most of the material moved was ammunition, followed by fuel for trucks. And the trucks moved ten times faster than the horses, allowing for more round-trips.

Trucks were also used on the battlefield, to move troops and weapons quickly to where they were most needed. Trucks were used as well in battle. During World War II, it was common for reconnaissance units to operate with heavily armed trucks. As recently as the 1980s, Chadian irregulars in Africa improvised combat vehicles using Toyota light trucks and defeated Libyan forces equipped with armored vehicles. The "Toyota War" was not an isolated incident, as U.S. forces still maintain thousands of armed Hummer trucks, as do many other nations.

• Armored fighting vehicles. Tanks and other armored vehicles (collectively called AFVs) were invented to overcome the defensive superiority of machine guns and rifles. The first armored cars appeared at the turn of the century, but these were restricted to the roads until tanks were invented during World War I. The tanks ran on threads, like bulldozers. The armor kept out the bullets, and the threads enabled movement across shot-up terrain. The first tank was created in July 1915, in Britain, by mounting the body of an armored car on the frame of a tractor propelled by treads. This was done, oddly enough, by the Armoured Car Division of the Royal Naval Air Service. This because the idea of the tank came from the First Lord of the Admiralty, Winston S. Churchill. By September 1915, work with this prototype led to the construction of the first tank design ("Little Willie"), and shortly thereafter a second model ("Big Willie") followed. In February 1916, the second design was accepted and a hundred tanks of this type (now the "Mark I") were ordered. At about the same time, the French were also working on tanks and ordered four hundred built in February 1916. But the British got their tanks into action before the end of 1916, while the French tanks weren't ready for action until the spring of 1917. By then, the Allies were using hundreds of tanks in single battles, and this was a major contribution to the collapse of the German army in 1918. Most of these AFVs were between six and fourteen tons, there being a greater need for speed than for thick armor. By the end of World War I, France and Britain had produced over six thousand tanks. Germany had produced only twenty. It took another twenty years of technological development before the AFV became a truly decisive weapon. This they have remained for the rest of the century, despite strenuous efforts to develop weapons that would make tanks obsolete. Technology may eventually nail tanks, but if the experience with horse cavalry is any indication, it may not happen soon. Many times over the past few thousand years, new weapons were developed that were seen as making the armed horseman obsolete. None really worked until the rifle and machine gun came along. The soldier on a horse made for a remarkably versatile and resourceful combination. Soldiers and their AFVs have reacted in the same inventive fashion to all attempts to make them obsolete. Armored vehicles will outlast the twentieth century.

- High-speed construction. Building things in a hurry has always been a military advantage. Over two thousand years ago, the Roman army established a building record that was not matched and surpassed until this century. And that happened because the twentieth-century builders had a lot of machines. A whole lot of machines. Trucks, bulldozers, cranes, forklifts, and many other heavy-duty construction vehicles made it possible to quickly build airfields, roads, ports, fortifications, and bases. American engineers pioneered most of these techniques, to the shock of their German and Japanese opponents and the admiration of the other Allied nations, during World War II. The most glaring examples were found in the Pacific. There, the Japanese had expected American troops to require about the same amount of time to build new airfields. But instead of the weeks it took Japanese engineers to build a new airfield in the jungle, American construction troops could do it in days. Since most of the new twentieth-century weapons require a lot of supplies (fuel, ammo, maintenance materials, etc.), the ability to quickly build the facilities that move supplies enables you to use all your wonder weapons before the enemy can use theirs. "Getting there first with the most" in the nineteenth century meant troops; in the twentieth century it means supplies and infrastructure. You can easily fly troops in, but most of your weapons and infrastructure are too heavy to be moved that fast. You need more ports and airfields to get the weapons in.

- Mines. Advances in technology made it possible, early in this century, to mass-produce naval and land mines. While mankind has for thousands of years been building traps and snares for human and animal prey, the twentieth-century mines were far deadlier, more reliable, and easier to use. Mines were given the highest accolade a weapon can receive when, late in the twentieth century, an international treaty was enacted that banned their use. It is unlikely that the treaty will work, for similar attempts in the past, while well intentioned, have all failed.

- Military medicine. In the twentieth century, soldiers were a lot more likely to survive their military experience because of advances in military medicine and in the speed with which this medicine was gotten to the injured. There have always been armies that have tried to take care of their sick and wounded troops. But until the twentieth century, more troops died of sickness and injury than of the results of battle. Indeed, it was common for large army units (over ten thousand men) to lose more than half their troops to sickness and injury in an eight-month campaign season, without even fighting a battle.

- Fire control. While firepower increased enormously during the twentieth century, it was the ability to better control it that made warfare so much more lethal. Fire control is much more than having telephones and radios available; systems had to be created that got the information about the targets to the weapons in a timely manner. The targets—be they enemy infantry, AFV, or aircraft—have a keen sense of self-preservation and will be devilishly clever in avoiding your attempts to destroy them. World War I saw the first use of modern fire-control systems with the introduction of battlefield telephones, radios, and aerial observers. The major problem was coordination, and not a lot of progress in this department was made until the 1930s. It was American artillery officers who then developed techniques for meshing radio and telephone reports from front-line observers with fire control centers farther back and the big guns themselves. A lot of math had to be done, and done quickly, to calculate which guns had to fire in which direction and when to bring maximum firepower to bear on a target. New communications technology helped, but so did variable-time (VT) fuzes for the shells. The VT fuze allowed the gun crews to quickly adjust the fuze so that the shell would explode a certain number of seconds after being fired. If the calculations were done correctly, hundreds of shells would explode simultaneously over the target, showering the enemy with a lethal rain of fragments that was difficult to avoid. This simultaneous attack was important, because once the enemy knew they were under fire, they would take cover. By having the shells explode at the same time, the enemy was taken by surprise, and much greater damage was done. The United States was also in the lead with fire-control methods for aircraft. Ground troops were equipped with radios that could talk to the aircraft overhead, and specially trained observers expertly directed the aircraft to hit enemy targets. This was much more effective than the usual method of leaving target selection to the fighter-bomber pilots (who were often too high and moving too fast to spot an elusive enemy on the ground). At sea, U.S. naval officers perfected the use of radio communications, radar, and, for shore bombardment, ground observers to greatly increase the effectiveness of naval firepower (both guns and carrier aircraft). Development on all these techniques went on throughout World War II and after. By the late twentieth century computers were common components of fire-control systems, and it was possible for one observer to call down enormous firepower in less than a minute. These developments had an enormous impact on tactics and the way wars are fought, an impact that continues to change the way we fight.

- Radio nets. Electronic communications changed warfare in many ways throughout the twentieth century. Initially this was simply seen as a more efficient way to send the usual military messages on the battlefield. Earlier, this had been done using messengers, flag signals, musical instruments, carrier pigeons, and the like. But telephones and radios were much faster and, when they worked, more reliable. It soon became obvious, especially with radio, that you had to work out better techniques to prevent everyone from talking at the same time and at cross purposes. This gave rise to the creation of "communications nets" and rules for their use, which eventually changed everything. Not just how the combat troops moved and fought, but also how the support units operated. Radio networks used the many different frequencies radios could operate on (conversations on one frequency would not be heard on another frequency) and sternly enforced procedures for everyone using the net. The procedures covered more than the obvious use of terms like "over" when someone was finished talking (to let the other fellow know it was his turn), but also priorities, so that someone with a more important message could get everyone else off the frequency so the more important message could get through. Effective radio nets required reliable technology and disciplined users to make them work. But it was now possible to coordinate units spread out over a vast area and perform maneuvers that would have been impossible without all those radio networks. Information on the situation flowed back to commanders over these nets, and orders to take advantage of that information went out from the commander.

• Tactical mobility. The twentieth century brought an unprecedented ability to move quickly around the battlefield. Before tanks were developed during World War I, there were armored vehicles, namely armored cars. But these could move easily only on roads. World War I made it clear that future wars would be fought over rough terrain, especially ground torn up by all the artillery fire now available. Thus the tank was developed. By World War II, there were armored vehicles for infantry, artillery, and supplies. At the end of World War II, the helicopter came along, and twenty years later this "flying truck" (as the troops came to call it) provided the ultimate in battlefield mobility on a wide scale. But all of this high-speed tactical mobility came at a price. Tracked vehicles and helicopters are expensive; not everyone can afford them. Given a choice between buying basic weapons and providing more tactical mobility, you have to go for the basics first. But those that can afford the high-speed gear buy themselves a significant combat advantage.

- Air support. Aircraft appeared at the beginning of the twentieth century, and the capabilities of aircraft grew with the century. Initially, aircraft were barely able to get off the ground and fly for an hour so at an altitude of a few thousand feet. But this was enough for aircraft to do what the troops wanted most: find out what the enemy was up to. Naturally, it was also valuable to keep the enemy from looking down on your movements, so the first scout aircraft were soon shooting at each other with pistols and rifles. This quickly escalated to lightweight machine guns and then specially designed scout aircraft that became known as "pursuit" or "fighter" aircraft. These airplanes found that they could attack ground targets with their machine guns. Infantry were hard to hit, but trucks or horse-drawn vehicles were much easier targets. It wasn't until the 1930s that aircraft became powerful enough to carry a lot of bombs, but from then on, more and more aircraft became "bombers." Millions of tons of bombs were dropped during World War II, then again during the Korean War, and a record tonnage was dropped during the Vietnam War. Despite all that, there is still some controversy over just how decisive bombing can be. Meanwhile, there is less dispute over aircraft used as scouts, for keeping enemy aircraft out of the way, and for moving troops and material quickly. Overall, aircraft have changed the way battles are fought. If you do not control the air, you have to sneak around at night and take more losses from constant air attacks. No one has been defeated by aircraft alone, but no army has won a war without controlling the air. You can get a stalemate without air superiority, but not victory. So far, anyway.

- Logistics. This means having lots of stuff, knowing where it is needed, and getting it there in time. Warfare has always depended on supplies of food to keep the troops going. But until the last century, it was possible to obtain most, or even all, of those supplies locally. You "lived off the enemy's land." At the beginning of this century, this was much less the case. Armies were much larger now, and used a lot more ammunition and other equipment that could not always be obtained locally. Logistics had been important in the past, if only to make sure that troops were moved through areas that contained a lot of food. As the century went on, logistics became even more important. By World War II, logistics was often the decisive element in many victories, and defeats. Gone was the day when an army could be launched into enemy territory without trucks, ships, and cargo planes streaming behind, to keep the troops supplied. Those commanders who have not mastered logistics are defeated before they begin to fight.

- Electronic warfare. When radios and telephones became commonplace tools for most armies early in this century, it was only natural for each side to seek ways to disrupt the enemy's use of these devices. This wasn't really new, for warfare had always included attempts to disrupt the other side's communications. But as the number of electronic devices proliferated during World War II, a new name for this sort of thing—electronic warfare—came into use. Electronic warfare was as old as electronic communications; there had been a lot of games played with telegraph communications in the last half of the nineteenth century. But in the twentieth century, electronic warfare exploded, and in ways that we are still trying to understand. While electronic warfare was first confined to the battlefield, the spread of the Internet and satellites has made everyone vulnerable to electronic attacks.

- Professional soldiers. In 1900, most of the millions of troops ready for war were not full-time professionals but reservists. There were men who had served two or more years on active duty and were then sent back to civilian life. But these fellows were still in the army. They still had their uniforms and were assigned to a local combat unit. Several times a year, the reservist would train with his unit and thus retain many of his military skills. In wartime, the reservist would be mobilized, along with the reserve unit he belonged to. In this way, you could have a small number of troops on the full-time payroll in peacetime, but a much larger army, trained and ready to go in a few weeks, if war broke out. The reservist was king for the first half of this century, but it soon dawned on the generals that this was a system good mainly for getting a lot of people killed, and not always the best way to win a war. The units that were the most lethal were the ones that had the most training. The more professional, full-time soldiers you had, the better your regulars and reservists did in wartime. This pattern was noted, and in the second half of the century, more armies depended largely on full-time professionals who trained hard and stayed on top of their profession. Looking back, it is clear that even those reserve-based armies early in the century were better, or worse, depending on the quality and quantity of the professionals they had running them.

——The Great Ideas That Weren't——

The twentieth century saw changes in warfare that were beyond imagination in 1900. Or were they? Airpower, tanks, and information warfare are three of the major revolutions, and all have been misinterpreted, and misapplied more often than not.

Now, that's an interesting concept in itself, but let us take a look at how each of these three items misfired, or simply were misinterpreted.

Airpower was still an infant technology when World War I broke out in 1914, but most armies already had aircraft. Never had a new technology been so quickly embraced by the generals. And they had these machines for one reason: to find out what was happening on the battlefield. In a word, reconnaissance. It didn't take a lot of insight to appreciate how easily someone in one of these primitive aircraft could see what was going on down there and then quickly report it.

Aircraft reconnaissance did indeed work, but since both sides had it, neither side had a decisive advantage. So it was not enough to have your own recon aircraft up there; you also had to keep the enemy planes out of the air. Thus was born the fighter aircraft. And so it went throughout the war, with both sides sending up swarms of fighters to struggle for control of the air. Whoever was able to control the air could see what the enemy was up to, while keeping the enemy from doing the same.

Toward the end of World War I, it became apparent that one could achieve air superiority by attacking enemy air bases. At first this was done with fighters, using their machine guns to shoot up aircraft on the ground. Ammunition and fuel supplies were also hit, as well as support troops needed to keep the aircraft fighting. Small bombs were also dropped, but these proved too small to do any significant damage. Multiengine bombers were built toward the end of World War I, but they were not effective, and were very vulnerable to attacks by fighters. Ground fire also turned out to be very lethal against aircraft.

Despite the inability of aircraft to do much beyond reconnaissance in World War I, the early 1920s were ablaze with new and ambitious plans for combat aircraft. This was the weapon of the future that would change war as had no other weapon before it. Compelling books and articles were written describing how bombers would pulverize enemy cities and compel surrender without the millions of dead infantry suffered in World War I.

Sound familiar?

This formula was tried in World War II, Korea, Vietnam, and Iraq. Didn't work as predicted.

Why?

The resources available were not up to the task. It was not for want of trying. The Allied air campaign against Germany pitted 1.5 million Allied airmen and 69,000 aircraft against 2.2 million German troops (plus 2 million civilians repairing the damage) and 61,000 Nazi aircraft. The aerial fighting started off slowly in 1939, but was a massive operation by 1943. The four-engine strategic bombers dropped 1.5 million tons of bombs; all other combat aircraft (single- and two-engine) dropped another 1.1 million tons. Losses were heavy, as 159,000 Allied airmen became casualties. Aircraft losses were enormous, with 21,914 bombers and 18,465 fighters lost. The bombers flew 1.5 million sorties and had a loss rate of 15 aircraft per 1,000 sorties. The fighters flew 2.7 million sorties, for a loss rate of 7 per 1,000 sorties.

The Germans, and the Japanese, managed to survive the bombs for several reasons, all of which still apply today. First, no one has yet figured out how to do effective BDA (bomb-damage assessment). After half a century of developing better cameras and other sensors, the people on the ground still have the advantage in this game of hide-and-seek. If you cannot confirm what you have hit and to what extent, how can you destroy what the enemy has? Until this problem is solved, the bombers will always be attacking with very unpredictable results. Then there was the problem of what to attack in the first place. This was similar to the BDA situation. The enemy on the ground has an easier time keeping his secrets than the air force does in revealing them. If you have a hard time finding what to bomb in the first place, and then are not sure if you hit what you thought was the proper target . . . well, you get the picture.

Not that all that bombing wasn't useful. It's just that it rarely did exactly what it was intended to do. But the bombs did hit something, and often they hit what they were expected to. Although the bombing campaign against Germany, Japan, North Korea, Vietnam, and Iraq did not go according to plan, damage was done. Exactly how much damage has not yet been discovered in all cases. Because we occupied Germany and Japan after World War II, we were able to send in survey teams to see exactly what had happened on the ground. This was a demoralizing experience for the Allied bomber generals. It's actually worse than that. The main reason we built all those heavy bombers early in World War II (and helped Britain do the same) was that it took less time to build aircraft than it did to build ships or create ground forces. America had tremendous industrial capacity, but the only way to use it against Germany immediately was to build aircraft. Not the sort of thing the air-force generals want to admit to.

Expediency was not the reason air power was used in Korea, Vietnam, or Iraq. In World War II, it was understood that victory was ultimately won when ground troops occupied the enemy capital. This option was not available, for political and diplomatic reasons, after World War II. So the air force stepped up and said, in effect, "We can do it from the air." This was an attractive option to the politicians. No one wanted to hear about what was known about airpower's failings during World War II. The air force assured everyone that the technical problems had been fixed, or soon would be. The problems were never fixed, and still aren't.

So what's going on here?

Politics, and public relations. Airpower is a clean weapon. Few of your troops are likely to get killed or captured. You can also fight as little, or as much, as you want to or can afford to politically. As the century went on, especially after the Vietnam War, the public became less accepting of wartime death and injury to our troops. Aircraft were the perfect weapon when you wanted to make war without risking many of your troops.

But "warfare lite" does not bring victory.

Airplanes look impressive as hell, though. And this brings us to the public-relations angle. Aircraft were the most visually striking weapon of World War II, even more so than tanks. And the Air Force grew to enormous size during the war and became a third service, after the Army and Navy.

Everyone wanted combat aircraft. In America, as in most other countries, the post–World War II services each had its own air force. America actually had five: the Air Force itself, the Naval Air Force, Marine Corps Aviation, Army Aviation, and the Coast Guard. The Army actually had more, although much less expensive, aircraft than the Air Force.

Aircraft was the single most expensive item the armed forces purchased. The post–World War II defense budget was a very political pile of money. The generals and admirals caught on real quickly that if they wanted votes for their budgets, they had to make sure that things were built in the districts of key legislators. Since over a third of the defense budget went for aircraft, a lot of powerful legislators would stand together against any plan that would threaten all those aircraft-manufacturing jobs in their districts. But Congress deals not only in dollars but in favorable press coverage. The two went together, and sexy combat aircraft were an easy item to get behind. The problems airpower had in the real world were treated as deserving of more billions to make them right. And over the decades, airpower has become more and more effective.

But airpower cannot do what armies and navies can do: defeat a hostile nation. Armies are the most effective, for they can march in and occupy the enemy territory. Navies can isolate, and starve out, territories that depend on sea transport for food and other materials. This takes longer, cannot work against all nations, but risks fewer troops. The air force can hurt the enemy but cannot by itself defeat the enemy. But since the 1920s, the air-force generals and their political allies have maintained that, if not right now, then in the near future, the air force would be able to do the job. Someday, but we could use another hundred billion dollars to make sure it happens.

And then there was the second most impressive new weapon of the twentieth century: tanks. These armored behemoths get the credit for revolutionizing ground combat. Nope, that honor really goes to the truck and a bunch of Army officers who, between World War I and World War II, figured out how to make war on the ground, at high speed. Actually, these lads were not the first to do it. The thirteenth-century Mongols, among others, had also discovered how to apply speed to combat operations. But machine guns were lethal to horses, and the care and feeding of these animals made them much less effective when used with the huge armies of the twentieth century. Some new ideas were needed. In the middle of World War I, the Germans took the lead in developing new infantry tactics that could get around the machine-gun problem. Non-Germans came to call this new approach infiltration tactics. The Germans just called it infantry tactics, updated to deal with new weapons. It was these new tactics, not the newly invented tanks, that broke the deadlock of trench warfare in World War I. There's no secret to this; it just gets downplayed by historians. The generals—some of them anyway—were quite impressed by the tank. It wasn't just the fearsome appearance and sheer firepower of tanks, but the fact that with this new vehicle they could leave behind the bloodbath of infantry fighting that had characterized World War I.

Most of these generals missed the lessons of World War I. Tanks did not eliminate the bloodbath of infantry combat, the new German tactics did. What tanks turned out to be good for was quickly getting through a hole in the enemy line and tearing up the growing number of supply and maintenance units behind the lines. Without food, fuel, bullets, and communications, the front-line troops quickly lose their combat power. Tanks are not even the best antitank weapon. Mines are most effective, followed by special infantry weapons. To punch a hole in the enemy lines you use not tanks but infantry, artillery, and careful planning. But to many generals the tank seemed to be a super-weapon. It wasn't. Tanks, despite their speed and armor, are very vul-nerable. Sending tanks into a city without infantry to protect them will lose you a lot of tanks very quickly.

Sure, large numbers of tanks can be thrown into a battle and you'll see results, but even during World War II, tanks were expensive, costing half a million to over a million dollars each. But if you had a lot of tanks, and no other way to get some things done, you could send in several hundred or several thousand of them. And lose a lot, sometimes most of them. The British did this toward the end of World War II, as they ran short of manpower and used more tanks instead. They did have fewer troops killed or injured when using tanks. On average, about half the crew would survive a tank's being lost. The Russians also used masses of tanks, and lost 96,000 (out of 131,000) as a result. The Rus-sians were never as skillful as the Germans when fighting a mobile battle, so they compensated with mass. This strategy cost 30 million Russians their lives, and without those 131,000 tanks, the Germans would probably have won. But it was still an infantry war, and whenever tanks have had to duke it out with infantry, the infantry usually wins. In effect, tanks are best used for the sucker punch. Run past all the infantry doing all the heavy lifting and go after the relatively defenseless rear-area troops. Not very glamorous, but that's how tanks contribute to winning. Don't let their sleek looks fool you.

When the Cold War ended, America needed a new villain. Drug lords and terrorists didn't quite do it. So in the early 1990s, information warfare was invented. What is it? Basically, it's Internet warfare, elec-tronic warfare, and hacking. But best of all, since it deals with high tech (all those computers and electronic gadgets) and something most people also use (PCs and the Internet), it's easy to snag some really scary head-lines. That gets the attention of Congress, which, in turn, gets you more money to fight the new enemy.

The information-warfare threat conjured up visions of terrorists or enemy cybersoldiers marauding through the Internet, bringing our economy to its knees. Hasn't happened yet. It might. But don't hold your breath. The most successful use of information warfare to date has been the clever, and quite scary, campaign to convince everyone that information warfare is real and that if we don't spend a lot of money on it, we're toast.

So at the end of the century, the United States was spending over $5 billion a year to defend us all against a threat that is overblown and overwrought. To understand why this is so, you have to realize how this kind of stuff actually works. First, information warfare is nothing new. As long as armies have had to rely on communicating with their own troops and with the folks back home, there have been opportunities to mess with the other guys' messages. Stealing them, sending false ones, or doing seemingly silly things to confuse the other guy—all have been staples of warfare for thousands of years.

When the first electronic-communications medium arrived in the 1850s, in the form of the telegraph, it wasn't long before it was being used to wage electronic warfare. As more electronic gear became available in the twentieth century, the number of games that could be played with it increased. Electronic warfare is not a late-twentieth-century thing. All the hocus pocus that took place in the 1991 Gulf War had already been done (with more primitive equipment) during World War II. Jamming radars, electronic navigation, spoofing sensors, and even cruise and ballistic missiles were used during the 1940s. What is different today is that we have a new name for an old game.

And like a lot of deceptive advertising, that does cause a problem, because what is really going on here is a lot scarier than the official line. The most common horror stories have to do with nasty people getting into vital computer systems and then doing stuff like shutting down the telephones, electricity, or air-traffic-control system. Or perhaps looting the bank, or bringing down the entire financial system. All of these systems have had problems, and some have been entered by people who shouldn't be there. But the unauthorized entry is usually by someone who had access codes or someone who took advantage of sloppiness by the people running the system.

It's usually an inside job, just like a lot of low-tech crime. There's nothing to prevent some hostile power from trying to bribe a user to gain access to some vital computer network. This is an ancient approach. Several thousand years ago, some astute general noted that the easiest way to take an enemy fortress was with a "loaded [with gold or silver] donkey." That same ancient general probably also knew that many a fortress or walled city fell not because its defenses were inadequate but because some of the sentries fell asleep while on duty. Or, in perhaps the most famous story of information warfare, we find the wooden Trojan horse left outside the walls one night, and the Trojans, unaware that the huge horse was full of enemy soldiers, taking the thing into the city, thinking it meant that the Greeks had given up and left it as a gift to their betters. And that was the end of Troy.

Getting betrayed or being sloppy is an ancient recipe for disaster, and that's what information warfare is all about. Because there are more toys to play with, there are more ways to get into trouble. Yes, it's high tech, and the one useful message from the information-warfare crowd is to not take gadgets for granted. Complex gear can, and does, fail. Of course, we witness that every day. We are surrounded by high-tech toys that fail at what appears to be random intervals. Manufacturers get around this by building things to be disposable or easily repaired by low-skill technicians or by the users themselves. Cheap digital watches and one-use cameras are examples of the disposable approach. Copy and fax machines are examples of easy-to-maintain items. But computers in general, and computer networks in particular, are neither disposable nor easy to maintain. The number of computer networks grew enormously during the last two decades of the century, and the number of people competent to maintain them did not keep pace. This became the main source of information-warfare opportunities. The software that allowed individual PCs to talk to networks, and local nets to larger nets, was put together in a hurry as the network grew rapidly. There were flaws in the software that allowed anyone with a knowledge of the flaws and a bit of patience to break into other people's computers. As soon as the flaws were discovered, the software was fixed. But there were millions of computers out there running networks connected to the Internet. Not all the people running the smaller networks kept their software up to date. So people with time on their hands and malice in mind would wander the Internet looking for systems with out-of-date software and exploit the situation. This is the source of most of the horror stories. The other source is rarer, and it happens at places where the software is kept up to date, usually at sites that contain very important stuff (banks, military, laboratories, etc.). Here the biggest source of trouble are people on the inside using their access to do damage or simply to do something that will benefit themselves.

But the military is talking about more than the usual Internet mayhem. They are talking possible world war, with hostile cyberwarriors swarming through the Internet and inflicting terminal damage on American civilian and military targets. What's wrong with this picture? Lots. First it assumes there is a foe out there as technically adept and as well equipped as the United States. Sure, as the most advanced cybereconomy, the United States has more targets, but we also have most of the people who know what this stuff is all about. The rest of the world has more to fear from an American information-warfare attack than the other way around. Perhaps we should just drop the pretense and run a global protection racket (against cyberattack).

Perhaps more important, all this talk of information warfare distracts attention from the most common form of war in the future. Bosnia, Kosovo, various wars in Africa, and so on are real and ongoing. There has been no information war yet. Peacekeeping in the Balkans and Africa is less popular to a high-tech military than future combat using impressive new technology.

This is one reason information warfare is so popular in the military. The American armed forces are in the forefront of converting themselves to fight "network-centric warfare" (NCW). This form of combat ties all units (ships, planes, tanks, infantry platoons, artillery, support units) into one big network. Information on what everyone sees goes back to the commander, who quickly issues orders to move and fire. The historical basis of this is sound. Many armies in the past have won largely because they acted fast, and at the end of the twentieth century, the American armed forces expect to achieve this decisive speed via networking and computers. This is the main reason for the interest in information warfare. A new form of warfare brings with it new vulnerabilities. But no one is sure how vulnerable NCW is to enemy action.

We had similar situations earlier in the century, when new forms of warfare were not sorted out accurately until after actual combat. Taking another look at the historical experience, it's interesting to note that the nation with the most resources came out on top. As Napoleon noted, "Victory goes to the big battalions." America had by far the biggest battalions in terms of NCW and information warfare.

Yet it is another fact of military history that if you don't anticipate what the enemy might do, you are vulnerable to a nasty surprise. Like Pearl Harbor. This is the great fear of the information-war crowd, a cyber–Pearl Harbor. Where it all becomes a bit absurd is when you realize that in 1941 it was known that the Japanese definitely had the means to pull off a devastating surprise attack. It was their custom. They had done it many times before. But with information warfare, there is nothing like the Japanese carrier fleet out there.

Perhaps in recognition of all this, the U.S. Air Force has been directing its actual information-warfare efforts at the real problems described above. Getting system managers to keep their software up to date and keeping an eye on the users is a more pragmatic approach to winning any information war.

The lesson here is to be wary of pundits bearing revolutionary new developments in military technology. Combat is the final arbiter of what works and what doesn't. And throughout the twentieth century, combat experience has often been at odds with the predictions.

Take a closer look at these things. And ask questions. You can't be too careful with this stuff.

Little-Recognized Weapons and Equipment That Changed Warfare

Think of twentieth-century warfare, and tanks and aircraft come to mind. While these changed warfare a lot, there were many other weapons that had an equal, or greater, impact that have largely been overlooked. These were the things that revolutionized land warfare, and it

WEAPON	NATION	TYPE	INTRODUCED	WEIGHT	ROF
Maxim	Germany	Machine gun	1901	58.3	400
Gewehr 98	Germany	Rifle	1898	9.2	20
Lee-Enfield	U.K.	Rifle	1895	8.2	30
MP-18	Germany	Machine pistol	1918	9.3	400
M-1	U.S.	Rifle	1936	9.5	40
MG-42	Germany	Machine gun	1942	25.4	600
PPSh	U.S.S.R.	Machine pistol	1941	8	500
AK-47	U.S.S.R.	Assault rifle	1947	9.5	400
M-16	U.S.	Assault rifle	1966	6.3	400
Bazooka	U.S.	Antitank	1943	Light	2
Mortar	France	Artillery	1915	40–200+	8
Nightscope	U.S.	—	1965	Light	—
Flak jacket	U.S.	—	1942	Light	—
Radio	Many	—	1910s	Light	—
GPS	U.S.	—	1990	Light	—
Land mine	Many	—	1930s	Light	—
Computer	Many	—	1960s	Light	—

"Nation" is the country that first introduced the weapon. "Introduced" is the year it was first used. Weight is in pounds. "Light" means under ten pounds. "ROF" is rate of fire in rounds per minute.

is on the ground that most of the fighting takes place and ultimate victory is achieved.

The Maxim MG08 was the original modern machine gun, of which Germany was the most enthusiastic proponent before World War I. The MG08 was a "heavy" machine gun, in that it had a heavy barrel and a water jacket around the barrel to prevent overheating when the gun was fired continuously. This made for a heavy weapon, with wheels or runners to make it easier to drag around. During World War I, the need for lighter machine guns was noted, and while the weight could be cut in half, the lack of water cooling cut down firepower considerably.

A few hundred rounds would make a light machine gun too hot to continue operating.

The Gewehr 98 rifle was designed by Peter Paul Mauser, whose work influenced most of the world's weapons designs in the late 1800s. An easy-to-use and robust rifle, it was the standard infantry weapon for the Germans for nearly half a century (until 1945). It had a 5-round magazine and fired a 7.92mm bullet.

Lee-Enfield. An improved version (mainly to take advantage of smokeless powder) of the earlier Lee-Medford rifle, this was the only weapon to really challenge the Mauser in terms of ease of use and reliability. In addition, the Lee-Enfield had a 10-round magazine, making the fast and accurate fire of the British infantry a formidable force. Early in World War I, Germans coming up against British infantry armed only with Lee-Enfields often thought the British had machine guns, so rapid was the fire from the British rifles. The rifle fired a 7.7mm bullet. Used by the British into the 1950s, and still found in many less affluent parts of the world.

MP-18. This was the first modern assault rifle. Developed during World War I, by the end of that conflict, in 1918, about 30,000 MP-18s were in use. Had there been ten or twenty times as many MP-18s available a year earlier, they might have changed the outcome of the war. As it was, the MP-18 demonstrated the devastating effect of automatic weapons in the hands of infantry. The MP-18 fired the standard 9mm pistol round and used a 32-round drum magazine. Using the blowback (simpler version of the recoil system) method to quickly eject shell cases and load new rounds, 400 bullets a minute could be fired. The Germans kept developing this type of weapon, and by World War II, they had the MP-38 and MP-40 (erroneously called the "Schmeisser," after a designer who had nothing to do with it). The short range (50 to 100 meters) of MP series 9mm pistol round prevented the Germans from attempting to rearm all their infantry with this weapon. There was also the shortage of production facilities to build that many MP-38s. It wasn't until they saw the Russians use similar weapons on a mass scale during World War II that the Germans realized that the short range of the 9mm pistol round was not as great a shortcoming as they thought.

M-1. This was the first widely used automatic (or "self-loading") rifle to arm a large army. Mauser had produced a workable self-loading rifle before World War I, but it was too expensive to mass-produce. Some were used in aircraft before special models of machine guns were developed for airborne use. Weapons designers in the United States continued working on automatic rifles. During World War I, America produced the Browning Automatic Rifle (BAR), which fired like a machine gun but looked like a rifle. It weighed 20 pounds and had a 20-round magazine. It continued to be the squad "machine gun" into the 1950s. It wasn't too much of a stretch to produce a smaller version of the BAR that was just self-loading (or "semiautomatic"). By 1932, the M-1 design was perfected, and it reached the troops (in small numbers) by 1936. The M-1 fired the standard .30-caliber U.S. rifle bullet and had an 8-round magazine. It was an enormously successful weapon, although quickly eclipsed by the fully automatic infantry weapons developed during World War II (which replaced the M-1 in the U.S. Army thirty years later). U.S. troops with the M-1 facing Germans armed with the bolt-action Gewehr 98 had a considerable advantage, one that saved many American lives. The success of the M-1 convinced a generation of U.S. infantry officers that having rapid-fire weapons for every soldier was an advantage. This led to much effort to develop a fully automatic infantry rifle after World War II, which produced the M-14 (a fully automatic M-1) in the 1950s and the M-16 in the 1960s.

MG-42. The ultimate light machine gun of the twentieth century. An improvement over an earlier 1930s weapon, the MG-42 was well designed. Easy to use and robust, its most useful feature was the ability of the operator to quickly change an overheated barrel. Light machine guns had one disadvantage versus water-cooled heavy machine guns, and that is the overheating of the barrel after a few hundred rounds have been fired. The quick-barrel-change feature solved that problem, although the machine-gun crew was vulnerable for about ten seconds while the hot barrel was removed and a fresh, cool one installed. This was mitigated somewhat by the German practice of setting up their MG-42s behind a mound of earth and firing at an angle. Several MG-42s would cover each other's front. The enemy would find themselves shot at from the side, rather than in front as one would expect. One or two spare barrels would be carried by the crew (five or six men), as well as much belted ammunition (over a thousand rounds) as they could carry. In a defensive position, more ammunition would be available. After World War II, many other nations, including the United States, built clones of the MG-42, and Germany, for the last half century, has continued to use the MG-42. No one has come up with anything better.

PPSh. This was the most widely produced (over 6 million) machine pistol in the twentieth century. A Russian design of the 1930s, it was influenced, in different ways, by three other machine pistols. The main inspiration was the German MP-18 of 1918. U.S. designers also developed the Thompson machine pistol in the 1920s, and this in turn influenced the Finnish Suomi Model 31 of the early 1930s. Being eager to keep up on all military technology, the Russians had developed their own machine pistol, the PPD, in the 1930s, but had not produced many of them. The 1940 war between Russia and Finland changed this. The Russians won a negotiated victory but were generally beaten on the ground. One of the major factors for this defeat was the Finnish use of their Model 31 machine pistol. The next year, the Germans invaded Russia, and all of a sudden the Russians needed a lot of very cheap and very effective infantry weapons. Within months, a cruder (easier to manufacture), but still very effective version of the PPD was being mass-produced. This was the PPSh. It used box and drum magazines of various capacities, the most popular one being a drum holding 71 rounds. About 20 percent of these weapons were actually a slightly different design called the PPS. By the late 1950s, the new AK-47 finally replaced all the PPSh's in Russian service. These machine pistols were not put in storage or destroyed but were sent to other communist countries, or communist revolutionaries. A lot of PPSs showed up during the Korean War. The combat experience with the PPSh was compelling. When entire platoons were armed with the PPSh, you had a unit with unheard-of firepower. Such a unit could fire off 1,700 9mm bullets in five seconds. And since you had about two dozen troops firing individually, the bullets were going everywhere, not just where, say, an individual machine gun would send them. By 1945, the Germans had developed a weapon to match the PPSh, the StG 44 (Assault Rifle 44). This was basically the AK-47, having the same shape and, more important, using a "short" rifle cartridge instead of a pistol round. This gave the StG 44 (and the AK-47) more range, while still providing a 30-round box magazine and lighter ammunition.

AK-47. The Russians had been working on a short rifle round but had not decided to design a weapon for it until they saw that the Germans had introduced a similar round in the StG 44. So the Russians quickly designed the SKS carbine (short rifle) for it. You can always pick out an SKS, for it has a bayonet permanently attached to the barrel (but usually folded back toward the trigger). Millions of SKSs were produced, but largely for use by support troops or guerrillas. After World War II, work on short rifle rounds continued, and the result was the AK-47. A very well thought-out design, the AK-47 was rugged and easy to take care of. Although its ammunition was heavier than the 5.56mm stuff used in the M-16, this did not make that much difference in performance. The AK-47 became the most widely produced infantry weapon of the twentieth century, with over 50 million produced.

M-16. Not so much an improved AK-47 as it was a competing design for the ideal infantry automatic rifle. Lighter than the AK-47, with a higher rate of fire and a more lethal and accurate round, the M-16 was enough of an improvement that all the major armies of the world eventually adopted it (or a similar design). The Russians replaced their AK-47 with the AK-74, a design almost identical to the M-16. The key factor in the M-16 design was the use of the 5.56 (.22-caliber) round. This bullet design had been around since before World War I, mainly to provide a lightweight, highly lethal, and accurate round for hunting small animals. In the 1930s, when the M-1 design was set, it was proposed that a lighter and equally powerful weapon could be built around the .220 Swift (civilian predecessor of the 5.56mm M-16 bullet). But war was looming, and money was short to change course. Had the M-1 used the 5.56mm round (and that was essentially what was proposed), the rifle would have weighed a pound or two less and been a little shorter. More important, the magazine would have held 10 or 12 rounds, and the troops could have carried twice as much ammunition. Many American lives would have been saved as a result. But there was a lot of resistance to anything less than the standard .30-caliber rifle round in the Army ordnance establishment (the people responsible for developing new weapons). When the 5.56mm round came up again in the 1950s, the ordnance opposition kept it out of the troops' hands until the Vietnam War came along and forced them to adopt the M-16.

The bazooka was an American innovation. The basic idea was to use the long-known, but little-used, "shaped charge" effect, otherwise known as the "focused explosion." The front part of the shell is hollow, the rear half is an explosive with a cone-shaped depression (open side facing the front of the shell). When the warhead hits, a detonator is set off at the rear of the explosive. This creates a metal-penetrating stream of superhot gas. This plasma jet burns a small hole in the armor and, once inside the tank, will ignite something else, like ammunition, fuel, and/or crew. It is not always fatal, as the plasma jet is only 10 to 20 percent the width of the warhead and dissipates quickly. The rule of thumb is that a shaped charge can penetrate armor equal to five times the warhead's diameter. The original bazooka had a 60mm-wide warhead that could go through 300 millimeters of armor. The Germans knew about shaped charges, having used them as demolition charges for penetrating enemy bunkers. They knew that spaced armor would defeat most of the shaped charge's effect. This worked because the plasma jet exists for only a fraction of a second, burning through whatever is in front of it. If thin armor is placed 300 millimeters from the tank's main armor, the warhead explodes and burns through 300 millimeters of air before it reaches the armor. Shaped-charge warheads also need a fraction of a second for the explosion to form the plasma jet. The bazooka was simplicity itself. A rocket containing a shaped-charge warhead was fired out a metal tube. The accurate range was only about a hundred meters, and this was short enough for most infantry users to obtain a hit most of the time. Unfortunately, the rocket could also hit the tank armor at an angle, thus sending the jet through more armor and perhaps not even penetrating to the interior of the tank. The infantry also found the bazooka useful for attacking bunkers. The Germans were quick to realize what the Americans had come up with and came out with two superior bazookas of their own. One was like the American weapon, but firing an 88mm warhead. The other was even more effective, the one-shot Panzerfaust ("armor fist"). This weapon had the 88mm rocket on the end of a narrower tube through which the rocket exhaust would exit. With a range of only about 50 meters, the one-shot/throwaway aspect of the weapon was popular with the users.

Mortars are artillery weapons that fire a round nearly straight up, and this over obstacles. Mortars were invented in the sixteenth century, but these were quite heavy. Early in World War I, several nations saw how useful a lighter mortar could be for the infantry. By World War II, three different classes of mortars had been developed. Light (50–60mm, up to 45 pounds firing a 2- to 3-pound shell up to 2 kilometers) and medium (81mm, weighing up 200 pounds firing a 10- to 15-pound shell up to 6 kilometers) were used by the infantry. Heavy mortars (107mm and up) were used as artillery, and not hauled around by the infantry. The light and medium mortars could be hauled around by the infantry to give them more firepower when they needed it. This made infantry a lot more flexible and lethal. You could no longer expect to stop infantry with your own, for a barrage of mortar shells would enable the advancing infantry to punch a hole in your defenses. Mortars were even more useful when defending, putting a lot of firepower down on attacking troops before your more distant artillery could respond.

The nightscope was an American invention. It was an electronic device that looked like a handheld telescope. It was used at night to allow the user to see things as if it were daylight. Available light (mainly from the moon and stars) was increased by the electronics to, in effect, turn night into day. First used in Vietnam, it gave American troops a tremendous advantage, for by seeing the enemy before he could see you, surprise is achieved (or avoided, if the enemy is trying to sneak up on you for an attack). In the subsequent three decades, the devices were made smaller, lighter, and more powerful. At the end of the century, they could be worn like goggles. A similar device, which detected differences in heat, worked even better, for it could see through smoke and smog. The heat-sensor device was heavier, so it was used on vehicles. By stripping away the cover of darkness, troops using these devices ruled the night. Against troops not equipped with similar devices, the results were usually disastrous for the guys who could not see in the dark. For thousands of years, soldiers feared operating at night. No longer, if you have the right equipment.

The flak jacket was first widely used by U.S. bomber crews during World War II. Thus the name; it was for protection against enemy anti-aircraft fire (called flak). The World War II jacket was heavy, as it used steel to provide the protection. It was usually worn only by the crewmen sitting down, especially the pilots. The jacket was very popular. Attempts to use flak jackets for ground troops had been made as early as World War I, but only for troops in fortifications. It was simply too much weight (40 to 50 pounds) and too cumbersome for a soldier to move around in. Moreover, the earliest flak jackets provided protection only from shell fragments, not machine-gun bullets. After World War II, new, lighter materials were developed for flak jackets, and they became practical for infantrymen to wear. Soldiers had been wearing steel helmets since 1915 to protect their heads from shell fragments, but the flak jackets greatly expanded the area protected. Infantry casualties, while still high, were reduced by about 25 percent when troops wore flak jackets. They would have been reduced a lot more were it not for the vast increase in the volume of firepower on the battlefield. But for the infantryman, any protection was appreciated. The flak jacket was as much a morale booster as it was a form of protection. At the end of the century, flak jackets have gotten lighter and are better designed to handle the heat troops in tropical climates have to deal with. Infantry feel very exposed when they go into combat, knowing that all those bullets and shell fragments can tear them up. But with a flak jacket, they know that they have a degree of protection. This makes a big difference when you're going into harm's way.

The radio revolutionized warfare more than most people realize, especially ground combat. Getting the word out on the battlefield has always been a serious problem. For thousands of years, generals who could best run a battle in spite of not getting timely and accurate reports from subordinates, nor being able to issue orders to those same people, won more than lost. Musical instruments, flags, and couriers were all used with varying lack of success. Fortunately, until the last century, most battles were fought in a small area, usually small enough for the commander to view most of the proceedings from a hill. But in the nineteenth century, armies began to sprawl out. Larger economies and longer-range weapons caused armies to spread out to the point where the guy in charge could barely hear what was going on up and down the several miles of battle line, much less see most of it. Telegraph, appearing in the middle of the nineteenth century, and telephones, showing up about thirty years later, helped somewhat. But only if you could string wire in a timely fashion, and then keep the wire intact amid all those bullets, shells, men, and horses. Wire-dependent communications were generally effective only when the battle line stood still for a few days and was quiet. This lack of control during the movement of battle, as much as the increased firepower from machine guns and better artillery, caused battles to degenerate into stalemates.

When radio appeared shortly after 1900, its military potential was seen immediately. But the technology was limited during World War I. The radio sets were heavy, and large antennas were needed. By the end of World War I, radios were smaller. You could get one into an airplane, but not on the back of an infantryman. You could put one in the back of a truck, but that helped only the headquarters troops, who could just as easily run a telephone line. Even without a lot of mobile radios, the "wireless" proved useful, but not for running battles. All that changed during World War II. Twenty years of technical progress brought forth lighter and more reliable radios. There were forty-pound radios for company and battalion commanders. The United States also developed the walkie-talkie. Although slightly smaller than a loaf of bread and as heavy as a laptop computer, it allowed troops in the thick of it to communicate to mortars and superiors a mile or so to the rear. Tanks and aircraft had longer-range radios, making it possible for a commander to communicate with the smallest units in his army. No longer was the battlefield such a murky place for the guy in charge.

But all was not perfect. Radios got damaged on the battlefield, done in by bombs and bullets or simply rough treatment. Operators were killed or injured. The portable ones ran out of batteries. The recon aircraft got shot down or found the battlefield concealed by fog, clouds, or night. Some armies could not afford as many radios as others. The Russians, with the largest army in World War II, had a radio for only one in every ten tanks, and rarely for company commanders. But still, the Russians found the radios invaluable. Without them, they could not have defeated the Germans.

Despite these problems, radios in World War II changed the way battles were fought. Artillery fire and airpower could be rapidly moved from one part of the battlefield to another. Reinforcements could quickly be sent to hard-pressed troops or to exploit a breakthrough.

But there were other limitations. At the lowest levels of combat, with the infantry squads (ten men) or platoons (thirty men), you often had to keep your voice down lest the enemy detect you. Hand signals were the preferred method of communication. Besides, even a walkie-talkie was too cumbersome for many front-line combat situations. But commanders of companies (three to four platoons) or battalions (three to four companies) found the radio invaluable for keeping in touch with their superiors and the people who controlled the artillery, air strikes, and resupply. While company and battalion commanders still spent a lot of time running around to check personally on their subordinates, in the thick of battle they were now just as likely to be standing in front of a map yelling into the radio mouthpiece.

For the rest of the century, everyone tried to improve on this new style of warfare. Radios got lighter, more reliable, and longer ranged. By the 1960s, radios were light enough to give one to each platoon, or each squad-size patrol. The widespread use of helicopters allowed battalion commanders to fly over the fighting and, radio in hand, direct their troops below. Or at least try to. The guy in the sky often became a problem, for the view from up there often missed vital details about what was going on down below. Moreover, the brigade commanders (three to four battalions) and division commanders (three brigades) might also be overhead in their own helicopters. Too many cooks in that kind of kitchen only increased the confusion, the number of friendly casualties, and the frustrations of the grunts on the ground.

Then came the 1990s and the Gulf War. The U.S. Army, a pioneer in the use of radio on the battlefield, added two more innovative communication devices to make the soldiers' job easier still. Both were complete surprises to the civilians who watched the war unfold. The devices were still in development, but the need was great, and both were sent to war. First there was the GPS (global positioning system), which provided precise location information (to within 25 meters or less) via a handheld satellite-signal receiver. Not all the needed satellites were in orbit when war began, but there were enough up there to give coverage over most of the gulf except for a few hours in the late afternoon. For an army operating in the desert, GPS was literally a lifesaver. It is very easy to get lost while traveling over (usually) unfamiliar terrain. Maps only appear to add to the confusion, and in desert operations, "navigation" becomes a major matter of life and death. All that was changed in the Gulf War because of the GPS. This system provided precise location information to anyone with a battery-powered SLGR (small, lightweight GPS receiver, or "slugger") unit. The smallest version weighed two pounds. Knowing who (and what) is where on the battlefield is absolutely crucial. Calling in artillery fire or air strikes depends on the ground observer (who is often not far from the target) knowing exactly where he is so that the shells or bombs hit the enemy and not friendly troops. Reconnaissance is much more effective with GPS, as the location of the target can be recorded with precision. Marking the location of enemy minefields, a common occurrence during the Persian Gulf War, was much more effective with GPS-equipped units. Some 4,500 GPS receivers were in the gulf by the end of February 1991, plus several hundred civilian versions bought by the troops (or their parents) at up to $4,000 each. At the end of the century, you can buy a GPS receiver for $100. Basically the GPS is nothing more than a radio receiver that uses the signals from distant satellites to tell the user where he is.

And then there was the other radio, or rather radar, device that made the soldier's life easier. This was a four-engine, downward-looking, radar-equipped jet aircraft called J-STARS. Radar had never been particularly useful to the ground troops, mainly because there was so much stuff on the ground to show up on the radar screen. But more powerful computers made it possible to sort out all the vegetation, hills, buildings, and vehicles and show the J-STARS radar operators what they wanted to see. And what they wanted to see was vehicles, especially armored vehicles, moving about below them. The radar has two modes: wide area (showing a 25-by-20-kilometer area) and detailed (4,000 by 5,000 meters). Each J-STARS had radar displays on board, plus more on the ground with Army headquarters units. All the radar displays could communicate with each other. The radar simultaneously supported both modes and several different chunks of terrain being watched at the same time. While an operator might have to wait a minute or two for an update on his screen, this was not a problem because of the relatively slow pace of ground operations. The radar could see out to several hundred kilometers, and each screenful of information could be saved and brought back later to compare to another view. In this way, operators could track movement of ground units. Operators could also use the detail mode to pick out specific details of ground units (fortifications, buildings, vehicle deployments, etc.). For the first time in history, commanders were able to see and control mechanized forces over a wide area in real time. But more important, they could see the enemy vehicles too. And it all worked.

With the Cold War over in the 1990s, the only remaining superpower, the United States, moved ahead with still more radio support for the ground troops. The two new items were digitalization and PLRS. Digitalization meant putting everyone with a radio onto a form of battlefield Internet. Information could be quickly, and sometimes automatically, transferred from, say, the fire-control system of a tank to the fire-control system of a bomber flying overhead. The bomber would then take care of the target while the tank took care of something else. Simple in function, somewhat more complicated in execution. But digitalization would strip away even more of the fog of battle. The side that has the clearest view of what is going on in combat will generally win.

And then there is PLRS. Another radio. PLRS (Position Locator Reporting System) tackles one of the premier problems of modern warfare: Where is everybody? Platoons tend to stick fairly close together, but individual platoons quickly become scattered all over the battlefield. A battalion has about 20 platoons, a division has over 250. There are actually twice as many separate entities running around, if you include antiaircraft and antitank missile teams, aircraft, individual vehicles, patrols, and so on. PLRS equips the division with 600 to 900 PLRS user units and up to a dozen base units. The user units are about the same size and weight as portable radios and broadcast a secure signal (difficult to jam or intercept) that base units can use to precisely locate all nearby user units. PLRS gives you some of the capabilities of J-STARS. You don't get the J-STARS view of the enemy, but you know where your own troops are. Thus in one century, the battlefield has been made far more visible than it ever was in the past. All because of radio.

Land mines are the twentieth-century version of the ancient traps and snares that hunters, and soldiers, have used for thousands of years. The ability to cheaply mass-produce these simple devices (a wood, metal, or plastic container of explosive with a motion- or pressure-sensitive device on top to set off a blasting cap, and thus the explosive, if the mine is disturbed) made them very popular with, and feared by, the troops. Mines enabled a weaker force to better defend itself against a more powerful foe. Going through a minefield, especially when the enemy was shooting at him, was the most horrific situation an infantryman could find himself in. At night it was worse, for the well-hidden mines were even harder to detect. Larger mines could disable or destroy tanks. After World War II, guerrillas found that they could also use mines to harass their foes and terrorize the local population into giving support. This last angle led to a treaty to ban land mines. But the treaty is largely a feel-good measure. Land mines are too easy to make, and too useful on the battlefield, to disappear. Especially once the shooting starts in earnest and the troops complain that they don't have mines to defend themselves.

Computers have been doing military work from the beginning. The first modern computers were invented for wartime tasks. Computers became more and more a part of military equipment as they got smaller and cheaper. When the personal computer came along, it was often the troops who were sneaking them into their units to make their paperwork easier. At the end of the century, computers are everywhere in the military, at least in the armed forces of the industrialized nations. But the low cost of microcomputers has allowed many low-tech nations to make use of computers in warfare. Even if it is only troops using their (computer-driven) cell phones out in the bush, the computers are everywhere.

No nineteenth-century soldier could have imagined how different ground combat would become at the end of the twentieth century because of the handful of items described here. But it happened, and a similar revolution could occur in the twenty-first century. Who knows? No one did last time around.

——The Camp Followers Take Over——

One of the more remarkable, and largely unnoticed, twentieth-century military developments was that, after thousands of years, we finally put the camp followers into uniform. Unfortunately, the camp followers appear to be increasingly running the show.

Camp followers usually are thought of as loose women following an army to service the troops. There was always some of that, still is, but historically camp followers have largely been male and mainly there to do the housekeeping and keep the troops alive in the field.

Battles have always been relatively rare, but the health hazards of camping out with thousands of men and horses are constant and abundant. The troops knew this, and until the last few centuries, most soldiers were volunteers of one sort or another, and few generals could get their lads to rough it without a lot of camp followers to keep everyone in good health.

There were usually more camp followers than troops, with the ratio of helpers to fighters as high as ten to one. There was a lot for camp followers to do. Pack animals had to be cared for, tents pitched, water carried, wood chopped, food stolen or bought from the locals and cooked. Then everything had to be packed up for the next march. During battles, the camp followers stayed behind in the camp, often fortifying it and using a few weapons and their bare hands to defend it against any enemy troops who got that far. After the battles, camp followers tended the injured, buried the dead and plundered the enemy corpses, or were killed or sold into slavery if their boys lost.

While it was much more efficient to have the troops do their own housekeeping in the field, few armies were disciplined enough to pull this off. The more successful armies did, like the ancient Romans, who traveled light. When a Roman army of ten thousand showed up, there were some eight thousand fighters with it. Most other armies could produce only a few thousand warriors. Since armies normally lived off the land, and this often limited the size of the army, the force that hauled along the fewest camp followers had a substantial military advantage.

This lesson eventually was relearned, and camp followers began to thin out in most Western armies. A century ago, support troops amounted to less than 15 percent of an army. But in the twentieth century, a lot more equipment has been added. Not just things like trucks, trains, transport aircraft, and cargo ships that civilians could be hired to run, but weapons and other gear close to the front that needed soldiers to take care of them. Now the camp followers comprise about 85 percent of the troops. Yet everyone wears the same uniform and gets the same pay. Combat troops get a small bonus when they are in a combat zone, but that's about it. Combat officers still get most of the senior positions, but that is starting to change because of the sheer number of noncombat officers versus the warrior types.

This change has been going on for several generations, and, more and more, the generals think less like fighters and more like bureaucrats. In the past, whenever bureaucrats have been appointed to run an army, disaster arrived along with the next war. As the century ends, it is still unclear how the struggle between warriors and camp followers will play out. It's another one of those things to watch out for in the twenty-first century.

——A Century of Infantry Rifles——

The infantry soldier has been around since the beginning of time. And throughout the twentieth century, no matter how much technology you had, victory wasn't won until your infantry occupied the enemy heartland. Getting there will always involve a lot of detail work that only the infantry can perform. The truth of this can be seen by comparing the infantry of 1900 and 2000. Despite a century of unparalleled technological progress, the infantry of 1900 was not that much different than that of today. Then and now, it was training and leadership that counted most for the successful ground soldier. Although today's infantry has a lot more equipment to fight with than their 1900 counterpart, they do a lot less of the killing and still take most of the casualties. The 1900 rifles have been replaced by assault rifles, yet well-trained infantry with rifles can still be more lethal than ill-prepared opponents with AK-47s. The twenty-first century may be different, with the growing use of robots. Then again, perhaps not.

In the twenty years before 1900, the infantry rifle underwent enormous changes and emerged a weapon so superior that it is still used to this day, virtually unchanged. There were three major changes that brought this about. First, engineers and rifle designers, especially Peter Paul Mauser, developed very easy-to-use and reliable mechanisms for loading bullets into the rifle from a magazine (holding five to ten rounds). Second, chemists developed a "smokeless gunpowder" (which was not a powder, but it was smokeless). These new propellants were not only smokeless (keeping the battlefield free of all that smoke), but they were cleaner and capable of moving the bullets along at higher speeds and longer ranges. Third, advances in metalworking allowed more precise parts to be made and assembled faster and more cheaply. Soldiers could now fire faster (up to twenty shots a minute), farther (a thousand meters or more), more accurately (no smoke), and with more lethality (faster bullets do more damage). But even with this enormous increase in efficiency, the impact of the rifle on the battlefield diminished throughout the twentieth century. Much of the same technology made machine guns, artillery, and aircraft even more lethal weapons.

But the modern rifle changed warfare in many ways:

- It further strengthened the defense. The modern rifle could regularly pick off enemy soldiers several hundred meters away. A group of riflemen firing together could "cover" an area over a thousand meters wide. This was a major change. Gunpowder weapons had, when they first appeared five hundred years earlier, made it easier to attack. But in the middle of the nineteenth century, a French officer realized that if you used a conical (with a point) bullet with the rear portion hollowed out, the thinner metal in the rear of the bullet would expand, wrap around the rifling in the barrel, and spin, not to mention that it kept the hot gas from getting out the barrel before the bullet. This made it easier, and faster, to load a musket (which required powder to be poured down the barrel and then a round bullet rammed down with, of course, a ramrod). With the "Minie ball" (named after the inventor) the bullet was just dropped down the barrel, and because it gave a better gas seal and spun rapidly coming out of the barrel, it went farther and with more accuracy. The effective range of muskets went from one hundred meters to over a thousand. This meant that artillery could no longer be brought up and used to blast infantry formations a few hundred years distant. With Minie bullets, the artillery crews would be picked off before they got close enough to use the "shotgun" (grapeshot) rounds that tore infantry units apart. In the space of a few decades in the mid-nineteenth century, the rifleman had become king of the battlefield. But only while defending. The range and accuracy advantage of the new Minie bullets did not help when attacking.

• It made sniping more common. Before the Minie ball, troops skilled at hitting distant targets were limited to using rifled (spiral grooves inside the barrels) muskets. These weapons took longer to load (because of a tighter fit for the musket ball to ensure that the rifling would work to impart the accuracy-enhancing spin to the projectile). Even then, it took a lot of practice, and expensive ammunition, to turn a soldier with a talent for accurate shooting into a lethal sniper. The Minie ball gave snipers some more range and accuracy, although the lack of smokeless powder exposed the sniper's location after the first shot. The modern rifle changed everything. More accurate, with a longer range and smokeless powder, it allowed a single sniper to keep dozens, or even hundreds, of enemy troops busy. Snipers have become one of the most frightening aspects of the twentieth-century battlefield. Unlike the random firepower troops face most of the time, you know that a sniper will take a personal interest in killing you.

• Irregular warfare became more lethal. Before modern rifles came along, the only irregular troops (guerrillas and the like) you had to worry about were the ones that were warriors to begin with.

These chaps knew how to use their weapons, they usually already had weapons, and they were experienced fighters. But the weapons were usually primitive (bows and arrows). Even when the irregulars had modern weapons, the hard-to-load and inaccurate muskets did not give them a lot of effective firepower. Modern rifles changed all that. Now any bloody-minded malcontents could get their hands on rifles and be quite lethal. Sniping was particularly popular with irregulars.

• Troops were more easily trained. The modern rifle was such a breakthrough largely because it was simpler to use and more durable. This made it easier to train new recruits and resulted in fewer weapons' being out of action from operator error on the battlefield. With the rifle, millions of troops could be put into action in weeks. This is what Russia did in 1941, much to the surprise of the invading Germans. It should not have surprised the Germans, as they had shocked the French in 1914 when the German reserve troops, carrying their Mauser rifles, proved more capable than expected.

With all the rifles available (well over 100 million) in this century, it has become much easier to raise an effective armed force. The most chilling aspect to this has been the arming of younger and younger children. Physical strength is no longer a prerequisite as in the past, only the ability, and willingness, to pull a trigger. Children as young as ten have been seen throughout the century carrying, and using, a rifle. While the rifle made it easier to arm more fighters, the same technology with metals and industrial design made other weapons far more destructive than the now mature rifle.

The rifle was largely replaced by automatic assault rifles in the second half of the twentieth century, but the damage was already done. Not so much the casualties, as artillery, bombs, and machine guns were weapons that killed more people. But the biggest killers in wartime were disease and starvation, and these were brought about largely because so many people were running around with rifles plundering and terrorizing the civilian population. As the century ends, millions of civilians are still suffering, and dying, from this, the deadliest legacy of the rifle. In the past, people could effectively resist men with spears or bows, but not men with rifles.

——Never Throw Anything Away——

For thousands of years, it was customary for weapons to be kept in service for as long as they would last. Metal weapons and armor, if carefully maintained, lasted for generations. Wooden warships armed with cannon often lasted over a century. This was mainly because weapons were relatively more expensive than they are today, and technology did not change as quickly in times past. Indeed, many weapons remained technologically current for centuries.

That changed, in some respects, during the twentieth century. High-tech weapons and equipment had to be discarded as new and improved ones came into service. After World War II, the pace of weapons technology increased so much that new weapons were developed, built, handed over to the troops, and then, a decade or so later, withdrawn from service as even more effective versions were developed. This was unheard of in times past.

But in many cases, older weapons have soldiered on for decades. Before World War I, modern battleships and several types of new infantry weapons were developed. Many of these served through World War I and then through World War II as well. Many pre–World War I infantry weapons (bolt-action rifles and machine guns) continued in service for decades after World War II. Actually, a lot of these hundred-year-old rifles can still be found in out-of-the-way areas. North Korea is known to equip its numerous reserve forces with some World War I–era rifles. These ancient weapons can still kill, and they still do.

You would think that aircraft would not last all that long. While they are light and take a beating during operation, airplanes are built to be maintained and updated. The most notable American example is the B-52 heavy bomber. Those currently in service were built in the early 1960s. But the all-time champ is the two-engine military transport, the DC-3 (or C-47, during World War II). The air forces of

Rwanda and Zimbabwe still operate DC-3s, and hundreds more still operate as commercial air transports around the world.

Artillery is another weapon that lasts and lasts. Many nations still use thousands of World War II–era guns. Denmark, a wealthy nation that could afford more recent stuff, still has over 200 1940s-era American artillery pieces. Chile has nearly 100. Egypt has over 300 Russian World War II–era guns. Even Israel has about 100 American 105mm and 155mm guns from the 1940s in reserve. Just in case. Neighboring Jordan also has 80 of these older guns in service. Uganda has about 60 Russian 1940s-era guns.

Pakistan has over 300 World War II–era U.S. guns, and Turkey uses not only some 1,300 World War II–era guns but also 128 150mm guns purchased in the 1930s.

Also popular are smaller antitank and antiaircraft guns. When the Haitian dictatorship was overthrown in 1994, it was found that the troops were still equipped with World War II–era 37mm and 57mm antitank guns. But most popular are 40mm antiaircraft guns from the 1940s. Basically, this was an excellent design that no one has really been able to improve on all that much in the last half century. Greece and Jordan still use them, and many other nations did not replace them until the 1980s.

You would think armored vehicles would be updated frequently, as these wear out quickly with use. But, no, Argentina still has nearly 100 World War II–era M-4 Sherman tanks and M-3 halftrack armored personnel carriers. Chile also still has some 100 of the Shermans, as do Brazil and Israel. Several nations still have U.S. and Russian 1940s-era armored cars. There may still be a few World War II–era Russian tanks in service, but the Soviet Union was so generous in giving away this old stuff that, even by their standards, it was easy to dump those old T-34s. Even so, T-34s were still seen in service into the 1970s.

Many half-century-old warships serve on. Certain 1940s-vintage U.S. destroyers and landing craft are particular favorites. I guess they don't make them like that anymore. Users include Greece, Turkey, Israel, Oman, and Pakistan.

The Norwegians, awash in oil revenues for the past few decades, know how to economize on weapons. Their tank crewmen still use

German World War II MP-38/40 submachine guns. And the king of Norway's Royal Guard is still equipped with U.S. 1940s-era M-1 rifles.

While we hear most about obsolete weapons, there are many more that remain sufficiently lethal to soldier on into the twenty-first century.

——Death from Above——

Airplanes did not exist in 1900. But by 1910, a few years after the Wright brothers invented a practical flying machine, soldiers were finding a way to use this new invention to deliver death from above. World War I saw thousands of fighter aircraft in action from 1914 to 1918, trying to keep enemy reconnaissance planes at bay, while letting their own aerial observers operate. There were a few bombers, and not many attacks on ground troops. The primitive aircraft technology of the period did not allow a lot of firepower to be delivered from the air.

But in the 1920s and '30s, there was tremendous progress in aircraft technology. By the start of World War II in 1939, new generations of warplanes could put a lot more bombs and machine-gun fire on ground troops. Many people saw this coming, and ever since the early 1920s, an increasing number of generals and admirals bought into the concept of "victory from the air." Didn't work out that way, but World War II was a golden age for bombers, and we've been paying for it ever since.

During World War II, Germany and Japan were bombed to rubble from the air. America built 33,000 four-engine bombers during that war, but found later that the damage was not as decisive as originally thought. It just looked that way from the air. The enemy on the ground kept things going until our ground troops showed up. This was not what the Air Force wanted to hear.

This was a problem encountered again in Korea, Vietnam, and Iraq. But in 1945, we also had the atomic bomb, which was delivered by a bomber. So after 1945, we kept in service 4,000 of the largest bombers, mostly B-29s that could carry A-bombs.

For the rest of the century, work was always under way on new bomber designs. Most of these have been forgotten, but here they are (plus year in service) to jog your memory: B-32 (1945), B-50 (1947),

B-45 (1948), B-36 (1948), B-49 (canceled 1952), B-47 (1952), B-52 (1955), B-58 (1960), FB-111 (1969), B-70 (1970, kept going for research, combat version canceled in early 1962), B-1 (1985), B-2 (1992).

The newer aircraft became much more expensive, not just because of technology but also because fewer of each were built. Each B-29 cost about $9 million. Each B-2 cost $2 billion, although if 4,000 B-2s were built, they would still cost about $500 million each.

At the end of the century, the United States will have only 181 heavy bombers in service, but they will cost more than the 4,000 bombers in service at the end of World War II.

In 1960, we had 1,951 heavy bombers, and it was in the 1960s that the intercontinental ballistic missile (ICBM) came into use. This was the perfect means to deliver nuclear weapons, for there was no way to intercept it and there was no friendly crew put at risk.

So by 1970, we had 600 bombers, and in 1980 only 411. But we also went into the 1980s with three different models of heavy bomber (B-52, FB-111, and B-1 in development).

More money was spent on bombers in the 1980s than on ICBMs. If the ICBMs were so good at delivering nuclear weapons and we had thousands of shorter-range aircraft to deliver regular bombs, why have three different heavy bombers? Politics and, for want of a better word, tradition. Building bombers meant big money, which the Air Force carefully spread around in the districts of legislators they thought would vote for more whatever the Air Force wanted. The Air Force also knew that once a defense factory was up and running, it was politically difficult to close it.

And then there was the tradition angle. Big bombers had "won World War II" and "dropped the A-bomb" to end that war. The Air Force was part of the Army until 1947 and still is a bit insecure about its independent status.

This insecurity was cured somewhat because of the Air Force's relationship to nuclear weapons. The bomber generals who ran the Air Force through the 1980s felt that the only reliable way to deliver nukes was via bomber. No one had ever used ICBMs in combat, but bombers had successfully delivered atomic weapons. Perhaps more important, ICBMs were essentially robots, while bombers had humans at the controls. Generals have not yet warmed to the concept of commanding robots rather than people.

The missile robots eventually became too efficient and cheap, while the bombers just got too expensive. But for fifty years, heavy bombers ruled the imaginations, and budgets, of the U.S. Air Force. Expect to see this pattern again.

——Still Walking After All These Years——

Tanks and trucks revolutionized warfare in this century, right? Well, yes. But most of the fighting in this century was done by armies that walked to work and hauled their heavy equipment behind teams of horses. Hard to believe, isn't it? But it's true. World War I armies were almost entirely horse-drawn, and most of the World War II troops were also. The United States and Britain were the only major armies in World War II that did not use horses to haul the big guns and supplies. We tend to look at twentieth-century military history as it reflects on our own troops. But American soldiers did a very small portion of the fighting in this century. You have to put it in perspective for things to make sense.

The first ten years of this century saw many technical breakthroughs that would have a big impact on the battlefield. The airplane and the battleship were both invented in the first ten years of the century. Also introduced on a large scale were trucks and agricultural tractors using a tracklaying (like a modern bulldozer) system. These were sturdy vehicles, designed to operate in muddy farm fields and terrain otherwise hard to cross in a truck or even on foot. After about a year of trench warfare during World War I, the British realized that these tractors, with a bit of armor and some machine guns added, would be a formidable weapon. Something along those lines was needed to break the otherwise impregnable trench lines stretching across Europe. The English referred to their new weapon by a code word, "tank." The code word stuck.

In reality, the tank did not turn out to be a decisive weapon, at least not by itself. The tank did become an important part of a new system of warfare: mechanized warfare. With infantry in similar armored vehicles and fast-moving artillery pulled by trucks or tractors, you could practice high-speed warfare in the face of all those machine guns. But it took another twenty years to work out all the details.

There were a lot of details. In 1900, a revolution in artillery was under way. The result, by World War I, was artillery that was more numerous and that fired quicker, farther, and with greater accuracy than ever before. For the rest of the century, artillery ruled the battlefield, inflicting most of the casualties and dominating the battlefield as never before. While the armored vehicles were important for getting the troops from one point to another while all those bullets and shell fragments were flying about, fancy footwork alone does not win wars or battles. The major wars of this century were won by infantry on foot. Millions of men carrying rifles, machine guns, and mortars, slogging across the landscape.

While much is made in the history books of the lightning thrusts of armored divisions, without support and follow-up from masses of infantry, those armored divisions get ground to bits fighting the enemy infantry. You don't hear many of those stories, for defeats are not nearly as entertaining as victories. But it was all too common during World War II, and after, for mechanized units to plunge into the thick of things by themselves and never be heard from again.

In the 1950s, the Russians motorized their entire army. China and India, possessing the world's two largest armies, are still in the process of motorizing at the end of the century. Even the high-tech armies still have a lot of troops who are expected to do a lot of walking while they are fighting. Commandos, paratroopers, and Marines are all expected to spend a lot of time on their feet. But because the actual fighting troops are such a small proportion of armed forces these days, you mainly see all the noncombat folks running around in their vehicles.

So let's hear it for the unheralded foot solider.

He may not be the king of the battlefield, but he runs things out there anyway.

And he still walks to work.

——Moving the Wounded——

On the highway, speed kills. On the battlefield, it can save lives, especially if soldiers are wounded.

Consider the increasingly shorter times between a soldier's being wounded and getting him to a field hospital (where extensive surgery can be performed). During World War I, it took fifteen hours to get a wounded man back to a field hospital. In World War II, this was reduced to nine hours. By the Korean War, it was only three hours, and during Vietnam it averaged thirty minutes. This makes all the difference to a badly wounded soldier, for once a soldier reaches a hospital, his chances of surviving are over 97 percent. Without immediate hospital-level care, the death rate goes up rapidly for each hour the wounded soldier is not in a hospital. Several additional hours of travel time can kill over 10 percent of the wounded and mean a longer hospital stay for those who do survive. Throughout this century, as the travel time to hospital care was reduced, the survival rate of the wounded went up.

——Send in the Droids——

That staple of science fiction, the combat robot, finally showed up in the second half of the twentieth century. But this most radical development in twentieth-century warfare went largely unnoticed.

For example, over a thousand computer-guided cruise missiles were used in the 1990s. These are high-tech weapons. The missiles are one-ton aircraft that can find their way over hundreds of miles of land or sea and then hit a target the size of a small barn. No pilot needed; onboard computers take care of all the decision making. The ultimate killer droid.

But these missiles are nothing new in this century. In the 1940s, the Germans fired some 9,000 V-1 cruise missiles at Britain. The V-1 was primitive, but it was the ancestor of today's cruise missiles. Some 5,000 V-1s managed to hit London.

A few months later, the V-2 ballistic missiles appeared. These used a complex guidance system to come down on a distant target.

More than 4,000 were launched, and unlike the V-1, they could not be shot down. In the 1980s, some 600 Russian Scud missiles, based on the V-2 design, were fired during the Iran-Iraq war. Iraq used about 70 Scuds during its 1990–92 war, and thousands of Scuds are still available for use.

Descendants of the V-1 and V-2 have become combat robots, and these droids are the unknown weapon of the twentieth century. More battlefield robots are showing up each year.

Starting with mines and torpedoes at the turn of the century, World War II saw technology moving ahead swiftly. By 1945, there were torpedoes that could follow a ship's noise. Naval mines could detect ships using magnetism (all that steel) or pressure (all that weight in the water). The air war saw the introduction of many new electronic weapons that would soon turn into missiles that could think for themselves.

After World War II, missiles became smarter every year. The goal was "fire and forget" missiles, and these have been a reality for decades. When microcomputers became available in the 1970s, robotic weapons suddenly became really, really smart.

Now there are antitank weapons (the WAM—wide area munitions—system) that listen for sounds and ground vibrations that indicate a particular type of vehicle. Then a coffee-can-size weapon is fired more than 300 feet into the air. On board are radar, a heat sensor, a computer, and a warhead that will punch through the top armor of any armored vehicle detected.

The robots will not replace all human soldiers anytime soon. People are smarter and more adaptable. But the droids are relentless and fearless. The robots work, they're cheap, they've been here for most of the century, and more are on the way. Year by year, the battlefield has more droids and fewer people on it.

Warfare will never be the same.

——Nuclear Weapons——

Nuclear weapons were the one unique new weapon of the twentieth century. All the other new weapons had a past equivalent, and even combat aircraft were predicted by some pre-twentieth-century theorists. But no one imagined something as destructive as the atomic bomb.

Over $10 *trillion* has been spent on developing and building nuclear weapons in this century. A little over half of this was spent by the United States. When the Cold War nuclear-arms race peaked in the late 1980s, there were some 50,000 nuclear weapons in existence.

The theoretical foundations for the atomic bomb were thought up in the nineteenth century and brought forward to the level of practical demonstrations early in the twentieth century by scientists like Albert Einstein. According to Einstein's theories, converting matter to energy released a tremendous amount of force. For example, one ounce of matter, if converted completely into energy, could produce the equivalent of 687,000 tons of high explosives. By 1939, with the help of German experiments that had split the uranium atom, physicists were able to explain the process of nuclear fission. When a large, unstable atomic nucleus splits (fissions), the result is two or more smaller, more stable nuclei accompanied by the release of tremendous amounts of energy and radioactivity. This was the atomic bomb, complete with deadly, lingering radiation. When World War II broke out, many of these scientists realized that it was likely that, with enough engineering and specially built equipment, an atomic bomb could be made. The calculation was that a bomb weighing ten tons could have the effect of tens of thousands of tons of explosives. Starting in 1942, and several billion dollars and much effort later, the United States had working atomic bombs. Two were dropped on Japan to end World War II in the Pacific. No more have been used since then.

In 1949, Russia exploded its first atomic bomb. Britain developed the atomic bomb in 1952. France did so in 1960, followed by China in 1964, India in 1974, and Pakistan in 1998. But there were other nations that developed nukes while denying (for various political and diplomatic reasons) that they had done so. The first nation to do it this way was Israel, which developed a nuclear-weapons capability in the 1960s. But Israel kept this quiet. Just before the 1967 Arab-Israeli Six-Day War, Israel hastily assembled two crude but deliverable nuclear weapons. At the time, Shimon Peres, who would eventually become prime minister, led a group of politicians suggesting that Israel conduct a nuclear test to demonstrate to its enemies that Israel had nukes and would use them. Cooler heads prevailed, and the Israeli government policy became one in which their nuclear weapons would be used only as a last resort, when all other options failed. But every time Israel is in a war, the atomic bombs are made ready.

Israel never has used or tested its nuclear weapons and hides its precise nuclear capability behind a wall of secrecy. Even the United States intelligence agencies, during the late 1950s, took three years to figure out that the industrial complex being built in the southern Negev desert town of Dimona was actually a nuclear-weapons-research plant. In 1963, the United States demanded that Israel keep America informed about what kind of nuclear-weapons program the Israelis had. The United States did not want to see Israel armed with nuclear weapons, but Israel was able to procure much of the technology it needed in Europe, particularly from France. In the 1970s, the United States accepted the fact that Israel would continue to have nuclear weapons and ceased pressuring Israel over the matter. Israel has never acknowledged that it has nuclear weapons, but has emphasized that it would not be the first to use them in the region. So far, Israel is the only nuclear power in the Middle East and has a significant number of weapons and the means to deliver them.

South Africa also developed nuclear weapons in the 1980s and apparently tested one. This nuclear-weapons program was dissolved before the white minority government turned over power to the black majority in the early 1990s.

Pakistan also has had weapons, untested, since the 1980s, and was prepared to use them against India in a war. Pakistan is also the first Islamic country to build nuclear weapons. A poor country, with a powerful Islamic-fundamentalist movement, the fear is that Pakistan would let money or religious fervor cause it to sell nuclear-weapons technology, or the weapons themselves, to countries or organizations that would use them for terrorist acts.

While nuclear weapons have been the main reason there has not been a war between nuclear-armed nations since World War II, as more nations get nukes, the odds of their being used again increases. We have already seen desperate nations like Iraq use chemical weapons in the

1980s. The efforts of Iraq, North Korea, and Iran to make nuclear weapons is not just a matter of aggressive nations' wanting the ultimate weapon to achieve their grand designs. After World War II, the knowledge of how to build nukes became widespread. But it was the details that made the difference, and decade by decade, more details became known. More important, the complex chemical and engineering equipment required became available (for nonnuclear uses) or easier to build. It's inevitable that more and more nations will be able to build their own nuclear weapons.

Historically, long periods without wars between the major powers eventually come to an end. Now all the major powers have nukes, and we must wonder whether these nations could go to war with each other without using their most powerful weapon. If the major powers don't, a lot of scrappier lesser nations probably will.

SEVEN

POLITICS

POLITICS got a bad name in the twentieth century. Never before have there been so many savage totalitarian governments in one century. Ironically, many of these governments were set up in reaction to previous rulers accused of repression and misrule. But the new governments turned out to be much, much worse. Over 100 million people were killed by their own governments, and late in the century, most of the world's nations were run by dictatorships, some of them quite brutal by any standard. But at the end of the century, things turned around. Either by force or sheer popular will, most of the world's dictatorships were overthrown. Or tamed to a degree. Democracy, or at least less repressive governments, replaced the dictators. This was a truly unprecedented historical event. A worldwide revolution took place, and did so with relatively little violence.

Just one more remarkable aspect to a remarkable century.

Note: All dollar amounts are given in terms of year-2000 dollars. That is, they are adjusted for inflation and represent the dollar value at the end of the twentieth century. If you want to see what the actual money values were for a year, see the Appendix.

——Democide——

Democide is governments killing their own people. What do you think killed the most people this century? Epidemics, war or democide? If you took a chance and choose democide, you were right. Only at the end of the century, when the truth has finally came out about the mass murders committed by the communist governments, has it become clear that democide was the great killer. Russia and China alone killed over 100 million of their own people (or "enemies of the people") in their drive to remake their nations. Communist Cambodia killed over a million, and, at the end of the century, communist North Korea was in the process of killing an equally large amount of its citizens. All communist nations had unusually high death rates, mainly for political reasons. The Nazis and other fascist nations also killed their own people, but at nothing like the rate at which the communists did.

But you don't have to be a communist or Nazi to be a mass murderer. The twin afflictions of nationalism and ethnocentrism can still kill on a large scale. In 1994, tribal and political rivalries in the African nation of Rwanda led to a few months' killing that left over half a million dead. There were several other massacres like this in the twentieth century, and many more in centuries past. But never so many in our own century.

Most of these wars are about money. Sad, but true. These slaughters are often justified with some trumped-up reason that sounds more high-minded. But it's generally about land, money, or both. The communists were all about state ownership of everything. Naturally, the state was run by a small group of very well taken-care-of politicians. The more the state controlled, the better off the politicians were economically. Saying this at the time could get you killed, and a lot of perceptive but indiscreet people met their end this way. At the end of the twentieth century, Chinese and Russians who speak out about the economic rapacity of the people in power are still getting put away, or killed. The most infamous of the twentieth-century democides, the Nazi use of death camps to slaughter over 12 million of their own subjects, was basically about money. The Nazi political doctrine held that some people were "useless" and others the cause of economic and social problems.

Because the Nazi democide program was based on race, rather than the communist "social good" excuse, the Nazis reaped a far greater share of justly deserved vilification. It was a distinction without a difference, for the Nazi and communist victims were equally dead. Yet this distinction was an important cause of many deaths. The communists managed to hide many of their atrocities behind very effective propaganda. The horrors of the Soviet Union's democides in the 1920s and '30s were largely unknown outside Russia because of the false front the communists erected. Posturing as the defender of the working class and champion of socialist revolution, the communists were seen by many intellectuals and journalists in the West as social progressives. Survivors of these democides who made it to the West were generally discounted as malcontents.

Many in the West did know that something terrible was going on, but the communists had built the most effective police states the world had ever seen. It was with shock, and no small degree of chagrin, that many in the West greeted the opening of the communist archives at the end of the Cold War. Many true believers in the West still make excuses for the communist democides. That is somewhat horrifying in itself, for it was that kind of moral blindness that allowed the democides to happen in the first place. For example, after World War II, many Soviet Union nationals (prisoners of war, refugees) who came under the control of Allied troops when Germany collapsed, were turned over to the Soviet Union. Most of these people did not go willingly, and many committed suicide instead. Those who did return knew what they were in for. Most ended up in labor camps, and about a million died. But apologists in the West concentrated on the small percentage of the returnees who had collaborated with or fought for the Germans. In the West, the frequently lethal nature of the Soviet labor camps was played down: "It was an internal matter." Besides, it was an article of faith among many in the West that the Soviet "workers' paradise" was incapable of such savagery.

The same blind faith was accorded the communist democides in China, where in the late 1940s over a million "landlords" were executed. What the Chinese communists were really doing was eliminating any local resistance of their rule. Successful farmers were more likely to become the center of opposition to communist rule and collectivization of agriculture. The Russian communists had killed over 20 million of their own people in the 1920s and '30s as they eliminated private farming and local leadership. But the Russians were outdone by their Chinese brethren in the 1950s, when a disastrous industrialization program led to over 30 million deaths.

But you didn't need a highly efficient police state to achieve a high death toll. In 1971, when Pakistan broke apart, the West Pakistanis killed some two million Bengali nationalists in East Pakistan. You don't even need a lot of weapons to do it. In 1994, Hutu nationalists killed over half a million Tutsis in Rwanda, using machetes, rocks, clubs, and fire.

The worst aspect of democide is that it will not go away. It is still with us, and will be for a long time.

——Nongovernment Governments——

Governments were invented to run things. Not just inside a country, but also outside their own borders. Governments were particularly good at handling relationships with other governments. For the last few centuries, that's how it has worked, and if you wanted to get anything done, you did it through a government organization.

That changed in the twentieth century.

At the end of the century, we have a new form of government organization, the NGO (nongovernment organization). These international organizations operate independently to achieve humanitarian and political goals, push their own agendas, or simply encourage international relations and the flow of information. NGOs are not unique to the twentieth century; they have existed for many centuries. But at the end of the twentieth century, there are over five thousand of them, far more than at any time in the past. Far more than the few dozen or so that existed in 1900. And at the end of the twentieth century, the NGOs have become a major factor in international relations.

The first NGOs were religious organizations that appeared some seven centuries ago. Initially, they were not truly independent of any government, for most were Roman Catholic and thus subject (but not always obedient) to the governing organization of the Catholic Church and the pope. After the major Protestant sects began to appear in the sixteenth century, there was an opportunity for more independent NGOs, and over the next few centuries, these began to appear. They were mainly missionary groups that also performed humanitarian work while seeking to gain new converts.

It was in the nineteenth century that the first of the modern NGOs emerged. These were also humanitarian in their goals, but they also had no reluctance to use diplomatic and political muscle to achieve them. The Anti-Slavery Society was such an organization, and in the early nineteenth century it was instrumental in getting slavery banned in most parts of the world. The society is still around, because slavery has not completely disappeared. A more recognizable organization is the Red Cross (and later Red Crescent) societies. These were first formed in the 1860s to campaign for more humane treatment of prisoners, the wounded, and civilian victims of warfare. The Red Cross was instrumental in getting the various Geneva Conventions (the "rules of war") accepted by most major nations. By the twentieth century, the Red Cross was also active in all manner of humanitarian activities. A century ago, the Red Cross was the most effective, powerful, and recognized NGO that ever existed. But it was only the beginning.

The massive death and destruction of World War I led to an attempt to create a super-NGO to prevent future major wars. Thus was born the League of Nations and, up through the late 1930s, hundreds of new NGOs. But the League of Nations did not work, World War II came, and in the wake of that war was an even greater resolve to do something about these disastrous wars. Thus was born, in 1945, the United Nations, a more effective successor to the League of Nations. There was also another explosive growth in NGOs. By 1960, there were a thousand of them, by 1970 two thousand, by 1980 four thousand. The growth sprang from two major sources: more money and more mass media.

The world economy grew continuously from the late 1940s through the 1970s. Prosperity returned to Europe, and with all that money came greater capacity to support charitable organizations. The United States was already creating hundreds of NGOs, but many of these were trade organizations, for in the latter half of the twentieth century, America was the largest exporter in the world. About one sixth of the NGOs are trade organizations, and while they prefer to operate quietly, they have done much to mold government policies. There was a lot of money involved in overseas trade, and these trade organizations had no trouble meeting their budgets.

About 20 percent of all NGOs are scientific or technical organizations. The twentieth century has been the century of science, and scientists learned early on that they had to work hard to get their message out. Science is not simple, and the media generally either get it wrong or depict a beneficial new development as something more sinister. The scientific NGOs not only worked to get scientific information and cooperation going around the world but also put their considerable stature and lobbying muscle toward getting more government money for scientific research.

One in seven of the NGOs deals with medical matters. Not just providing medical care and information where it is most needed, but expediting the exchange of medical information among the international community of medical professionals. These were among the earliest NGOs, as the twentieth century saw an unprecedented number of cures to ancient diseases. The medical NGOs had a lot to do.

Sports NGOs grew with the reintroduction of the Olympic Games in 1896. Although comprising only about 8 percent of all NGOs, these are the ones that most people will come into contact with.

The rest of the NGOs cover a wide range of activities. You name it, there's an NGO for it. Religion, culture, labor relations, world affairs, education, and all manner of special interests are playing the NGO game. And it's a very serious game.

The mass media made it all possible, for most NGOs live or die by the amount of attention they get in the press. While many NGOs deliver services, the money to keep them going comes from those who see those services being delivered. NGOs are pressure groups, and with so many of them out there hustling for a headline, the pressure has some strange results. Because most of these NGOs have an international outlook, and an agenda, they want to get their point of view across worldwide. And many NGOs with a lot in common will pool their resources to exert tremendous pressure to do just that. There have been many good examples of how this works, especially late in the century when the number of NGOs became so great. The 1997 international treaty to ban land mines was the result of hundreds of NGOs applying political pressure to do something they wanted. No government by itself could have pulled this off. Because the NGOs were international, not affiliated with any single government, and pushing a humanitarian measure few could oppose (except on the pragmatic grounds that it was unenforceable and likely to be counterproductive), they got their way.

More common is the call by NGOs for military intervention into some war-torn area. The NGOs have a vested interest in such intervention, for the United Nations and many wealthy countries hire NGOs to deliver humanitarian services in disaster areas. While other NGOs come in on their own, using funds they have collected to deliver aid, all NGOs in a crisis area still need military protection. And at the end of the century you will find up to several hundred NGOs operating in an area beset by some armed conflict. Each of these NGOs is spending some of its resources lobbying for government intervention to protect its staff in what is usually a very dangerous area. The NGOs also know that securing any media attention for their efforts will not only increase pressure on governments to get more involved but will make it easier for the NGOs to raise money.

The NGOs have come to be so active in all these trouble spots not just because there are more NGOs but because there is more trouble out there. The number of conflicts like those in Afghanistan, Sudan, the Balkans, and South America (just to name those active in the 1990s) grew from 36 in the early 1960s, to 55 in the 1970s, 62 in the 1980s, to 70 at the end of the century. Aside from millions of dead and injured, these conflicts generate millions of miserable refugees. This problem became particularly acute in the 1980s. There were 8.2 million refugees in 1980, 11.6 million in 1985, and 17.2 million in 1990. The number went down about 20 percent by the end of the century, but it was still huge. And many governments were only too happy to pay NGOs to help bring the misery index down a bit.

Many of these crises are civil wars or ethnic conflicts or both. Very dangerous. What the NGOs did not promote was what happened afterward, and now in the long term, the outside intervention serves mainly to keep the combatants supplied so they can keep on fighting, as well as giving them more people to shoot at and plunder.

In the 1990s, even the NGOs began to say openly that the aid they supplied was prolonging these wars. True, the aid was alleviating suffering, and it was a painful paradox. For if nothing were done, people would suffer, and the fighting might end sooner. While with the aid, people were helped in the short run, but the fighters were supplied also, and the mayhem continued. Foreign governments found themselves in a difficult position. If they continued subsidizing and at times protecting the NGOs, the problem would go on and on. This had been the case with Sudan and Somalia throughout the 1990s. But, unlike government employees, the NGOs could not just be ordered out of an area. Governments could cut off the money they were giving to the NGOs, but not the private contributions they received. While many NGO employees were there because it was just a job, many more were true believers in their mission. True believers are hard for government bureaucrats to push around.

The NGOs are also very media savvy. They know what kinds of stories the TV and radio crews are looking for and will provide them in return for a little favorable coverage. The media often found that the NGO staff was the best source of leads and stories in crisis zones. The NGOs didn't work for any government, so they had less reason just to dish out the official version of what was going on. The NGO people were pushing their NGO, but the press generally didn't mind, for the NGOs were doing good works, and who could criticize that?

But criticism did begin to show up when it became obvious to media and government officials that too many NGOs were trying to control media coverage of the areas they were operating in and the foreign policy of many nations sending support to these crisis zones. The media began to realize that they were being used rather shamelessly to promote whatever the NGOs were pushing. And at the other end of the media pipe, the governments were faced with voters up in arms about this and that humanitarian crisis that was all over the news and, by God, someone should do something about it. But people were getting wise to the tricks, with unfortunate results. In 1998, Hurricane Mitch, a massive storm, ravaged much of Central America. In order to speed up the flow of relief, local governments and NGOs inflated the numbers of people killed. The media ran with the story at first, and the aid came. But other journalists eventually discovered the truth, and that story soured a lot of people who were ready to help out.

By the end of the nineties, the media and the voters were a little more skeptical, which was unfortunate, as there are still a lot of disasters out there with people in need. And there are a growing number of NGOs ready to help. But after half a century of rapid growth, many of the NGOs have gotten fat with bureaucrats. Many of the humanitarian NGOs are increasingly staffed by careerists. While many NGO staffers are just young folks out for a little adventure and good works, then to go on to a more conventional life, the proliferation of NGOs has created an NGO culture. Fans of world government will find this to their liking, for one attitude many NGO staffers share is that there is the need for some kind of world government.

As the twenty-first century opens, more showdowns among increasingly powerful NGOs and governments and media trying to avoid being manipulated will take place. The governments and media thought they knew how to handle the conventional lobbyist NGOs, but found themselves bumped around by the even savvier, and more self-righteous, humanitarian NGOs. It will be an interesting struggle, one of the first interesting events in the twenty-first century.

The Religious Wars of the Twentieth Century

We don't generally think of the twentieth century as being a time of vicious religious wars, but such was the case. Over 100 million people died in the twentieth-century religious wars.

In the last few centuries, religion has been the driving force in some of the most devastating wars. In Europe, the Thirty Years' War

(1618–48) devastated much of central Europe. In the mid-nineteenth century, over 20 million Chinese died in the religion-inspired Tai-Ping Rebellion. But the twentieth century dawned with traditional religions on the defensive as a major force. But the new political movements, communism and fascism, took on all the appearance, intolerance, and fanaticism of a new religion. Fascism tended to ignore traditional religions, although the German version (nazism) promoted its own pagan form of worship. The communists went further, suppressing religion as much as possible and replacing it with a "worship of the state," replete with new ceremonies to replace the traditional ones for marriage, death, and Christmas.

As was common with new religions, there was intolerance for existing faiths and a belief that the new believers were on a mission from a higher power. This meant that the normal rules did not apply and the usual result was a lot of dead bodies. Such was the case with the communists and fascists. Between them, they managed to kill over 100 million people. All for "the cause," of course. The communists were more subtle and were better at controlling the media. Thus the fascists got most of the hate mail for their dirty deeds, at least until the end of the century. When most of the communist dictatorships fell apart in the late 1980s, the archives opened, and a lot of ghastly evidence came to light. The slaughter turned out to be worse than anyone had imagined or predicted. Worse still was the evidence of how extensive the operations of the secret police had been in all the nations run by communist governments. Wives had spied on husbands, children on parents, teachers on pupils, doctors on patients, and any other combination you could imagine. Most of these spies were not true believers, but they had seen how brutal the secret police could be and were convinced that resistance was futile. The totalitarian governments made excellent use of the media to convince their subjects that the state's power was total and not to be resisted.

But like all false religions, the communist and fascist true believers eventually realized that there was no there there. But in their early days, these new beliefs energized millions of true believers to do the most horrible things in the name of their new cause. Where did all this come from? And will it return?

Communism and fascism were similar in many ways, but they came from, and were headed in, different directions. What both had in common was a belief in socialism, centralized political power, clever use of mass media, hostility toward established religions, murderous ruthlessness, and dictatorship. What made these two systems different was the communist belief that they owned the future and had discarded the past. The fascists were much more interested in reviving ancient history and adapting it to the present and future. The communists were also in favor of eliminating private property, while the fascists generally protected it.

Communism was developed by Karl Marx, a nineteenth-century philosopher who studied history and insisted that he had determined how the future would unfold. His analysis held that current economic (capitalism and free markets) and political (monarchy in particular) systems were dying. He proposed that a new economic/political system, communism, would take over. Communism was based on the state's owning all economic assets (all businesses), with economic activity directed by a central planning authority. The state (eventually there would be one world state) would be run temporarily by a "dictatorship of the proletariat," until such time as democracy could be implemented. There would, however, always be just one political party: the Communist party. The political leadership would be politicians, but Communist-party politicians selected to lead by senior party members. The principle of "from each according to his abilities, to each according to his needs" would eliminate poverty, as well as wealth.

Communism was a radical new way to run a society. It had never been done this way before. Neither had there ever been as much economic and political change as occurred in the nineteenth century. After thousands of years as farmers, people in the newly industrialized nations were moving into cities and working in factories and offices. People were better educated than ever before, and more conscious of their potential political power. New problems called for new solutions. Communism was the most radical solution, and many self-proclaimed "progressive thinkers" embraced communism, even if it was uncertain how it would all turn out.

The fascist movement grew out of the same rapid economic and social change that spawned the communists. But rather than studying the past in order to design a radical new future, the fascists sought to re-create the past using the new technical and social tools at hand. Germany called their new government the Third Reich (empire). The first one being the Roman Empire as presided over by the medieval German emperor Charlemagne, and the second one being the wholly German one created in 1870 and swept way by the aftermath of World War I. The German fascists (Nazis, short for National Socialists) dismissed Christianity as a weak-willed modern religion that had failed the German people. The Nazis preferred the ancient German gods, who were certainly more fearsome and colorful than the somber deity of the Christians. But aside from some odd religious proclivities and a desire to restore long-lost glories, the fascists were quite practical. They generally left private property and business alone, as long as the owners toed the party line. Unfortunately, the main party lines were world conquest and mass murder.

But there was more variation in how fascism was practiced. There was only one communist state initially (Russia, renamed the Union of Soviet Socialist Republics). But there were many fascist governments formed in the 1920s and '30s. Each was different, often quite different, from the others.

The first major fascist government to gain power was in Italy. The Italian fascists did not overthrow the king of Italy, although that king was turned into more of a figurehead than he usually was. Nor did the Italian fascists get into quarrels with organized religion. While rough and nasty with political opponents (particularly communists), the Italian fascists turned out to be "fascist lite," at least compared to their counterparts in Germany and Japan.

The German and Japanese fascist movements shared a fondness for using racial hatred to propel them into power. The Germans and Japanese were both obsessed with racial purity. For the Germans, the "master race" included other Europeans who were members of the "Aryan race." For the Japanese, the master race meant just the Japanese. In both cases, everyone else was considered expendable. Naturally, the Japanese and Germans had to accord each other "honorary" racial status. The Germans made the Japanese "honorary Aryans." While Nazi academics worked out the twisted logic of this, the Japanese simply considered the Germans useful allies who, while racially inferior, should be dealt with politely.

The racial angle was one that the Germans had for the past century or so tried to put behind them. The Nazis knew that many Germans still believed in racial superiority and exploited that attitude to gain power. It was political expediency, as well as acting on a belief held by many Nazi-party members. You still see the racial-animosity angle exploited by unscrupulous politicians today, and will continue to see it in the future. But the German Nazis were unique in making it a principal national policy to murder millions of non-Germans simply because they were not German. Or not German enough, which was the reason for murdering over a million German citizens. Jews, Gypsies, homosexuals, and political opponents were all killed for not being German enough.

The Japanese were equally brutal with their neighbors. Anyone who was not Japanese was considered expendable, and Asians by the tens of millions, mainly Chinese, were killed in the course of Japanese military operations in the 1930s and '40s. Japan, however, practiced a somewhat different kind of fascism. Japan was taken over by a military dictatorship in the 1930s, but it was a dictatorship that had a lot of political support. In effect, it was a military-led political party. Like the German Nazis, the Japanese fascists used terror as well as conventional political techniques (patronage and propaganda) to get control of the government. This led to many changes in Japanese attitudes, just as the Nazis changed the attitudes and behavior of the German people when they took over. Before the fascist governments assumed power in both countries, Germany and Japan were both committed to the general trends in Western culture.

The Japanese were playing catch-up, as they had only decided to move from a medieval society, in the late 1800s, to one comparable with Western industrial society. During the Russo-Japanese war (1904–5), for example, the Japanese treated captured Russians according to the European conventions for the humane treatment for prisoners of war. While the Japanese were ferocious and crafty fighters, they did nothing that Western observers could not admire. All this changed when the Japanese fascists took over. Preaching a doctrine of the Japanese as a "warrior race" destined to conquer all about them, they determined that other nationalities were to be treated as subhuman and murdered out of hand. In some respects, the Japanese were more brutal than the Germans. While the Japanese did not establish death camps, they were far more likely to kill Chinese civilians casually. Bayonet practice on live Chinese was all too common. Japanese military surgeons frequently practiced their surgical techniques on Chinese (and American) prisoners. The subjects were often not given anesthesia and were always killed afterward.

Both the German and Japanese fascists saw themselves as above the laws and restrictions that other nations followed. Anything was permissible if it contributed to the victory of the master race. They were on a mission from God, and not answerable to those who were not.

The communists, however, were worse. But the communists had one major advantage, in that they professed (even if they did not practice) a more humane and "progressive" doctrine. The communists preached the brotherhood of man and worldwide revolution in the name of the universal good. Hard to argue with that. But in practice, the communists were more ruthless than anyone could have imagined. The Russian and Chinese communist governments used mass murder of their own people to achieve economic and political goals. When the peasant farmers of Russia and China resisted collective farming and the strict discipline the communists advocated, they were killed and starved in the tens of millions. Yet while this was going on, these same governments cranked up the propaganda machine to tell the world that everything was fine and that the farmers were cheerfully going along with the plan. Food was plentiful and the farmers were smiling, at least in those locations set up for Western (and communist) journalists to see for themselves how socialism was going to save the world.

Enforcing "correct thought" was a primary objective of both communists and facists. The Japanese went so far as to set up a special "thought police" organization to monitor public thinking and weed out those who thought otherwise. This was obvious and abhorrent to foreigners (and many Japanese). The communists had a more deft touch, and better techniques for controlling public opinion. They developed a nationwide network of informers and secret police who operated with somewhat more subtlety than the Japanese, and they got away with it for many decades. It wasn't until the last few decades of the twentieth century that many Westerners caught on to how things really worked behind the Iron Curtain.

While the fascists were seen for what they were early on, and condemned for it, the communists managed to keep their crusade going for another four decades. Not that fascist governments have disappeared. It depends on how you define fascist. But history has seen few dictatorships as vile and murderous as the Nazis and World War II Japanese. Many less bloody-minded fascist governments continue to operate, though. Think about it. There are still governments that rule via political terror and perpetuate the idea that their nation is composed of people who are special, to the extent that others may be massacred with impunity. The mass murders in Rwanda and Yugoslavia in the 1990s sprang from that mind-set. Purely religious (and a bit of ethnic) fascism still pops up in the Muslim world. And there is great fear that China or Russia might blunder into a fascist direction.

When dealing with a population's emotions, you have to be ever mindful that there's always the chance things can go very, very wrong.

——The Terrorism Business——

Terrorists blowing up American embassies in Africa or skyscrapers in New York are nothing new. Terrorism has been around for thousands of years. Today, however, it is different. It's more organized. It has to be. Unlike in the past, police are now plentiful.

But still the bombs go off.

It was after World War II that terrorism as we know it showed up, a new form of international terrorism unlike anything seen before. Modern terrorism is most likely to succeed if there are well-educated, trained terrorists who are backed by a network of safe houses and special services for forged identities, intelligence, transportation, weapons, and safe contacts overseas. Funds are needed to pay the terrorists, for they often have families dependent on them. Modern terrorism is run like a business, which is the key to whatever success it has.

The principal backer of modern terrorism was the Soviet Union. It wasn't until after the Soviet Union collapsed that it became widely known just how much money and effort the communists poured into producing professional terrorists.

But money and training facilities are not enough. Eager volunteers are required for the extremely dangerous missions. Since terrorism is the only practical form of warfare for vastly outnumbered factions, volunteers must be inspired to step forward. The Soviets developed effective techniques for producing volunteers, then indoctrinating and training them. The Soviet support for international terrorism was just another Cold War tactic for them.

Meanwhile, most of the world's terrorists did their work at home and were rarely heard about abroad. Terrorism is based on illusions. Despite the tens of thousands of terrorists trained and equipped over the last three decades, only a small percentage ever get into action. Yet each successful terrorist mission has the desired effect of making many people terrified at the prospect of further atrocities.

In reality, international terrorism is very difficult to pull off. It has become more difficult throughout the twentieth century, as police achieved more technology and greater numbers. Had it not been for the Soviet contribution of technique, technology, and organization to the terrorist's arsenal, there would have been a lot less terrorism at the end of the century.

What the Soviets provided was a systematic, very professional approach to terrorism. Dozens of operations are planned, then aborted as too risky, for each operation that actually comes off. But each act of terrorism does indeed terrorize, for the attacks seem to occur despite energetic precautions. The nations targeted for this terrorism have reacted strongly to the attacks, so strongly that it is now standard for most terrorist acts to go unclaimed by any traceable organization. Even nations that rather openly support terrorist organizations—such as Iran, Lebanon, Syria, and Afghanistan—publicly deny any such support. But this has not stopped the terrorism.

With the demise of the Soviet empire, the most effective way to deal with international terrorists is to destroy their training bases and make their movements more difficult. Bases are hard to get at; it is easier to foil the movements of the terrorists. False passports can be detected; satellites can use cameras and eavesdropping equipment to detect terrorist movements and plans. Good intelligence and police work in the target countries are the most common means of stopping and catching terrorists.

From a public-relations angle, antiterrorism measures are a hard sell. Target countries cannot show what they are doing, lest the terrorists see what to avoid as they sneak in and set up their operations. Even the police work can backfire when they make the wrong moves with an immigrant population (usually Muslims these days) that might provide some support to terrorists.

The terrorists don't have an easy time of it doing what they do, and the potential victims are not helpless. But the war against terrorism takes place largely in the shadows, where a lot of murky business is taken care of. What you see about it in the news is only a tiny portion of the business being transacted.

Twentieth-century terrorism makes full use of mass media and propaganda. These terrorists are unlike anything seen in the past. They need few successes to keep them going. Even failures are hailed as heroic blows against the enemy du jour by martyrs for the cause. And this terrorism works because it does terrorize. Security precautions are constantly added, often just on suspicion of terrorist activity.

But with so much money available, and international travel so accessible, all you need are a few dozen true believers to get a credible terrorist organization going. But the most common sources of terrorist support are governments that want to make war against their real, or perceived, enemies. Usually it is impossible to make war in the traditional sense, because the foe is so much stronger. But terrorism still works. It's relatively cheap and makes great headlines. Of course, you cannot take credit for these acts of terrorism, but you know you did it. And often your enemies know it too.

This is the kind of information warfare that is real. And it's not going away anytime soon.

Storm Troopers Are Bad, but It's Been Worse

Let us end all of this with the reminder that, as bad as things were in the twentieth century, they could have been worse. And have been in the past.

As bad as the Nazi and communist slaughters have been in the twentieth century, they were not the worst mass murders in history. Although more people were killed by war and organized violence in the twentieth century, that's mainly because there were more people to kill and more efficient tools to kill them with. The Nazis and communists were responsible for killing some 4 percent out of an average world population of 2.5 billion early in this century. But seven hundred years ago, the Mongols managed to kill 12 percent of the world's people (nearly 50 million, when the planetary population was only 360 million). The Mongols were four times as murderous as our twentieth-century butchers. One can take some comfort in that, but at the same time it would be unwise to ignore the circumstances that put a bigger dent in the human population than anything since. What's also amazing is the number of parallels between what has been happening in this century and the more gruesome events seven centuries ago. There are lessons to be learned here, as well as some insights into how much the world has changed in the past millennium.

The leader of the Mongols, Genghis Khan (or Temujin), was known as a great conqueror. But he was more than just a conqueror; he killed people on an unprecedented scale (before or since).

In the table on page 300, note the population changes in areas where Mongol armies campaigned.

Back then, many areas were very thinly populated by twentieth-century standards. China, for example, now has twelve times as many people as it did seven hundred years ago. Japan's islands were uncrowded, with only 7.5 million people, versus over fifteen times as many today. All of Southeast Asia had only 7 million people. Iran had a highly civilized and well-armed people. Afghanistan had a population of fierce tribesmen. Iraq's population was largely concentrated around Baghdad.

POPULATION CHANGES (in Millions)			
REGION	A.D. 1200	A.D. 1300	A.D. 2000
China	115	86	1,300
Korea	4	3	70
Iran	5	3.5	69
Afghanistan	2.5	1.75	23
Iraq	1.5	1	11
World Total	360	360	6,000

China was hit the hardest by the Mongol conquests, and this was so for carefully calculated reasons. Temujin knew that serious attempts to conquer China would always rally the Central Asian tribes behind him, but the Chinese could also be expected to put up a fierce, bloody, and prolonged resistance. Thus the high death rate. Korea, although populated by people more ethnically similar to Mongols than Chinese, was a Chinese satellite and also resisted Mongol conquest. There was less resistance, and less bloodshed, in Manchuria (northern China) and East Turkestan (now western China). These areas were populated largely by people similar to the Mongols and were won over to the Mongol cause with a minimum of fuss. In the first half of this century, the Japanese tried a similar divide-and-conquer strategy with China. Like the Mongols, the Japanese ultimately failed.

The basic motive for the Mongol invasions, like the Japanese and German ones of World War II, was greed. The Mongols were relatively poor nomads, while most of their victims were wealthier farmers and city dwellers. The Mongols were direct in their methods, using superior military power, terror, and strong-arm diplomacy to take over populations more than a hundred times larger than their own.

While the Mongols carried out mass slaughters, the historical record is a bit vague on how many of their victims died from Mongol swords and arrows and how many perished from the aftereffects of Mongol terror and destruction. Disease and starvation always followed in the wake of Mongol armies. Houses and farm equipment were destroyed on a vast scale.

Medieval farmers lived on the edge of survival. One or two bad harvests and there was massive starvation and death from disease. The Mongols knew this and saw such destruction of agricultural resources as a means to prevent their victims from recovering and fighting back. In parts of Iran and the Middle East, it took centuries for the elaborate irrigation infrastructure to recover from Mongol destruction.

World War II was little different in terms of the huge number of civilian deaths created as a by-product of the military operations. Russia lost 10 million soldiers during the World War II fighting, while 20 million civilians died amid the fighting. Most of the civilian deaths in China were a result of deliberate Japanese tactics (like advancing just to steal the harvest, then retreating to let the civilians starve to death).

But the wide-ranging campaigns of the Mongols brought an even deadlier weapon into play. Epidemic diseases that had long stayed in one region were now carried by Mongol armies to places where the locals had no resistance to these alien plagues. The Black Death in Europe is the best known of these afflictions carried vast distances by the Mongols.

World War II saw the introduction of antibiotic medicines at the same time the troops were providing epidemic diseases the chance to spread further. As a result, there was no great increase of disease deaths. But in World War I, there was an epidemic that was spread by the war-related movement of people. A particularly lethal strain of influenza got going in 1919, quickly circled the globe, and killed 20 million people in the process. Since World War II, we have seen the spread of disease made easier by the movements of refugees.

Epidemic diseases were most devastating in densely populated China, both then and now. It is known that these epidemics occurred in China in the wake of the Mongol campaigns and contributed to the severe population declines there. Elsewhere, the Mongol effect on local politics was even more severe. Iran was shattered as a regional power by the Mongols, and one could say that Iran has never really recovered. The same thing happened to Iraq, whose principal city, Baghdad, had long been a center of Muslim Arab power. The destruction of Baghdad by the Mongols was a blow the city, and the region around it, still felt to this day. Then again, many of the Mongols converted to Islam during the course of the thirteenth century, firmly establishing Islam among the Turkish peoples of Central Asia.

Back in Mongolia, in one of the ironic twists of history, Buddhism eventually became the new religion, and remains the principal faith of Mongolia to this day. Russia was also permanently changed by the Mongol invasions. The centuries of Mongol rule turned Russia away from the West, a condition that Russians feel still persists.

In the latter half of the twentieth century we were faced with potentially catastrophic deaths from weapons of mass destruction (nuclear, chemical, and biological). These threats are still with us. Should a latter-day Mongol horde arise, armed with these weapons, another slaughter of thirteenth-century proportions could happen. This is why most people are properly terrified of these weapons, and of more nations' getting their hands on them. Given the record of the Mongols, and less successful conquerors, it could happen again.

On the positive side, the Mongol campaigns in China united the nation once more. China, until then, had gone through periods of unity followed by breakdown into several smaller kingdoms. The Mongol conquest brought a unification that lasted until the present. The Mongol dynasty itself did not last long, with Chinese rebellions in the fourteenth century reestablishing local control by 1364. In the 1380s, Mongolia itself was invaded, although Chinese control did not last.

The major twentieth-century wars also produced some positive effects. Europeans have lost their taste for war, and edge ever more closely to economic and political unification. Russia, China, and Japan all lost their totalitarian governments, some more quickly than others, and their potential for wars of conquest. But if we have learned nothing else from the past, it is that what happens once can happen again, only more so.

APPENDIX:
Inflation Multiples

Below are the multiples applied to dollar values in years past in order to translate them to year-2000 dollars.

YEAR	MULTIPLE	YEAR	MULTIPLE	YEAR	MULTIPLE
1900	25.24	1919	9.94	1938	12.20
1901	24.25	1920	8.58	1939	12.38
1902	23.00	1921	9.61	1940	12.26
1903	23.12	1922	10.26	1941	11.68
1904	22.82	1923	10.08	1942	10.55
1905	22.70	1924	10.06	1943	9.94
1906	22.03	1925	9.81	1944	9.77
1907	21.15	1926	9.72	1945	9.55
1908	20.57	1927	9.90	1946	8.80
1909	19.55	1928	10.04	1947	7.70
1910	18.65	1929	10.04	1948	7.14
1911	18.85	1930	10.30	1949	7.21
1912	17.77	1931	11.29	1950	7.14
1913	17.34	1932	12.59	1951	6.62
1914	17.11	1933	13.27	1952	6.48
1915	16.94	1934	12.84	1953	6.43
1916	15.75	1935	12.53	1954	6.40
1917	13.41	1936	12.41	1955	6.42
1918	11.42	1937	11.98	1956	6.33

(continued)

YEAR	MULTIPLE	YEAR	MULTIPLE	YEAR	MULTIPLE
1957	6.11	1972	4.11	1987	1.51
1958	5.95	1973	3.87	1988	1.45
1959	5.90	1974	3.49	1989	1.39
1960	5.81	1975	3.19	1990	1.32
1961	5.75	1976	3.02	1991	1.26
1962	5.68	1977	2.84	1992	1.23
1963	5.62	1978	2.64	1993	1.19
1964	5.54	1979	2.37	1994	1.16
1965	5.45	1980	2.09	1995	1.13
1966	5.30	1981	1.89	1996	1.10
1967	5.15	1982	1.78	1997	1.07
1968	4.94	1983	1.73	1998	1.05
1969	4.69	1984	1.66	1999	1.03
1970	4.43	1985	1.60	2000	1.00
1971	4.25	1986	1.57		

INDEX

Heterosexuals, 21
High-tech weapons, 277
Highways, 185, 188, 201, 277
Hip-hop, 89
Historians, 202, 247
History, 3, 4, 5, 14, 32, 46, 55, 68,
    73, 83, 119, 137, 147, 169,
    172, 182, 198, 209, 214, 234,
    251, 252, 264, 266, 275, 276,
    282, 292, 296, 299, 300, 302
HMOs, 18, 19
Hobbies, 109
Hobbyists, 51, 109, 217, 221
Hollywood, 57, 58, 60, 61, 62, 63,
    64
Holographs, 76
Homeopathy, 14, 16
Homosexuals, 20, 21, 80, 294
Hoover, J. Edgar, 69
Horse-drawn transport, 213, 241
Horseman, 237
Horses, 139, 140, 142, 184, 185,
    203, 212, 214, 235, 237, 247,
    250, 261, 266, 275
Hosiery, 39
Hospitals, 13, 14, 15, 17, 18, 277
Households, 8, 34, 37, 98, 100,
    107, 112, 119, 125, 126, 127,
    141, 164, 169, 170, 174, 181,
    182, 212, 232
Housekeeping, 125, 181, 182, 266
Housewives, 125, 135, 169, 181, 213
Housework, 43, 181
Hovels, 126, 172
Humanitarian, 285, 286, 288, 289,
    290
Hungarians, 24
Hunters, 93, 265
Hunting, 46, 93, 161, 216, 257
Hurd, Earl, 58
Hygiene, 20
Hypertext, 112

IBM, 8, 218, 219, 220
ICBMs, 274

ICQ, 123
Immigrants, 7, 21, 22, 23, 24, 25,
    27, 28, 29, 30, 124, 135, 149,
    298
Immigration, 21, 23, 29
Immunity, 19, 20, 21, 76
Impotency, 19
Ince, Thomas Harper, 60, 61
India, 13, 14, 30, 144, 145, 276,
    279, 280
Industrialization, 3, 6, 7, 13, 17, 31,
    48, 51, 52, 74, 83, 86, 103,
    124, 125, 129, 134, 135, 136,
    138, 142, 147, 155, 161, 164,
    170, 172, 184, 245, 265, 270,
    280, 285, 292, 294
Industry, 24, 28, 43, 55, 59, 73, 74,
    77, 78, 98, 100, 103, 115, 127,
    159, 188, 189, 200, 207, 221,
    229, 232
Infants, 101
Infections, 2, 11, 13, 15, 19, 20, 209
Infertility, 81
Inflation, 1, 47, 124, 125, 128, 130,
    131, 132, 133, 172, 173, 205,
    219, 234, 282
Influenza, 301
Infrastructure, 136, 238, 301
Injury, 5, 15, 238, 246, 248, 261,
    266, 288
Innovation, 37, 43, 59, 61, 72, 73,
    92, 139, 140, 141, 155, 157,
    159, 166, 167, 168, 174, 180,
    183, 195, 204, 214, 218, 226,
    232, 258, 262
Innovators, 55, 58, 190, 226
Insects, 93, 143
Insurance, 14, 16, 17, 18, 19, 128,
    149, 179, 269
Intellectuals, 284
Intelligence, 193, 280, 296, 298
Invention, 8, 9, 22, 36, 37, 39, 46,
    49, 50, 54, 55, 56, 59, 60, 72,
    73, 86, 89, 94, 95, 100, 109,
    110, 116, 154, 167, 168, 170,